# Love Jesus,
# Leave Church (ianity)

# Love Jesus,
# Leave Church (ianity)

how to leave organized religion
with a clear conscience
without losing your faith

Mark Clifton

ISBN: 979-8-218-14745-7
Library of Congress Control Number: 2023902280

Edited by Jared Clifton and Mike Zuehlke
First printed April 2023
Published by Jared Clifton

This book is dedicated to the memory of my parents, Howard and Jackie Clifton, who believed that the Bible was the sole basis for all Christian faith and practice, and from whom I learned to love the Truth. It contains the information I wish they could have had when they were married in 1947 and began looking for a Bible-believing church.

This book is also dedicated to you, my fellow believers who love the Truth, who believe that the Bible is inspired by God (2 Tim 3:16), and are unhappy with "church."

*-Mark Clifton (1950 - 2022)*

# Contents

# FOREWORD
by Jared Clifton

Jesus wants to have a personal relationship with you. He wants to know you on a deeper level.

The book you're about to read was written by my dad, who died just weeks after finishing it – I promised him I'd edit and publish it. This book is written for those of you who are not happy with what we call "church," but still want to have a relationship with Jesus. If you are happy with church, this book is likely not for you. But if you picked this up, you might be trying to figure out why you aren't satisfied, and why your heart tells you something should be different.

You've probably by this point read accounts in the New Testament of the miraculous power of the Holy Spirit. More than likely you've seen very few, if any, true miracles yourself. Perhaps you've been told that miracles aren't for today, but that isn't true. Why *did* worship look so different in the first century? How did relationship with Jesus become merely a list of rules? Why don't we see as many miracles? To put it bluntly, *who turned off the power?*

Something must have gone terribly wrong sometime between the first century and now. But how many of us know *what, when, why,* and *how?* That's what we're going to cover. I have to warn you – this isn't light reading. It reads like a textbook and is not meant to be read *quickly* – my father was very literal, technical, and thorough, although he also loved satire and dad jokes. I always warned my friends: if you ask my dad something, be prepared for the long answer; however, by the end you will have a firm understanding of the subject. He had that gift, if you had the time to listen.

During editing, I've left this book roughly as-is – I made the edits I believed necessary, but only those. I did not want to over-prettify the text as I felt it could inadvertently affect the information or general impact. I tried to present the information more clearly to the audience with the least amount of editing possible. We, the family, agree this is better considering the circumstances. I left it in his voice, his style – and I absolutely love it and back it 100%, but you've heard it here first: it's textbook-y!

I want to talk a bit about my dad and about this book. I think it will add some much-needed context. Before my dad died, he entered a state of complete surrender to our Lord Jesus. Not many know what this is, and at the end of the book, we will talk about it more. We call it *getting in the wheelbarrow*. In his notes, I found where he wrote, "Last chapter: the wheelbarrow – the goodness of the Kingdom of God & God's rest."

What is *the wheelbarrow?* I won't go into it now, because we will cover that at the end of this book. Suffice it to say that this note, as well as the conversations we had during his last days are some of the reasons I know he wanted this to be added, and why I feel the book is not complete without it. And who better to write it than our brother Mike who first introduced us to it.

When Mike first told Dad about *relationship,* Dad recounted that he was taught that God was the big policeman in the sky with a billy club and a list of rules eagerly waiting for you to step out of line so he can punish you. As he said, "Who would want a relationship with *that?*" He was brought up in an extremely religious household, with godly guilt-trips and holy burdens galore. Every time the doors opened at their church, my dad and his family would be there. That meant multiple times *every single week*, being stressed out and tired, they sat in a pew wearing their Sunday best, listening to sermons, singing hymns, putting money into the plate, etc. Being a voracious reader with a nearly eidetic memory (he could almost memorize books), he would keep reading whenever a verse was quoted during a sermon.

As he read on past the one or two verses the preacher used, he found most often that these verses seemed to be divorced from the larger context, and didn't appear to be saying what they were touted to mean. This began a journey at a young age, which eventually led to this book – a project which took around thirty years to complete. He and our family jumped around from church to church up until around the time I was born, before deciding to worship at home with family rather than *go* to church. Although sometimes Dad found amazing churches, he never found anything *lasting*. He was not happy with church, but separating the wrong God he was taught by churchianity from the real one wasn't easy. Learning who God is and how much he loves us took years, but he finally got there, and I am so proud of him. Not only that, the talks we had toward the end were never possible while he was mired in the teachings of organized religion. We became closer through relationship with Jesus.

Some four decades ago, ten years or so before he began work on this book, Dad was in the hospital. He was very sick, and knew he could die. Worse, he wondered how he would take care of his family. He was also terribly afraid of some things happening politically. He realized that he would not get well unless he put down his burden and rested. He did this, though he can't explain how. He describes feeling like he set something down beside his bed. He instantly felt the best he'd ever felt in his whole life. He was *light,* totally at peace, totally surrendered. He did not yet know how to fully trust God. At this point, he sensed God speaking to him in his spirit.

God said, "How do you feel?"

To which my Dad answered, "Great!"

God asked, "When was the last time you felt like this?"

Dad thought about it. He had *never* felt like this.

God continued and asked, "Wouldn't you like to feel like this *all the time?"*

Dad instantly thought of every reason *not* to feel this way. He had a family, he was sick, the world was going down the drain politically.

He asked God, "What about all *this?"*

God replied, "I have that all under control. I've *always* had it under control. I have it so under control, *I don't even think about it."*

Dad was aghast. He couldn't comprehend what God was saying, so he asked, "Well, what *do* you care about?"

This is where God got really quiet – then said, "Mark, how are things *between you and me?"*

The thing to note here is that God said *you and me,* not *me and you.* There was nothing between God and Dad. There never is, and there never will be. God loves us *unconditionally.* There was, however, a lot between Dad and God, which was hindering Dad from feeling that peace of surrender, making real relationship impossible. God had *no problem with Dad,* which is the opposite of what Dad had been taught by organized religion. It was only ever *the other way around.*

It was many years later through a series of extremely challenging life situations that Dad *had* to learn, and God was there every step of the way. It was our brother Mike who took him under his wing and taught him about *relationship.* That said, *we are all students,* and Mike is one of the most incredible students I know. He had a very difficult life - it was God who changed him, God who made him who he is. He has a job to do; to let you know about *relationship.*

To put it simply, this book is the way *out* of organized religion – but what then? If there's nothing else out there, you may simply return to the familiar routine. We want you to be aware of *relationship*, and how important it is. *It's all about relationship,* as Mike often says, and it's the truth. But like my dad, many of you are mired in organized religion, making it impossible to relate to Jesus in this way. What we want to do here is to be a signpost in the road, pointing you in the direction. However, there is no list of steps when it comes to relationship; and there are no rules. As Brother Lawrence so succinctly states in *The Practice of the Presence of God*:

> …our sanctification did not depend upon changing our works, but in doing that for God's sake, which we commonly do for our own. That it was lamentable to see how many people mistook the means for the end, addicting themselves to certain works, which they performed very imperfectly, by reason of their human or selfish regards. That the most excellent method he had found of going to God, was that of doing our common business without any view of pleasing men, (Gal 1:10, Eph 6:5, 6) and (as far as we are capable) purely for the love of God. That it was a great delusion to think that the times of prayer ought to differ from other times. That we are as strictly obliged to adhere to God by action in the time of action, as by prayer in its season.

> It is, however, necessary to put our whole trust in God, laying aside all other cares, and even some particular forms of devotion, though very good in themselves, yet such as one often engages in unreasonably: because those devotions are only means to attain to the end; so when by this exercise of the presence of God we are with Him who is our end, it is then useless to return to the means; but we may continue with Him our commerce of love, persevering in His holy presence: one while by an act of praise, of adoration, or of desire; one while by an act of resignation, or thanksgiving; and in all the manner which our spirit can invent.

If you've never read Brother Lawrence, you may want to pick it up. I highly recommend it. But for now, and until the epilogue, let's get *out of* organized religion. I recommend that you take your time reading this, and that you ask God for wisdom, for insight, and for discernment.

*~God's man Jared*

# PREFACE

If I were to identify a specific incident that explains how this book began, it would probably be the time when, at about age fourteen, I approached our pastor with a logical question. It came about like this.

In our church we hardly ever heard a sermon where Catholicism didn't come in for dishonorable mention. I had recently learned that Protestantism wasn't around before the sixteenth century. I had been reading and studying the New Testament. Connecting the dots, I reasoned that something must have gone wrong with Christianity sometime after AD 95 when the Apostle John wrote the *Revelation*. But *what* went wrong, *when* did it go wrong, and especially *why* did it go wrong?

Obviously our pastor would know the answer. So after one Sunday service, I waited in line and then asked him, "How did those first-century churches we read about in the New Testament become the Roman Catholic Church?"

And his answer was "Well, *we just don't know.*"

I was shocked and confused and didn't know what to say. As I walked away, inside my head red lights flashed, buzzers sounded, and all sorts of alarms started going off. "What?! You denounce Catholicism practically every Sunday and yet you have no idea how it got started? You're convinced that it's wrong but you have no idea what went wrong, or when, or why?"

To paraphrase Darth Vader: "I find your lack of intellectual curiosity. . . *disturbing.*"

The same sort of thing happened again a few years later. I was part of a group doing a ten-week Bible study in systematic theology. Everything went smoothly until we reached ecclesiology; the doctrine of church structure. I noticed two things:

Other doctrines had dozens of proof texts – which are biblical passages used as proof of an idea – but the doctrine relating to church structure had just a handful; and our study guide referred to the office of the pastor (singular), but the proof texts were all about elders (plural).

Puzzled by this incongruity, I approached our teacher after class and asked, "why do our notes say 'the office of the pastor,' but all the proof texts are about elders?"

And our teacher answered in a terse voice, "*That* was how they did it *then*, but *this* is how we do it *now*." I recognized that my question had just been dismissed with prejudice.

This sort of thinking, and these kinds of questions, tended to make me unpopular with church leaders. Yet it wasn't that I went around looking for hornets' nests of inconsistency to stick my logical hand into; I just wanted to know the truth. Webster's defines cognitive dissonance as the psychological conflict resulting from incompatible beliefs and attitudes held simultaneously. Cognitive dissonance was becoming the bane of my existence.

*Introduction*

# LOVE JESUS, LEAVE CHURCH (IANITY)

If you love Jesus but are unhappy, disappointed, frustrated, disillusioned, or just plain burned-out with church or religion, I have good news for you. There *is* a problem with church, but it's neither your fault nor God's fault and you're not required to "try harder" to fix it. Furthermore, you're not alone. More and more evangelical Christians sense that church and religion are somehow at odds with relationship with the Lord Jesus Christ.[1]

The answer to disillusionment is to leave organized religion without losing our faith. And no, that's not a trick statement: "leaving" doesn't somehow mean "staying."

Many Christians who become disillusioned with church naturally assume that the fault must lie with them. After all, didn't Jesus promise "on this rock I will build my church, and the gates of Hades will not overpower it" (Matt 16:18)? Didn't the apostle Paul refer to "...the house of God, which is the church of the living God, the pillar and ground of the truth" (1 Tim 3:15 KJV)? And doesn't Hebrews 10:25 command "forsake not the assembling of yourselves together..." (KJV)?[2]

If in fact God commands us to go to church, then dropping out amounts to rejecting God's Word and violating our conscience. Christians who do that are in danger of losing their faith. As Paul explained to Timothy: ". . . you must hold firmly to faith and a good conscience, which some have rejected and so have suffered shipwreck in regard to the faith," (1 Tim 1:19).

### THERE'S A WIN-WIN SOLUTION

When disillusionment becomes too great to ignore, Christians face a distressing choice: remain stuck in an intolerable situation, or drop out of church. Those who choose to remain may look for a different church; stay where they are and struggle to survive; or stay put outwardly but drop out inwardly. Christians who quit church may look for a way to still hold onto Jesus, or else throw out the baby with the bathwater and become agnostic or atheist.

All of these responses are "lose-lose": they all amount to choosing the lesser of evils. Wouldn't it be great if there was a "win-win" solution that didn't involve any evil at all! If only Jesus had an answer that resolved all our difficulties . . .

As a matter of fact, **He does**! There *is* a way out of church that does not require us to ignore or reject God's Word, violate our conscience, or "survive or die trying." But as Nicodemus asked Jesus in John 3:9, "How can these things be?"

### CHURCHIANITY: COUNTERFEIT CHRISTIANITY

Our problem—the cause of our disillusionment—is actually with what we know as "church." A better name for it is *churchianity*, aka organized religion. The name churchianity highlights the fact that there is something that claims to be Christianity but is different; something that professes to love and serve the Lord Jesus Christ but actually has an entirely different agenda.

Churchianity is hijacked Christianity. It's a counterfeit. Churchianity has been masquerading as Jesus' Ekklesia for about 1,900 years. If you love Jesus but are unhappy with church or religion, your problem is not with Jesus or His Ekklesia—his called-out people. Your problem is churchianity.

**CHURCH OR EKKLESIA?** Ekklesia is the English equivalent of the New Testament Greek word translated as church. In the New Testament, Ekklesia means the company of believers in Jesus. But today, after the third century, the word church generally means a building for religious meetings. So for the most part, I will use the word *Ekklesia* to denote what Jesus promised He would build (Matthew 16:18), and *church* to refer to churchianity.

### THE WAY OF ESCAPE

In order to leave organized religion—churchianity—without losing our faith, two things are required:

1. We must recognize and accept that there is a counterfeit version of Christianity - if Christianity really was hijacked, who hijacked it? And

when, why, and how did they do it?

2. We must be able to distinguish real Christianity from the counterfeit. We must understand what God *actually says*, and just as importantly, what He *does not say*. God has already told us how to escape from churchianity. The truth we need has always been right in plain sight in the New Testament. The reason we haven't seen it is because churchianity has taught us to read and understand the Bible upside-down (I explain this concept in chapter 3).

The New Testament tells us that there's a right way to understand the Bible. It also warns us against using the Bible the wrong way. Evangelical Christians have developed possibly the best principles for correctly understanding Scripture that anyone has ever seen: the 1982 *Chicago Statement on Biblical Hermeneutics* (and also the 1978 *Chicago Statement on Biblical Inerrancy*). These are the principles which I follow throughout this book.

Tragically, although in theory we know the right way to understand the Bible, in practice we still use medieval methods of mystical misinterpretation to read the Bible upside-down. The misuse of Scripture to justify teachings and practices that we *know* must be God's will but that cannot be found in the New Testament has unintended but terrible consequences:

- The Bible becomes hard to understand

- God doesn't make sense

- Our worship is meaningless

- The body of Christ is divided, immature, and powerless

- Christians suffer needlessly

And more and more Christians are becoming terminally disillusioned with church.

### FOLLOW THE BEREAN EXAMPLE

It is vitally important that this book accurately handle Scripture and the facts of church history. Much of what I present differs significantly from traditional evangelical thinking. When evaluating new ideas, there are two opposite errors to avoid: uncritical acceptance and unthinking rejection. As Dr. Randy Alcorn explains in his groundbreaking book *Heaven*,

Many things in this book will be new even to readers who are veteran students of Scripture. New ideas are rightly suspect because they are often heretical. However, when biblical truths have been long neglected or ignored, attempts to present them may sound far-fetched. They may appear to be adding to or misinterpreting Scripture, when in fact they are simply portraying what Scripture has said all along but we've failed to grasp.[3]

I encourage readers to follow the Berean example of principled skepticism (Acts 17:11). The Bereans listened carefully to the apostle Paul, but then examined the scriptures to see if he was telling the truth. I urge you to verify my references and examine my use of Scripture for accuracy and context. Judge for yourself if I'm telling the truth. The truth is all that matters; my opinions will not set anyone free.

### REFERENCES AND DEFINITIONS

Each chapter's endnote references are listed on a separate page at the end of the chapter. New Testament Greek word definitions are from the Bauer-Danker-Arndt-Gingrich (BDAG) New Testament Greek-English lexicon, third edition. I've included Strong's Concordance numbers with all New Testament Greek words. I've also included phonetic spelling in parentheses following Greek words and theological terms.

### THE NEW ENGLISH TRANSLATION (NET) BIBLE

I chose the NET Bible for nearly all of my biblical quotes. Unless otherwise stated, all Bible quotes are taken from the NET. I wanted a modern English translation with a good balance between word-for-word (formal equivalence) and thought-for-thought (dynamic equivalence) accuracy. The NET Bible more than satisfied my criteria, and I highly recommend it. *Editor's note: during the initial writing of this book, the NET also did not have any limits on how many total verses one can legally quote. Many Bible translations have limits, and now the NET does too, but this book still stays within those limits.*

### DISCLAIMER:

This book contains some few *misquotes* to illustrate a point. These misquotes will be formatted differently so you can more easily identify them, as they should not be taken as direct quotes. The purpose of these misquotes is to illustrate or drive home certain points. Since I don't want anyone to be confused, they will be formatted [like this, in brackets and in Times New Roman font.]

## HOW THIS BOOK IS ORGANIZED

**Section 1 - Organized Religion's Myth-theology:** Chapters 1-5 are the book's foundation. Chapter 1 explains churchianity's origin. Chapter 2 explains how churchianity keeps Christians trapped in organized religion. Chapter 3 explains how churchianity tricks us into misreading and misunderstanding the Bible. Chapter 4 turns the Bible right-way-up and explains how to correctly interpret the Bible. Chapter 5 busts the myths that have kept us trapped.

**Section 2 - Apostles:** How accurate and reliable were Christ's Apostles— the men who authored and approved the New Testament's twenty-seven books and letters? Did they know everything there was to know about Christianity? Or did they know only enough to design a temporary, baby church? Did they tell us everything we need to know, or did they leave out important parts—or maybe even get some things *wrong?* Spoiler alert: Jesus had a specific design in mind for His Ekklesia. His apostles were fully knowledgeable about His design and they implemented it perfectly right down to the smallest detail.

**Section 3 - Blueprint:** How accurate and reliable is the New Testament? Does it document the complete and permanent design of Jesus' Ekklesia, or are its instructions and examples partial and temporary? The New Testament clearly and thoroughly documents the Ekklesia's design and functioning, and that documented design makes church government impossible.

**Section 4 - Worship:** With the advent of a single, visible head over the church, worship had to be radically redefined and redesigned in order to agree with the new *organizational* function of the Ekklesia. The church was always meant to be an *organism,* with each part of the body of Christ functioning correctly. In this section we will cover how it changed, why it changed, what it changed to, and what it changed *from.* Far from being silent about worship, the entire New Testament is a worship manual.

**Section 5 - Busted:** God didn't give us organized religion and He doesn't require Christians to participate in it. God has already told us, in writing, in the New Testament, that He neither authorized nor does He approve of church government and its practices. The New Testament, correctly understood, makes organized religion impossible. Not only that, we can be certain that it was actually written during the first century and not changed afterwards. The New Testament itself contains the strongest possible evidence for its own reliability, but the information has been suppressed. Until now.

**Endnotes**

1    Steve McCranie's 2006 book *Love Jesus, Hate Church* cites the overwhelming statistical evidence from USA Today/Gallup polls and Barna Institute studies. Then there's anecdotal evidence such as Jefferson Bethke's video *Why I Hate Religion, But Love Jesus* being viewed over 16 million times in the two weeks following its release on January 10, 2012.

2    Although that's the way I always heard it misquoted, what the KJV actually says is: "And let us consider one another to provoke unto love and to good works: Not forsaking the assembling of ourselves together, as the manner of some is; but exhorting one another: and so much the more, as ye see the day approaching." (Heb 10:24-25 KJV).

3    Randy Alcorn, *Heaven*, xvi.

# Section 1:

# ORGANIZED RELIGION'S MYTH-THEOLOGY

Organized religion, or churchianity, encompasses some doctrines and practices, such as church government and worship, that Christians consider central and even vital to the Faith—but that cannot be found in the New Testament. The Westminster Confession of Faith of 1646 admitted as much:

> Nevertheless, we acknowledge . . . that there are some circumstances concerning the *worship of God*, and *government of the Church* . . . which are to be ordered by the light of nature, and Christian prudence, according to the general rules of the Word . . . (Westminster Assembly, emphasis mine)

So on the one hand, the Confession acknowledges that the New Testament is silent about church government and worship; but on the other hand, both are mandatory: they "are to be ordered." This contradicts Protestantism's formal principle of *Sola Scriptura*: that the written Bible is the only authoritative source for all Christian faith and practice; that only God's Word, not unwritten traditions, may bind a Christian's conscience.

The obvious question, then, is: if churchianity's practices really are central and vital to Christianity, why aren't they documented anywhere in the New Testament's twenty-seven books and letters? And since they aren't, why do we nonetheless accept and practice them, and why are we averse to the thought of abandoning them?

The answer ought to be equally obvious, but we're reluctant to speak or even think about it because acknowledging it threatens to expose a flaw in the foundation of our faith. We Bible-believing Christians lack the courage of our convictions: we're less than one hundred percent certain that the New Testament tells us everything God wants us to know about Christianity. To put it bluntly, we're double-minded about the Bible.

Something has afflicted our minds with confusion, doubt, and unbelief about the Bible generally and the New Testament in particular. Whatever this something is, we're afraid to talk about it or even think about it. That means something besides God's Word is binding our conscience. And this non-biblical something that makes us doubt God's Word is what keeps us trapped in organized religion.

What is this unspeakable, unthinkable, unbiblical something that exerts such power over our minds?

1,900 years ago when organized religion was just getting started, it faced a seemingly insurmountable obstacle: the twenty-seven books and letters that Christ's apostles had written or approved. Correctly understood and believed, these inspired writings made organized religion impossible. In order to succeed, churchianity had to get around, circumvent, nullify, and explain away nearly everything that Christ's apostles believed, practiced, taught, and documented. The problem was, *how?* How could Christians be duped into ignoring and disobeying God's clear, written instructions?

Yet there was a way for churchianity to accomplish its objective: a tried-and-true technique as old as the Garden of Eden, when the serpent beguiled Eve into ignoring and disobeying God's clear, verbal instructions. Eve was duped into doubting and disbelieving God's Word by means of a lie—a lie with just enough truth thrown in to make it appear plausible.

Organized religion is likewise based on a lie—a *myth-theology*: mostly mythology with just enough bad theology thrown in to make it appear plausible as long as we don't look too closely. And historically, Christians have been afraid to look too closely. We've all been convinced that organized religion must somehow be God's will. Thus, questioning or doubting churchianity would mean opposing God, violating our conscience, and possibly losing our faith. Myth-theology plus fear have kept Christians trapped in organized religion for almost 1,900 years.

To leave organized religion with our faith intact, we're going to have to bust churchianity's myth-theology. We're going to have to expose and reject the lie. We need to understand how churchianity has seduced and deceived us. We can't bust the Myth until we know what it is and how it operates, so let's dive in.

# Chapter 1

# CHRISTIANITY'S TROJAN HORSE

Jesus said "My sheep listen to my voice, and I know them, and they follow me" (John 10:27). If you attend church and are happy and satisfied, you probably shouldn't read this book. I wrote it for Christians who love Jesus but are dissatisfied with church. My goal is to help my fellow believers who have serious questions and are searching for answers. If you're unsure whether or not to proceed, take Mary's advice to the servants at the wedding at Cana. Ask our Lord what He wants you to do, and then: "Whatever he tells you, do it" (John 2:5).

There. You've been warned. Here we go.

If you love Jesus but are unhappy, disappointed, frustrated, disillusioned, or just plain burned-out with church or religion, I have good news for you. There *is* a problem with church, but it's neither your fault nor God's fault and you're not required to "try harder" to fix it. Furthermore, you're not alone. More and more evangelical Christians sense that church and religion are somehow at odds with relationship with the Lord Jesus Christ.[1]

This is not a new problem. Ever since the second century, groups such as the Montanists, Novations, Donatists, Waldenses, Paulicians, Albigenses, Lollards, and Hussites[2] believed something was wrong. Even during and after the Protestant Reformation,[3] the Puritans, Anabaptists, Baptists, Pietists, United Brethren and others kept looking for the answer. Evangelicalism itself, beginning with the first Great Awakening around 1740,[4] was another step in the search. So if you're still searching, you're in good company historically speaking.

Christians who become disillusioned with church may naturally assume that the fault must lie with them. But the problem actually is with what we know as "church." A better name for it is *churchianity*, aka organized religion. The name *churchianity* highlights the fact that there is something that *claims* to be Christianity but is different; something that professes to love and serve the Lord Jesus Christ but actually has an entirely different agenda.

Churchianity is hijacked Christianity. It's a counterfeit. It's the World System[5] of 1 John 5:19 masquerading as Jesus' Ekklesia.[6] It's been around for nearly 1,900 years. If you love Jesus but are unhappy with church or religion, your problem is not with Jesus or His Ekklesia—his called-out people. Your problem is churchianity.

Churchianity is the reason Christians are still searching for the real thing. Why, after so many centuries, hasn't anybody managed to find the answer? As influential philosopher and poet George Santayana explained, "Those who cannot remember the past are condemned to repeat it."[7] Christians have been repeating the past for about 1,900 years.

Because Christians don't remember the past, we can't tell real Christianity from the counterfeit. So we keep trying to fix the hijacked version. But all our attempts end up being about as effective as "rearranging the deck chairs on the Titanic."

Thankfully, grim death or bare survival are not our only options. Churchianity's Titanic can't be fixed, but God doesn't require us to go down with the ship. The correct answer is to leave churchianity without losing our faith. And no, that's not a trick statement: leaving doesn't somehow mean staying. But as Nicodemus asked Jesus in John 3:9, "How can these things be?"

To leave organized religion without losing our faith, two things are required:

1. Accept the fact that there is a counterfeit version of Christianity;

2. Learn how to distinguish real Christianity from the counterfeit version.

For now, let's start at the beginning. Step 1 starts by taking George Santayana's advice and remembering the past, so the past is where we'll begin. If Christianity really *was* hijacked by religion, who hijacked it? And when, why, and how did they do it?

### STEP 1: CHURCHIANITY'S ORIGIN

To complete step 1, accepting that there *is* a counterfeit Christianity, let's take a look at the start of churchianity. A decade or so after the Apostle John died in AD 100, a Christian leader wrote a series of letters. In these letters he advocated a slight change to the pattern of Christianity inherited from Christ's apostles. He believed this change would protect God's flock from false teachers. His "new, improved" design proved to be immensely popular. Within a couple generations it was accepted and practiced throughout the Roman Empire.

(*Who* was this man? We'll meet him later in this book. First we need to understand *how* Christianity was hijacked. So right now we're going to focus on *what* he taught.)

Nobody realized it at the time, but this *slight change* he advocated was a Trojan horse: it concealed an insidious agenda all its own. Once it was accepted, a whole series of subsequent changes became necessary and inevitable. Slowly, step by step, one change followed another. The entire process took almost 200 years. No single generation of Christians ever saw all of what was happening. By AD 300, nearly everything that first-century Christians believed and practiced had been altered or replaced. Christianity had been hijacked by religion.

In the Greek myth, the Trojan horse had a visible exterior and an unseen interior. On the outside, the horse looked impressive and seemed harmless. The people of Troy even believed that it would bring them divine protection. But the unseen interior held a deadly threat – a number of concealed Greek soldiers who climbed out in the night to take the City of Troy. The horse's true purpose was destruction. When the Trojans brought the horse into their city, they sealed their fate.

The slight change that Christians embraced after AD 100 also had a visible exterior and an unseen interior. The visible part was seductively attractive. Like the people of Troy, second-century Christians believed the change would bring them divine protection. But in the unseen realm, the "slight change" concealed a deadly threat. The true purpose of the change was destruction. And just as the deceived people of Troy brought the horse into their city, Christians brought stealthy destruction into Jesus' Ekklesia.

### FROM ORGANISM TO ORGANIZATION

The slight change—the horse's visible exterior—consisted of giving Jesus' Ekklesia a visible head:

> During the 2nd century the ministry was subject to a change. The ruling body of office-bearers in every congregation received a permanent president, who was called the pastor or bishop, the latter term being the commoner.[8]

First-century Christianity had no visible head: there was no single bishop, pastor, president, or CEO. During most of Christianity's first one hundred years after Pentecost, Jesus was the invisible head and the Ekklesia was His body on earth. The Apostle Paul refers to the Ekklesia as Christ's body fourteen times in his thirteen letters. And Paul meant that literally, not figuratively.[9]

Second-century Christian leaders never realized that by setting up a visible head they were establishing a rival to the Lord Jesus Christ. No one can serve two masters and no body can serve two heads. Making anyone else the *acting* head unavoidably made Jesus merely the *figurehead*.

Setting up one man as the visible head over every congregation brought political power and control into Christianity. Once second-century Christians accepted a visible head, everything else about Jesus' Ekklesia had to change to follow suit. Instead of an *organism*—the body of Christ—Christianity became a political *organization*. We call the visible part of the Trojan horse church government or organized religion.

### CONSTANTINE WASN'T THE CULPRIT

Protestants generally agree with step 1: that Christianity was hijacked but they mistakenly blame the Roman emperor Constantine. Constantine was born in AD 272 and ruled Rome from 312[10] to 337. The church's problems, we're commonly told, began when Constantine made Christianity the official religion of the empire. That would be a great explanation if it were true, but unfortunately it's mythology, not history. Constantine tolerated Christianity but *did not* make it the official religion of the empire.[11] That didn't happen until 380 under Gratian and Theodosius.[12]

Furthermore, the changes that hijacked Christianity all happened before Constantine became emperor. The most important ones occurred before he was born. And that's history, not mythology. Most church historians concede that the churches changed soon after AD 100. In his analysis of Christianity's first 300 years, Thomas M. Lindsay summarized the second-century changes:

> The beginnings of the change date from the early decades of the second century; by the end of the century it was almost complete . . . every local church came to supplement its organization by placing *one* man at the head of the community, making him the president of the college of elders.[13]

Lindsay's *The Church and the Ministry in the Early Centuries* was first published in 1903. It went through three editions and is back in print and still in demand today. It's even available free on the web.[14]

Nearly eighty years later, scholar and church historian Bruce L. Shelley agreed that Christianity began to change soon after the end of the first century. Shelley also noted that today those changes are almost universally acknowledged:

> These changes in the structure and functioning of the church, especially the role of bishops, raise crucial and controversial questions. Christians of nearly every denomination admit that these changes took place.[15]

Dr. Shelley's *Church History In Plain Language* has an entire chapter[16] on this subject. First published in 1982 and now in its fourth edition, it has sold over 315,000 copies[17] and is used as a college textbook.

Protestants naturally believe that the Reformation restored Christianity to its original, apostolic pattern. Church history, however, tells a different story. The Reformers rolled back the visible changes that occurred after about AD 220, but they kept all the earlier ones.[18]

Since historians have known better for over a century, why does Constantine still get blamed for hijacking Christianity? It's because that keeps the focus on what happened *after* Constantine while ignoring the changes that took place *before* AD 300.

Blaming Constantine lets us ignore the fact that we're practicing the "new, improved" version of Christianity. It lets Protestants continue to practice organized religion while simultaneously professing that the Bible is *Sola Scriptura,* that is, the sole authoritative source for all Christian faith and practice.

### NO CHURCH GOVERNMENT IN THE NEW TESTAMENT

Church historians know the facts. Look up church government in Nelson's Bible Dictionary and we find: "No single pattern of government in the early church can be discovered by reading the New Testament."[19] Fausset's Bible Dictionary doesn't even have an entry for church government, but the entry for "church" states: "No detailed church government is explicitly commanded by Jesus in the New Testament."[20] The International Standard Bible Encyclopedia explains it this way: ". . . to discover what kind of church government is mirrored in the New Testament . . . is, no doubt, quite impossible."[21]

Even the Westminster Confession of Faith of 1646 acknowledges that church government cannot be found in the New Testament. The full quote[22] is in the footnotes, but here's the condensed version:

> Nevertheless, we acknowledge . . . that there are some circumstances concerning the worship of God, and government of the Church . . . which are to be ordered by the light of nature, and Christian prudence, according to the general rules of the Word . . .

The reason that church government and worship must be ordered "by the light of nature and Christian prudence" is because the New Testament is silent about both of them. Yet somehow they're still mandatory; they "are to be ordered"!

Today few Christians remember the past. The organized version of Christianity is all we've ever known. We're not aware that there ever was anything else. We believe that organized, religious Christianity is "the faith that was once for all entrusted to the saints" (Jude 3). But that's mythology, not history. Jude never heard of church government. It hadn't been invented yet.

### STEP 2: RECOGNIZING THE COUNTERFEIT

The purpose of this book is to enable Christians to leave organized religion without losing our faith. So far, we've covered a brief history of churchianity in order to cover step 1: accepting that there is a counterfeit version of Christianity. We did this by detailing the fact that the New Testament is silent about the subject of church government and organized religion.

In order to leave organized religion while keeping faith in Jesus, we need more than simply recognizing that there *is* a counterfeit version of Christianity, we need to be able to tell the difference, which leads us into step 2: learn to distinguish genuine Christianity from the counterfeit version. To accomplish this, we merely must be able to distinguish what the New Testament actually says from what churchianity claims it says.

So far in this chapter we've identified *what* churchianity is and *when* it began. We now recognize there *is* a problem, but a brief history lesson will not be enough to distinguish real Christianity from its counterfeit.

Even if we agree with the scholars that (1) there's no church government in the New Testament; and (2) first-century Christian congregations had no visible head – that is, no single bishop or pastor - today virtually everybody is convinced, or at least strongly suspects, that organized religion is still somehow God's will.

The obvious question for Christians, then, is: how is it that we all know something that God never put in writing?

One of the enemies hiding inside the Trojan horse of organized religion was a powerful, deceptive myth. This myth keeps Christians trapped in organized religion. It keeps us from being able to tell real Christianity apart from the counterfeit. It makes us afraid that rejecting church government means rejecting Christ: if we leave churchianity we'll lose our faith.

What is this myth? Does it have a name? And how does it work? We're about to find out.

**Endnotes**

1    Steve McCranie's 2006 book *Love Jesus, Hate Church* cites the overwhelming statistical evidence from USA Today/Gallup polls and Barna Institute studies. Then there's anecdotal evidence such as Jefferson Bethke's video *Why I Hate Religion, But Love Jesus* being viewed over 16 million times in the two weeks following its release on January 10, 2012.

2    Various Christian denominations originating between the second century AD and 1170 AD that followed similar beliefs to the Baptists of today.

3    The movement of 16th century Europe whose followers believed in freedom to relate directly and individually with Jesus, which was in direct opposition to the Roman Catholic Church and subsequently caused another branch of Christianity called *Protestantism.*

4    Shelley, *Church History In Plain Language: Updated 2nd Edition,* 346.

5    Greek: *kosmos*: KAHZ-mahs; NT:2889

6    Greek: *Ekklesia*: ek-klay-SEE-ah; NT:1577 - the company of believers in Jesus. See also: Body of Christ.

7    Santayana [1905] 2006

8    Orr, *International Standard Bible Encyclopedia,* "Ministry"

9    With good reason: "Saul, Saul, why are you persecuting *me*?" (Acts 9:4, emphasis mine).

10    Constantine was acclaimed emperor by the army in 306; became the western emperor in 312; eastern empire 324.

11    Chadwick 1993, 127.

12    Walker et al, *A History of the Christian Church,* 144.

13    Lindsay, *The Church And The Ministry In The Early Centuries,* 169.

14    http://www.ccel.org/ccel/lindsay/early_church.html

15    Shelley, *Church History In Plain Language: Updated 2nd Edition,* 71.

16    Shelley, *The School For Sinners,* chap. 7.

17    Cited on the back cover, 4th edition, December, 2013.

18    ". . . the Reformed Church, in the sixteenth century . . . restored the bishops to their ancient position of pastors of congregations . . ." (Thomas Lindsay, *The Church And The Ministry In The Early Centuries,* 210, emphasis mine). Lindsay stated that the office of the bishop or pastor was invented in the second century (p. 169). So the position was "ancient" but not primitive or original. The Reformers retained the second-century form of episcopacy.

19    Youngblood, *Nelson's Illustrated Bible Dictionary,* "Church Government"

20    Fausset, *Fausset's Bible Dictionary,* "Church"

21    Orr, *International Standard Bible Encyclopedia,* "Church Government"

22    "The whole counsel of God concerning all things necessary for His own glory, man's salvation, faith and life, is either expressly set down in Scripture, or by good and necessary consequence may be deduced from Scripture: unto which nothing at any time is to be added, whether by new revelations of the Spirit, or traditions of men. Nevertheless, we acknowledge the inward illumination of the Spirit of God to be necessary for the saving understanding of such things as are revealed in the Word: and that there are some circumstances concerning the worship of God, and

government of the Church, common to human actions and societies, which are to be ordered by the light of nature, and Christian prudence, according to the general rules of the Word, which are always to be observed." (Westminster Assembly, 1646).

Chapter 2

# ORGANIZED RELIGION'S HOTEL CALIFORNIA

E ver since the second century, organized religion has been like the Hotel California:[1]

You can check out any time you like but you can never leave.

Once Christianity was hijacked by religion—once second-century congregations accepted a visible head—a number of other changes became necessary and inevitable. Here are seven visible changes that came in with church government (see Appendix for details):

- The office of the bishop or pastor
- Clergy and laity
- Ordination
- Salaried clergy
- Church buildings
- Worship services and the Order of Worship
- Sermons

Though these may look familiar, *none* of these practices can be found in the New Testament. All of them were invented after AD 100—after the lifetimes of Christ's apostles. First-century Christians never heard of any of them. Yet today, most Christians believe that these practices are authorized by God and vital to our faith.

What makes the counterfeit version of Christianity impossible to leave? How does it convince us that church government is God's will?

### CHURCH GOVERNMENT'S MYTH-THEOLOGY

Right from the start, organized religion faced one huge obstacle: how to get around the New Testament. Christians all agreed that God had spoken infallibly through Christ's apostles. Those inspired men had written or approved twenty-seven books and letters documenting everything they believed, practiced, and taught: everything that the Holy Spirit had revealed to them. And nowhere in any of those documents was there any mention of church government.

Not only that: the New Testament's instructions and examples clearly contradicted all the changes that church government required. For churchianity to succeed, it would somehow have to get around, circumvent, nullify, and explain away nearly everything that the apostles of Christ believed, practiced, taught, and documented. But how could Christians be duped into ignoring and disobeying God's clear, written instructions?

At the time, it wasn't that difficult. For one thing, Christianity didn't get organized all at once. Church government took nearly 200 years to fully develop. No single generation of Christians ever saw all of what was happening. And each small change seemed natural and reasonable at the time.

Furthermore, printing presses and paper didn't exist. Writing was done by specialists, on parchment scrolls, one letter at a time. Copies of the apostles' writings were scarce and costly. Besides, many Christians couldn't read anyway. That's why Paul told Timothy to "give attention to the public reading of scripture" (1 Tim 4:13). Publicly reading the scriptures aloud was particularly important given the historical context.[2]

The scripture that Paul was talking about was the Old Testament. The New Testament wasn't completed until AD 95 and wouldn't be arranged in its final form until the fourth century. During this time and for centuries afterwards, Christians were dependent on oral teaching.

Christian faith came to be defined as "what has been believed everywhere, always, by everyone."[3] Well, *always* since the second century anyway. But without literacy and access to a written New Testament, how would later generations of Christians ever discover that the faith had changed?

Under these circumstances, it was easy for Christians to be convinced that church government was authorized by God.

## THE MYTH'S ORIGINAL VERSION

Eventually a mythical explanation for the changes emerged. It explained and legitimized all the differences between New Testament Christianity and its counterfeit, *churchianity*. According to the myth, the first-century church—the one that's documented throughout the New Testament—was an infant that grew up during the next several centuries. Adults don't look or act like babies, so it was only natural that the grown-up, new and improved Christianity didn't resemble the New Testament's baby version.

The myth's name is *The Church's Infancy*. The International Standard Bible Encyclopedia provides a concise description of the myth's original version in its article on bishops:

> . . . the apostles and early Christians . . . were looking for the speedy return of Christ, and consequently did not *organize the church in its infancy*, as it was afterward found necessary to do.[4] (emphasis mine)

Churches whose form of government existed before the Protestant Reformation openly accept the notion that Christianity began as an infant. Catholic and Orthodox Christians believe that God authorized the changes after the first century:

> Still other Christians argue that the Holy Spirit so dwelt in the church and guided its decisions that the developments of the early centuries in doctrine and church structure were the work not of men but of God. They are, therefore, permanently binding for the church.[5]

In other words, the Myth's original version explains church government as follows:

1. Jesus' Ekklesia began as an infant;

2. The New Testament documents only the Church's infancy;

3. After the New Testament was completed, God authorized and guided the development of church government as the Ekklesia grew to maturity.

## THE MYTH'S STEALTH VERSION

At the time of the Reformation, however, a new version of the Myth became necessary. The Reformers didn't want to get rid of church government; they just wanted to change its form. But there was a problem: up to that time only one form of church government ever existed: the original one; the one Protestants wanted to change. See, if God really had authorized the original form, then Protestantism couldn't be legitimate.

According to the Myth's original version, God spoke through unwritten tradition and non-apostles (*church fathers*) to develop church government. But Protestantism proclaimed that the written Bible was the only valid source (Sola Scriptura) of divine revelation. So Protestants needed an explanation for church government that didn't require extra-biblical authorities - it had to come from scripture.

That's why church government of any kind still had to get around the New Testament, so a myth was still needed. But the Myth's new version couldn't depend on Holy Tradition or church fathers; it would somehow have to find church government in the Bible. Also, God would have to authorize church government but not require any particular form: one form was as good as another, and any form would do. Finally, the new version had to avoid mentioning infancy because the infancy myth contradicts the design that Paul and the other apostles of Christ put into writing. Second-century changes would require some other explanation.

The new version of the Church Infancy Myth is the stealth version; it's "the Myth that dares not speak its name."[6] Here's how one popular evangelical reference work affirms the Myth's stealth version without mentioning its name:

> At first, church organization and government in the New Testament was flexible to meet changing needs. But as the church became better established, it gave attention to the right structures and procedures that would help it accomplish its mission . . . Thus, numerous forms of church government are used today to provide order and structure for the work of churches.[7]

But that very first sentence is wrong and church historians know it; church government in the New Testament isn't *flexible*, it's *absent*! The truth is, *there is no church government in the New Testament*: zero, zip, zilch, nada, none. To quote still another church historian:

> One may account for this virtual silence by saying either that the writers did not regard such forms as important or that they took them for granted; but the silence itself is undeniable.[8]

According to the Myth's stealth version, church government is right there in the New Testament; it's just so flexible that we can't see it; it's stealthily hiding between the lines.

### HOW THE MYTH KEEPS US TRAPPED

The Myth keeps Christians trapped in churchianity by holding our conscience hostage. It makes us believe—or at least strongly suspect—that church government is commanded or approved by God. It makes us fear that rejecting

14

organized religion means opposing God, violating our conscience, and losing our faith.

Faith and conscience are inseparably linked. As Paul warned Timothy,

> . . . you must hold firmly to faith and a good conscience, which some have rejected and so have suffered shipwreck in regard to the faith. (1 Tim 1:19)

The Myth's original version keeps Catholic and Orthodox Christians trapped by claiming God's authority for unwritten tradition and the selected writings of men who were not apostles. The Myth's *stealth version* keeps Protestant Christians trapped by claiming that God permits and approves of church government. There are even proof texts, that is, Biblical passages adduced as proof, for most of the practices employed by church government.

Thus, although the Myth's two versions contradict each other, they both accomplish the same result: everybody believes or suspects that church government *is* God's will. If the thought of abandoning churchianity's practices makes us feel afraid, guilty, or defensive - that's the *myth's* power at work.

### HOW TO LEAVE WITHOUT LOSING OUR FAITH

To leave churchianity with our faith intact, we would need to be utterly convinced that organized religion is not God's will. Our conscience would have to be 100% clear. We could have *no* guilt, *no* qualms of conscience, *no* lingering doubts, *no* fear of God's disapproval. We would need to be absolutely, unquestionably certain that God neither authorized church government nor does He approve of its practices. We need to be able to completely separate real Christianity from the counterfeit version.

But is that kind of absolute certainty possible to attain? And even if it is, how could we possibly attain it? There's only one way we could be that unshakably certain: God Himself would have to tell us. Furthermore, His answer would need to satisfy three conditions: God would have to have told us:

1. already,

2. in writing,

3. in the New Testament.

### Q&A TIME

**1. Q: Why already?**
**A:** Because only Christ's apostles were authorized to speak for God (we'll explain this in the next section). John, the last surviving apostle of Christ, died

in AD 100. After that, God would have had to communicate via non-apostles or unwritten tradition. And as we will see, that path leads into, not out of, churchianity.

**2. Q: Why in writing?**

**A:** Because it's the only sure way to know what God says. Christians may disagree over whether the Bible is *sola* or *prima*, that is, whether the Bible is *the only* or simply *the primary* basis for Christian faith and practice, but we all agree that the written Bible is God's Word.

**3. Q: Finally, why only the New Testament?** Why *not* the whole Bible?

**A:** Because in the first mention of His Ekklesia in Matthew 16:18 Jesus said "I will build," not "I have built." Don't bother looking for Jesus' Ekklesia in the Old Testament; it hadn't been built yet.

Either God has already told us everything we need to know to leave organized religion, or else He hasn't. If He hasn't, then there's no escape from churchianity. But if He has, then the New Testament holds our only path to freedom.

Consider this radical possibility: what if God *has* already told us? What if the New Testament clearly and plainly tells us everything—and I mean *everything*—that we need to fully and finally escape from churchianity?

But if that's true (and it is, and we're going to prove it)—where is it stated? Why haven't we seen it? Is it possible we could have *mythed* it - excuse me - missed it? As one pastor I knew often put it, "Book, chapter, and verse, please?"

There are two ways God could tell us that He doesn't approve of organized religion. One way would be negative. Christ's apostles could have expressly prohibited putting a visible head over every congregation. They could have written something along the lines of "Thou shalt not have a presiding elder in thy churches."

The problem with prohibitions is that they need to be specific and comprehensive. They'd need to cover every possible thing that could go wrong. The result would be endless lists of rules.

The other way God could tell us would be positive. Instead of endless prohibitions, Christ's apostles could simply have thoroughly documented the design of Jesus' Ekklesia. They could have told us the Ekklesia's purpose and precisely how it functions. Then if anyone tried to alter their design we'd be able to spot the changes and reject them.

Does the New Testament thoroughly document the Ekklesia's design? Did Christ's apostles tell us its purpose and explain precisely how it functions? As a matter of fact, yes it does and yes they did. And their documented design makes organized religion impossible. But for about 1,800 years we've been unable to see what the New Testament really tells us.

The reason we think that organized religion must be God's will is because the Church Infancy Myth controls how we understand—or rather, myth-understand—the Bible. The Myth tricks us into looking in the wrong direction—looking for what isn't there. And when we look for what isn't there, what's actually there becomes invisible. In the next chapter, we will explore what myth-interpretation is and how it works.

## Endnotes

1    Don Felder et al. *Hotel California.* Asylum, 1976. Vinyl recording.

2    NET Study Note.

3    *"Quod ubique, quod semper, quod omnibus creditum est."* (Ramm, *Protestant Biblical Interpretation,* 43).

4    Orr, *International Standard Bible Encyclopedia,* "Bishop"

5    Shelley, *Church History In Plain Language: Updated 2<sup>nd</sup> Edition,* 72.

6    Paraphrased from Oscar Wilde's 1892 poem, *Two Loves.* Original: "The love that dares not speak its name."

7    Youngblood, *Nelson's Bible Dictionary,* "Church Government"

8    Niebuhr et al, *The Ministry in Historical Perspectives,* 3.

Chapter 3

# MYTH-UNDERSTANDING THE BIBLE

God has already told us, in writing, in the New Testament, that He didn't authorize organized religion and He doesn't approve of its practices. Christ's apostles documented everything we need to know in order to leave organized religion without losing our faith. The New Testament is our road map, compass, and GPS.

So where is all of this stated? If it's there, shouldn't it be obvious? Then why haven't we seen it?

We can't see it because the Church Infancy Myth controls how we understand the Bible.

Since the early third century (circa AD 220), virtually all Christendom has practiced some form of church government. For 1,800 years organized religion has had to keep Christians convinced that God authorized and approves of the counterfeit version of Christianity. But the New Testament poses a double obstacle to churchianity's deception:

1. It contains no mention of church government;

2. The documented design of Jesus' Ekklesia makes church government impossible.

In order to succeed, organized religion has had to trick Christians into seeing what isn't there—church government and "worship" services—and not seeing what is there—the design and functioning of Jesus' Ekklesia. That was easy when there were no printed Bibles and few people could read. But how is it possible today? Today we have printed Bibles in our own language and can read them. How can the Myth possibly keep us from seeing what is in plain sight, in black and white, right before our eyes throughout the New Testament? How can the Myth make God's words invisible?

The trick is mental misdirection. We can't see what the New Testament says because (A) we're not looking for it, and (B) we're looking for something entirely different, something opposite. The Myth tricks us into looking in the wrong direction. Like a skilled magician's sleight of hand, it directs our attention away from what is right before us. We've all been looking for what isn't there. And when we look for what isn't there, what's actually there becomes invisible.

### THE MYTH'S BIG LIE

Organized religion begins with a Big Lie: that church government is God's will. And how do we know it's God's will? That's easy: according to organized religion, it is because He *didn't tell us about it!* The fact that there's no church government or "worship" anywhere in the New Testament ought to make us question and doubt the Myth. But seduced by the Myth's Big Lie, we question and doubt the New Testament instead.

Both versions of the Myth create confusion, uncertainty, and doubt about the New Testament. Both versions claim that the New Testament doesn't tell us everything God wants us to know about Christianity.

According to the Myth's original version, Christ's apostles were short-sighted and incompetent. They failed to design Jesus' Ekklesia for the long haul. Their inadequate design had to be completely revised after AD 100. What they believed, practiced, taught, and documented in the New Testament was temporary, partial, and incomplete.

According to the Myth's stealth version, God wants us to have church government but He left the details up to us. In other words, the New Testament is a fill-in-the-blank divine revelation. That's what the Westminster Confession of Faith means when it says that church government and worship must be ordered "by the light of nature and Christian prudence" instead of, "expressly set down in Scripture," or . . . "deduced from Scripture."

When we can't find organized religion's teachings and practices, we blame the New Testament for being silent. But that's because we've fallen for the Myth's Big Lie. We've already accepted organized religion as the standard, the pattern, the frame of reference for understanding the Bible. But the New Testament's silence isn't an error or omission, it's a clue. It tells us we're looking in the wrong direction. We're looking for what isn't there.

### HIGHER AUTHORITY THAN THE BIBLE

When we accept the Myth's Big Lie, organized religion becomes a higher authority than the Bible.

Jesus is the Word, or *Logos*,[1] of God made flesh—God's Word in human form. The Bible is God's Word in written form. When second century Christian leaders made the bishop (or pastor) the visible, acting head of each congregation, that man became a higher authority than Jesus, a subject we'll come back to later. And when the bishop (or pastor) became a higher authority than God's word in human form (Jesus), organized religion became a higher authority than God's *written* word.

As the higher authority, organized religion is the standard by which we interpret and understand the Bible. The Myth tells us which parts of the New Testament to take literally and which parts to take "spiritually," (that is, mystically or non-normally); which parts are still in effect and which parts have been rescinded or revoked; which instructions and examples to follow and which to ignore because they're "not for today."

Organized religion has brainwashed Christians to believe the Myth and blame the Bible. It teaches us that the Bible must always be made to conform to organized religion, never vice versa. Whenever organized religion and the Bible disagree, the problem must then be with the Bible, not with organized religion. Any inconsistencies, discrepancies, disagreements, and contradictions must always be resolved in churchianity's favor, according to organized religion.

For this to work, organized religion cannot, however, appear to contradict the Bible; Christians may disagree about whether the Bible is *sola* or *prima*, but we all agree that it is God's written Word. We would never be fooled if churchianity openly opposed the Bible.

Organized religion must keep Christians convinced that the Bible agrees with its teachings and practices without appearing to contradict God's words. Getting us to *look* for what isn't there is only half the job, however. To succeed as a counterfeit, organized religion must also trick us into *finding* what isn't there. But since there's no church government in the New Testament, how can we find what doesn't exist?

The only way to "find" organized religion in the New Testament is to *myth-interpret* the Bible. We've all inherited a seductive deception about God's written Word. Organized religion claims that the Bible is so different, so holy, so spiritual, that it cannot be understood normally, the same way we interpret and understand all other written communication. Instead, it must be interpreted non-normally, or mystically.

Non-normal, mystical interpretation appears temptingly spiritual. It entices us by promising to reveal deeper meanings, hidden truths. But its true purpose is to create doubt and unbelief. It makes God's Word confusing, obscure, and hard to understand.

### FINDING WHAT ISN'T THERE

Have you ever thought that the Bible is hard to understand? Does it ever seem like a pile of doctrinal jigsaw puzzle pieces with no picture on the box? Why is the New Testament silent about church government and worship? Why are we left to infer the purpose, design, and functioning of Jesus' Ekklesia from "the light of nature, and Christian prudence . . ."?[2] Why are we forced to fill in the blanks from cherry-picked proof texts?

At my parents' church we called ourselves Bible believers. We held 2 Timothy 3:16 to be literally true: God so inspired the authors of the sixty-six books of the Bible that the very words they wrote were "God-breathed." We recognized that the Bible was divinely inspired in every thought and word:[3] infallible, inerrant, and the sole basis for all doctrine and practice, and which alone can bind a believer's conscience.

Yet as a teenager I had almost given up trying to make sense out of the Bible. At our church, sermons often hopscotched all over the Old and New Testaments, pulling out a verse here or part of a verse there, piecing together whatever it was that God wanted us to know. Instead of being stated clearly and straightforwardly all in one place, our doctrines often depended on hints and inferences scattered throughout the entire Bible.

The Bible appeared mystical, impossible to understand normally, the way I understood other written works. Inexplicably, proof texts often turned up in the middle of longer passages that seemed to be talking about something else entirely. Cherished denominational dogmas were frequently based on a single word or phrase completely divorced from the larger context. It seemed that the Bible's authors could hardly ever manage to stay on topic for even one sentence at a time.

Apparently God's idea of communicating was to break up His message into small fragments and then sprinkle them randomly throughout the entire Bible. The only way to figure out what God was trying to tell us was first to learn all my church's doctrines, then sift through the entire Old and New Testaments to find all the bits and pieces, and finally reassemble them all in the correct order.

Obviously when God said "For my thoughts are not your thoughts, neither are your ways my ways . . ." (Isa 55:8 KJV), *He wasn't kidding!* I was relieved that my church had all the correct doctrines because I could never have found them on my own.

What I didn't know then was that my confusion wasn't God's fault. The Bible isn't mystical and God can and does communicate clearly. My problem was that, at my church, we were still using mystical methods of myth-interpretation from the Middle Ages. Without realizing it, I had been taught to myth-interpret God's Word.

## MEDIEVAL MYTH-INTERPRETATION

As organized religion developed, medieval theologians found themselves between a rock and a hard place. The rock was the New Testament; the hard place was churchianity's doctrines. Taken literally, normally, at face value—the same way we interpret and understand all other written communication—the New Testament made organized religion impossible.

Their solution was to interpret the Bible non-normally. The Bible was so different, so holy, so spiritual, that it could not be understood literally or normally. Thomas Aquinas, the thirteenth-century philosopher and theologian, taught that "God was able to inspire men in such a way that they wrote not only literal and historical truth but spiritual and figurative truth."[4] But the only way to discover those non-literal "spiritual" meanings was to interpret God's words non-normally: to *myth*-interpret the Bible – to interpret the Bible in a mystical manner instead of a literal one. In his textbook *Principles of Biblical Interpretation* Louis Berkhof describes how this worked:

> During the Middle Ages, many, even of the clergy, lived in profound ignorance of the Bible . . . It was generally regarded as a book full of mysteries, which could be understood only in a mystical manner . . . it became an established principle that the interpretation of the Bible had to adapt itself to tradition and to the doctrine of the Church. It was considered to be the acme of wisdom to reproduce the teachings of the Fathers, and to find the teachings of the Church in the Bible . . . Hugo of St. Victor even said: "Learn first what you should believe, and then go to the Bible to find it there."[5]

Let's summarize churchianity's teachings regarding biblical interpretation:

- The Bible must be understood non-normally;

- Interpretation of the Bible must reproduce churchianity's teachings;

- First learn what you should believe, then find it in the Bible.

At my parents' church none of us had ever heard of Hugo of St. Victor.

But we were still following his wrong advice. We already knew what we should believe. And obviously the Bible had to support our church's teachings. So we found our doctrines the same way the medieval theologians found theirs: by interpreting the Bible non-normally.

But brother Hugo's method of interpretation is upside-down, backwards. It's wag-the-dog, cart-before-the-horse theology. It's like Alice in Wonderland's Red Queen demanding "Sentence first—verdict afterwards." And the notion that the Bible is so different, so holy, and so spiritual that it cannot be understood normally is sanctimonious nonsense. It's just circular reasoning posing as superior spirituality.

### ORGANIZED RELIGION'S VICIOUS CIRCLE

Myth-interpretation is a vicious circle: a self-reinforcing and self-perpetuating trap of circular reasoning. We myth-interpret the Bible because we believe it is mystical. But myth-interpretation is what makes the Bible mystical in the first place.

The unwritten rule is: the Bible must reproduce churchianity's teachings. So we myth-interpret the Bible to make it agree with churchianity's teachings. Then we believe those teachings because "the Bible tells us so." Christians have been repeating history, going round and round in churchianity's vicious circle since the Middle Ages.

We're going to have to break out of the trap. But how do we do that? Consider this radical possibility: what if we didn't have to make the Bible reproduce churchianity's teachings? What if instead of myth-interpreting the Bible, we understood it normally, the same way we understand all other written communication?

If we dared to do that, we might find—well—what we're going to cover in the rest of this book. The New Testament shows us the way out of churchianity's trap, but only when we understand it correctly—normally. To leave organized religion without losing our faith, we'll have to stop myth-interpreting the Bible and understand it as normal written communication.

That sounds simple enough. The problem is: we don't know how. We've never been taught to understand the Bible correctly, that is, *normally* and *non-mystically*. Ever since the third century, myth-interpretation has been the only game in town. After centuries of reading the Bible upside-down, we don't know there's any other way. We can't tell the difference; we don't even know there is a difference.

We can't stop myth-interpreting the Bible if we don't know we're doing it. So our first order of business is to learn to recognize myth-interpretation. We've already mentioned one type of non-normal interpretation: treating the

Bible as a collection of proof texts. Out-of-context (OOC) proof-texting is the most obvious way that churchianity turns the Bible upside-down. But there are other ways that are even worse but not at all obvious.

What is myth-interpretation? If myth-interpretation is the wrong way to understand the Bible, is there a right way? Do we know what it is? What is normal interpretation? How is it different from myth-interpretation? How can we tell the difference?

## Endnotes

1  Greek: *Logos*: LOW-gahs; John 1:14; NT:3056

2  "Nevertheless, we acknowledge... that there are some circumstances concerning the worship of God, and government of the Church... which are to be ordered by the light of nature, and Christian prudence, according to the general rules of the Word..." (Westminster Assembly, 1646).

3  The original words of the authors, not necessarily the words of copies or translations.

4  Ramm, *Protestant Biblical Interpretation*, 40-41.

5  Berkhof, *Principles of Biblical Interpretation*, 23.

Chapter 4

# THE BIBLE
# RIGHT-SIDE-UP

The New Testament shows us the way out of organized religion's vicious circle, but by teaching Christians to first decide what to believe, then look for it in the Bible, myth-interpretation keeps us from perceiving what it says by twisting it out of context. The myth tells us we must reach a conclusion first (the one Churchianity tells us is correct,) *then* read the Bible to find it. This is not just backwards - it's upside-down and mystifying at best. To leave organized religion without losing our faith, we'll have to turn the Bible right-side-up and understand it as normal written communication.

That sounds simple enough. The problem is, we've been reading the Bible non-normally for so long that we do it without realizing it. We can't stop myth-interpreting the Bible if we don't know we're doing it. In order to turn the Bible right-side-up, we must be able to recognize the difference between normal and non-normal interpretation. At the beginning of this book, I said we first needed to accept that there *is* a counterfeit version of Christianity, and then learn to distinguish the two; and that means being able to see what's actually there in the Bible, not what the Myth tells us is there. So our path out of organized religion continues by learning to recognize myth-interpretation.

What is myth-interpretation? If it's wrong, is there a right way to understand the Bible? Do we know what it is? Has God told us anything about it, or do we have to fill in the blanks?

### ACCURATE VERSUS TWISTED

There is a correct way to understand the Bible. We know this because the Apostle Paul told Timothy to use God's Word the right way:

> Be diligent to present yourself approved to God as a workman who does not need to be ashamed, *accurately handling* the word of truth. (2 Tim 2:15 NASU, emphasis mine)

Since there's a right way—an accurate way—to use the Bible, there must also be a wrong way—an inaccurate way—to use it. And the Apostle Peter warned us about it:

> Some things in these letters are hard to understand, things the ignorant and unstable *twist* to their own destruction, *as they also do to the rest of the scriptures.* (2 Peter 3:16, emphasis mine)

But what did Paul and Peter mean? How do we accurately handle God's Word? What does it mean to twist God's words, and how do we avoid doing it? Why didn't Paul and Peter explain what they meant?

They didn't explain because the answer is self-evident. It's so obvious that we miss it for the same reason that fish don't know they're wet. The answer is constantly all around us. We have always been surrounded by the answer.

Here's a clue: the Bible is *written*. It's *writing*. And there are only two ways to understand *any* writing: normally or non-normally. And everyone who can read already knows the normal way to understand writing. It's just the plain, normal, literal, at-face-value meaning of the words *in context*.

Myth-interpretation twists God's words out of context. We've already mentioned the most obvious way: treating the Bible as a collection of proof texts. But as mentioned, there are two other ways that are even worse but not at all obvious. That's because there are three types or levels of context. These three levels of context are how we understand any writing normally. Myth-interpretation violates all three.

We're going to identify each level of context and show how myth-interpretation twists it. I mentioned "book, chapter, and verse" previously and that's where we'll begin.

### LEVEL 1 CONTEXT: THE PROBLEM WITH VERSES

The first type or level of context is the physical one we're all familiar with. It consists of:

1. The text immediately before and after a passage;

2. The rest of the book or letter; and

3. The rest of the Bible.

Myth-interpretation violates level 1 context by means of chapters and verses.

Verses caused much of my youthful confusion about the Bible. Our church emphasized Bible memorization. That was good. But what we memorized were verses. With my mind focused on verses, the larger context became virtually invisible. Without ever being told to, I learned to view the Bible as a random collection of unrelated, numbered sayings. Our verse-based sermons reinforced my misunderstanding.

At our church we had a joke that illustrated the problem with verses:

> The Bible says Judas went out and hanged himself (Matt 27:5). "Go, and do thou likewise" (Luke 10:37 KJV). "That thou doest, do quickly." (John 13:27 KJV).

We laughed because we knew that God didn't want us to hang ourselves. Yet it seemed never to occur to us that our proof text sermons were often guilty of the same error.

And yet officially we've known better for at least seventy years. In his textbook *Principles of Biblical Interpretation*, published in 1950, Louis Berkhof pointedly explained:

> The absolute necessity of taking particular notice of the preceding and following, the near and remote connection of a passage, can scarcely be over-emphasized . . . And yet this is often neglected, especially by those who regard the Bible as a collection of proof-texts.[1]

To further illustrate the problem with verses, I want to point out that God didn't divide His written communication into chapters and verses. Chapters were added by Stephen Langton in 1205; verses by Robert Estienne-Stephanus-Stephens in 1551 while on a journey from Paris to Lyons.[2] Stephens' verse divisions defy logic, linguistics, and common sense. The joke among seminary students is that he did the work on horseback, and every bump or jolt in the road jogged his arm and resulted in a new verse in the Bible.

Viewing the Bible as a random collection of unrelated, numbered "Sayings of Chairman God," and then mixing and matching them to "prove" absolutely anything, is no joke. "A text without a context is a pretext"[3] for interpreting the Bible non-normally; for putting words into God's mouth; and for finding what isn't there—things that God never said. And many Christians do this without even knowing it.

Some years ago I was a guest at a Christian high school-aged youth group meeting. The teenagers were discussing problems they faced at church. One young woman complained that adults often dismissed young peoples' concerns and opinions as unimportant. This was wrong, she declared, because the Bible says "let no man despise thy youth."

Well, give her credit for knowing the Bible well enough to quote 1 Timothy 4:12. But her argument was a textbook example of using verses to take God's words out of context. It was also an example of *universalization*, a violation of level 3 context which we'll get to later in the chapter.

How did this young woman come to view the Bible this way? She couldn't have invented it because we were doing the same thing at my parents' church more than fifty years earlier. So she and her friends must have learned it. But how did they learn it? Who taught them to myth-interpret God's Word in this manner?

The answer is: nobody taught them. They learned it by osmosis, the same way I did, without ever knowing they learned it.

We know better than to do this with any other written works, yet we do it with the Bible, creating confusion and uncertainty. As Bernard Ramm observed in *Protestant Biblical Interpretation*:

> In view of the frequent neglect of context especially in preaching we may sympathize with Robertson's remark that "the first step in interpretation is to ignore modern chapters and verses."[4]

### LEVEL 2 CONTEXT: LINGUISTIC, HISTORICAL, AND CULTURAL BACKGROUND

The second type or level of context is the text's linguistic, historical, and cultural background. We call it the *grammatical-historical context*. It's how we understand any writing from other times and cultures. Accurately handling God's Word requires that we take into account the text's grammatical forms and historical, cultural background.

Myth-interpretation violates this second type of context via silence. By keeping us ignorant about the Bible's grammatical-historical-cultural background, organized religion dupes us into concluding that the Bible is hard to understand and that God cannot or does not communicate clearly.

For example, in Jesus' statement in Matthew 11:29-30, what do the words yoke and burden mean?

> "Take my *yoke* upon you, and learn of me; for I am meek and lowly in heart: and ye shall find rest unto your souls. For my *yoke* is easy, and my *burden* is light." (KJV, emphasis mine)

For most of my life I assumed Jesus was speaking metaphorically. A literal yoke is a wooden device used to harness animals together for the purpose of pulling a load. And Jesus implied that He was pulling a load: "my burden." So this passage meant that Jesus wanted me to get harnessed together with Him and help Him pull a load, but the load didn't weigh much and pulling it would be easy.

But *how* was I supposed to get harnessed up with Jesus, and *what* was the load He wanted me to help pull? That was never explained. I supposed that today Jesus' burden was my church's ministry and helping Him pull it meant supporting church programs and activities.

Eventually I learned the truth. Jesus wasn't talking about a metaphorical yoke or even about pulling a load. In first century Israel, yoke and burden were rabbinical figures of speech. A rabbi's yoke was his teaching. His burden meant his commands and prohibitions.[5] Because I had never been taught the linguistic, historical, and cultural context of these words, I never understood what Jesus meant.

### LEVEL 3 CONTEXT: NORMAL VERSUS MYSTICAL

The third level of context is the normal, literal, at-face-value meaning of the text as determined by the first two levels. This is distinctly different from mystical, or *non-normal* interpretation which we'll now address so you can know the difference. In his book *To Be Continued?*, Dr. Samuel Waldron notes three types of non-normal, or mystical interpretation common among evangelicals; these three types are:

1. Spiritualizing,

2. Universalizing,

3. Devotionalizing.[6]

We're going to consider how each of these techniques violate level 3 context. We'll start with spiritualizing, otherwise known as allegorical misinterpretation, because it's the most common.

**1. Spiritualizing (or allegorizing)** assigns to the text a symbolic meaning different from its literal, normal meaning. This is sometimes called the deeper or spiritual meaning. It's a seductive and insidious way to impose a foreign meaning on God's words; to put words in God's mouth; to make God appear to say things He never said.

In my parents' church the Old Testament book of Malachi was spiritualized to teach that Christians owed God ten percent of their income:

> Will a man rob God? Yet ye have robbed me. But ye say, Wherein have we
> robbed thee? In tithes and offerings. Ye are cursed with a curse: for ye have

robbed me, even this whole nation.

> Bring ye all the tithes into the storehouse, that there may be meat in mine house, and prove me now herewith, saith the Lord of hosts, if I will not open you the windows of heaven, and pour you out a blessing, that there shall not be room enough to receive it. (Mal 3:8-10 KJV)

Malachi's prophecy has a normal, literal meaning. Malachi's tithes consisted of crops and animals, not money. The storehouse was a building where the crops were stored. "Meat in mine house" meant literal food in a literal temple.

Tithing applied only to the nation of Israel, and *only in the old covenant* – that is, the Old Testament. The new covenant is quite distinct from the old covenant, and Christians are no longer bound to the old one. But the spiritualized version was applied to Christians. "Tithes" no longer meant crops and animals, but ten percent of our wages (before taxes!). The storehouse meant the church building. Meat in mine house meant money in my church. And failure to tithe was a sin: non-tithers were guilty of robbing God and were under a curse.

Churches that teach tithing are forced to allegorize the Old Testament book of Malachi because the New Testament is silent on the subject. Matthew 23:23 and Luke 11:42 are sometimes cited as proof that Jesus taught tithing:

> "Woe to you, experts in the law and you Pharisees, hypocrites! You give a tenth of mint, dill, and cumin, yet you neglect what is more important in the law—justice, mercy, and faithfulness! You should have done these things without neglecting the others." (Matt 23:23)

> "But woe to you Pharisees! You give a tenth of your mint, rue, and every herb, yet you neglect justice and love for God! But you should have done these things without neglecting the others." (Luke 11:42)

But to claim that these two passages prove Jesus taught tithing is another example of universalizing - our second type of mystical interpretation.

**2. Universalizing** is the notion that the entire Bible—every promise, command, prohibition, instruction, and example in the Old and New Testaments—applies to every Christian at all times. In our earlier example, the high school student who quoted "Let no man despise thy youth" was unwittingly universalizing Paul's instruction to Timothy, treating it as a general principle applicable to all Christians.

The most dangerous type of universalizing confuses the Old and New Covenants. It seduces Christians into placing themselves under Old Covenant law—the very thing Paul warned against in his Galatian letter.

Failure to distinguish the New Covenant from the Old causes us to misunderstand Jesus' teaching. Here's a trick question that illustrates the error: which covenant did Jesus teach? The correct answer is, He taught both. Jesus was born under the Old Covenant—under the law (Gal 4:4). The New Covenant didn't begin until He died:

> And so he is the mediator of a new covenant, so that those who are called may receive the eternal inheritance he has promised, since he died to set them free from the violations committed under the first covenant. For where there is a will, the death of the one who made it must be proven. For a will takes effect only at death, since it carries no force while the one who made it is alive. (Hebrews 9:15-17)

According to Matthew 23:23, tithing was part of the Old Covenant law. Citing that passage to prove that Jesus taught Christian tithing confuses the two covenants and puts Christians under the Old Covenant.

Universalizing includes using the Old Covenant as a pattern or template for Jesus' New Covenant Ekklesia. The Old Testament's temple, priesthood, and ritual worship practices are "Christianized" (i.e. allegorized) to supply those missing New Testament doctrines—organized religion's church buildings, clergy, and worship rituals. Yet Jesus told the woman at the well that God was no longer interested in temples and ritual worship (John 4:21-24).

**3. Devotionalizing** comes in two forms, both of which are also types of universalization. A *devotion* typically consists of a verse, a reflection, and a prayer. The problem occurs when the reflection ignores level 1 context. As Samuel Waldron points out:

> Many passages and promises addressed first or even exclusively to the apostles of Christ are spiritualized or devotionalized and applied to all Christians.

The other form of devotionalizing treats the Bible as a kind of divine Ouija Board or Magic 8-Ball: a mystic oracle that provides daily personal direction and guidance. Bernard Ramm gives the example of a pious Christian who is considering taking a trip:

> In his devotions he reads how the Church at Antioch sent Paul and Barnabas away on a missionary trip. So this Christian feels that God is speaking to him in that passage and it is now God's will that he should take the proposed trip.[7]

My favorite example of this second type of devotionalizing is the story of the Christian businessman who showed up at church one Sunday looking troubled. The pastor asked him what was wrong. He explained that his business was having serious financial problems and he just didn't know what to do.

The pastor told him: "When you get home, close your eyes and spin your

Bible around three times. Then open it, put your finger on a page, open your eyes, and do whatever it says."

The following Sunday the businessman showed up at church happy and smiling. The pastor asked him, "Did you follow my advice?" "Yes," replied the man, "and it worked! Everything's okay now."

"That's wonderful," said the pastor. "What did the Bible tell you to do?"

And the businessman answered, "Chapter 13!"[8]

### WE KNOW BETTER, BUT . . .

Twisting God's words out of context in the ways we've just reviewed can make the Bible appear to say anything churchianity wants it to say. Any written work, ancient or modern, would seem confusing, obscure, and hard to understand if misinterpreted in this manner.

We would never be so gullible if anyone tried to trick us into doing all this nonsense with any other written communication. So why do we think we're supposed to do it with God's written Sacred Communication? Because organized religion's unwritten rule is that the Bible must reproduce churchianity's teachings. And non-normal interpretation is the only way to make it do that.

Officially we know better. Evangelical Christians have developed possibly the best set of principles for correctly understanding Scripture that anyone has ever seen: the 1982 *Chicago Statement on Biblical Hermeneutics* (and also the 1978 *Chicago Statement on Biblical Inerrancy*).

Too many Christians are convinced that the Bible is hard to understand and that figuring out what Scripture teaches is best left to ordained experts. But God is confident in our ability to understand His written Sacred Communication. If He wasn't, He wouldn't have communicated in writing.

**Endnotes**

1    Berkhof, *Principles of Biblical Interpretation*, 104-105.

2    Stone, n.d. "Chapters and Verses"

3    The full quote, which Dr. Donald A. Carson ascribes to his father, a Canadian minister, was "A text without a context is a pretext for a proof text."

4    Ramm, *Protestant Biblical Interpretation*, 140.

5    "Yoke": Greek: *Zygos*. zoo-GAHS; Matthew 11:30; NT:2218

"Burden" (KJV); "Load" (NET): Greek: *Phortion*. far-TEE-on; Matthew 11:30; NT:5413

6    Waldron, *To Be Continued*, 23.

7    Ramm, *Protestant Biblical Interpretation*, 112.

8    From uscourts.gov: "A chapter 13 bankruptcy is also called a wage earner's plan. It enables individuals with regular income to develop a plan to repay all or part of their debts."

Chapter 5

# MYTHBUSTING
# ORGANIZED RELIGION

Now that we know how myth-interpretation works, we're ready to bust organized religion's myth-theology. We're going to show that the Church Infancy Myth is a lie from start to finish. Church government is not God's will. God neither authorized church government nor does He approve of its practices. Once we're certain of that, we can leave organized religion with a clear conscience and without losing our faith.

Organized religion's problem has always been the New Testament. Understood normally, it makes church government impossible. To keep Christians trapped in churchianity, organized religion has to contradict God's words without appearing to do so. Non-normal myth-interpretation keeps us from noticing the contradictions. It keeps us from seeing what God has already plainly told us, in writing, in the New Testament.

Organized religion accomplishes its sleight of mind through accusations disguised as explanations. I mentioned in chapter 3 that the first and greatest accusation is that the New Testament is silent about church government and "worship." That's true, but it's not because God somehow failed to tell us everything we need to know about the design and functioning of Jesus' Ekklesia.

The accusation of silence is a subterfuge, a smoke screen, a red herring. It focuses our minds in the wrong direction. It tricks us into looking for what isn't there instead of looking at what's actually there. It causes confusion, doubt, and unbelief about God's written Sacred Communication, the Bible.

In the rest of this book we're going to expose organized religion's accusations and show how they contradict God's words. We're going to bring to light what the New Testament tells us about Jesus' Ekklesia. We're going to see what the Myth has kept us from seeing.

### DISGUISED ACCUSATIONS

We'll begin by reviewing the Myth's two versions. First the original:

> . . . the apostles and early Christians . . . were looking for the speedy return
> of Christ, and consequently did not organize the church in its infancy, as it
> was *afterward found necessary to do.*[1] (emphasis mine)

Next, the stealth:

> At first, church organization and government in the New Testament was
> flexible to meet changing needs. But as the church became better established,
> it gave attention to *the right structures and procedures* that would help it accom-
> plish its mission . . . Thus, numerous forms of church government are used
> today *to provide order and structure* for the work of churches.[2] (emphasis mine)

On the surface, both versions of the Myth appear harmless and even help-ful. They're simply two different ways of explaining the New Testament's puzzling silence about church government and "worship." After all, doesn't everyone agree that churches need to be organized? As one of my college professors quipped, "people complain about organized religion. What do they want—*dis*organized religion?"

So what's the problem? How can these innocent-sounding explanations actually accuse the New Testament, Christ's apostles, and the Lord Jesus?

The original version's accusation is straightforward: Jesus' apostles failed to provide necessary organization.

The stealth version's accusation is deviously indirect. It claims that Jesus' apostles approved of and practiced church government but never managed to settle on a single design. Consequently their documentation doesn't clearly provide "the right structures and procedures" that the Ekklesia requires to accomplish its mission.

If that's true, then either the New Testament is confusing or else it's in-complete. But it gets worse: if the apostles' documented design wasn't *right*, then it was *wrong*. And if church government was necessary to provide order and structure, then what the apostles built and documented was *dis*ordered and *un*structured.

By making these accusations, the Myth implicitly claims to be a higher au-thority than the Bible. It claims to know what God intended but never put in writing. It claims the authority to correct the Bible's errors.

The Myth's explanations are actually insidious and pernicious. They seduce us into accepting and believing things that we would never tolerate if stated plainly.

### THE UNSPOKEN MEANING BEHIND BOTH OF THE MYTH'S VERSIONS

Jesus' apostles—the men He selected as His personal ambassadors—whom He commissioned to teach and make disciples for Him—whom He authorized and inspired to build His Ekklesia and record divine revelation in writing—didn't do a very good job. At best, their work was temporary and incomplete; at worst, short-sighted and incompetent. The churches they founded had to be totally redesigned after their lifetimes. The divine revelation they recorded was silent on vitally important doctrinal matters, and sometimes wildly misleading when it was not missing entirely.

**Not only that:** in AD 95 Jesus had a golden opportunity to correct all the errors and omissions of Matthew, Peter, James, John, Paul, Luke, John Mark and the rest when He gave His *Revelation* to John. Needless to say, He failed to do so, leaving Christians with a written divine revelation that was full of holes, riddled with errors, and dangerously confusing. It would now take the "church fathers" several centuries to supply the missing pieces and correct Christ's apostles' mistakes in teaching and practice.

Accusing and discrediting Christ's apostles creates doubt and unbelief about the New Testament. That's no accident. In order to legitimize church government, the Myth *has to* get around, circumvent, nullify, and explain away what is documented in those twenty-seven books and letters. It has to twist God's words to find what isn't there and keep us from noticing its own inconsistencies, discrepancies, disagreements, and contradictions.

What contradictions are we talking about?

### CONTRADICTIONS

Earlier we read Dr. Bruce Shelley's statement about second-century changes raising "crucial and controversial questions."[3] What sort of questions? Well, if God really did authorize church government, then here's what must also be true:

- Although He never said so and even stated the opposite on more than one occasion,[4] Jesus must have actually intended for His Ekklesia to have political control.

- When Jesus said "I will build my church" (Matt 16:18), He had no particular design in mind. The design and functioning of His Ekklesia wasn't important. One form of government was as good as another and any kind would do.

- In AD 95 when He gave His *Revelation* to the Apostle John, Jesus had a golden opportunity to tell us to put one man in charge, but He didn't mention it. Why? Did it just slip His mind?

- None of the apostles of Christ ever told us to put one man in charge of each local Ekklesia. Why? Couldn't they think of such a simple and obvious solution to false teaching?

- The Apostle Paul wrote ". . . like a skilled master-builder I laid a foundation, but someone else builds on it. And each one must be careful how he builds" (1 Cor 3:9-10). Obviously Paul thought there was a right way and a wrong way to build Jesus' Ekklesia. But according to organized religion, neither he nor the rest of Christ's apostles managed to get it right.

- Paul told Timothy that God's written Sacred Communication contained everything necessary for us to be wise for salvation and thoroughly equipped for every good work (2 Tim 3:15-16). But when it came to the matter of church government—the issue over which nonconformist Christians would be persecuted, tortured, and murdered for centuries to come—God's attitude was, "Oh well, that goes without saying: fight it out among yourselves"?

- Christ's apostles documented either a wrong design or else a partial and temporary one. Only after they died did Christian leaders, aka "church fathers," finally figure out the right structures and procedures that would allow Jesus' Ekklesia to fulfill its mission.

- The design and functioning of Jesus' Ekklesia documented in the New Testament by the apostles of Christ is not complete and permanent; rather, it is partial and temporary.

- If the New Testament presents only a partial and temporary plan for something as important as Jesus' Ekklesia, what other important things might also have been left out?

Thus if God really did authorize church government; if He really does approve of those seven practices listed in chapter two: then either the New Testament is temporary, partial, and incomplete, or else it's confusing, obscure, and hard to understand. If that's true, we're stuck with a written divine revelation that is full of holes, riddled with errors, and dangerously confusing.

And to figure out what God wants us to know, we would either need to turn to unwritten tradition and the selected writings of non-apostles, or else fill in the blanks from cherry-picked proof texts and then universalize, spiritualize, and devotionalize them as required to reproduce churchianity's teachings. That's one option.

## THE UNSPEAKABLE ALTERNATIVE

There is, of course, another explanation for the New Testament's silence about church government and "worship." This alternative explanation is simple and logical. It doesn't contradict the New Testament or accuse Christ's apostles. But its implications are—unspeakable! It's so unthinkable that almost no one in 1,900 years of church history has considered it: what if God is silent on the subject of church government because *there isn't supposed to be any*?

What if the New Testament isn't missing anything? What if it is neither temporary, partial, and incomplete, nor confusing, obscure, and hard to understand? What if it is perfectly clear and understandable and the problem is with organized religion?

What if the reason we can't find churchianity's teachings and practices is because Jesus' Ekklesia has nothing to do with political organization and control? What if the New Testament fully documents the design and functioning of Jesus' Ekklesia? What if that design is so different, so opposite from political organization that when we look for organized religion, the Ekklesia's design becomes invisible?

And what if the New Testament isn't silent at all about worship? What if the entire New Testament is actually a worship manual? What if the problem is that we're looking for organized religion's wrong definition of worship?

If these things are true, that would mean we'd have to stop requiring the Bible to reproduce churchianity's teachings. We'd have to reject the Myth as a higher authority than God's Word. We'd have to believe the Bible and blame the Myth. We'd have to resolve all inconsistencies, discrepancies, disagreements, or contradictions in the Bible's favor.

And we'd have to do all of this without twisting God's words out of context. We'd have to treat the Bible as normal written communication. We'd have to interpret and understand God's words the same way we understand all other written communication.

The problem is, the Myth tells Christians that the Bible *isn't* normal - so it can't be understood normally. So to fully and finally bust the Church Infancy Myth, we'll have to settle the question of mystical interpretation. Is the Bible really so different, so holy, so spiritual, that it cannot be understood normally? Does God intend for us to interpret His written Sacred Communication

41

mystically—or normally?

To fully and finally bust the Church Infancy Myth, we'll show that God intends His written Word to be interpreted normally, not mystically.

**Endnotes**

1    Orr, *International Standard Bible Encyclopedia,* "Bishop"

2    Youngblood, *Nelson's Bible Dictionary,* "Church Government"

3    Shelley, *Church History In Plain Language: Updated 2nd Edition,* 71.

4    Matthew 20:25-28; Mark 10:42-45; Luke 22:25-27; John 18:36. And in Acts 1:6-8, Jesus made it clear that His purpose was not to restore Israel's political kingdom.

# Section 2:

# APOSTLES

Our mythbusting starts with the apostles of Christ—the men who built Jesus' Ekklesia. They documented their design in the twenty-seven books and letters of the New Testament. The Church Infancy Myth claims that their design was shortsighted and incompetent, and that their documentation was partial and temporary, as stated by the Church Infancy Myth:

> . . . the apostles and early Christians . . . were looking for the speedy return of Christ, and consequently *did not organize the church in its infancy*, as it was afterward found necessary to do. (emphasis mine)

According to the myth, Christ's apostles were unaware that Jesus' Ekklesia was in for the long haul. They cobbled together an unstructured and disordered baby version of Christianity. After they died, Christian leaders had to figure out the "right structures and procedures that would help it (the church) accomplish its mission." Over the next few centuries these "church fathers" corrected the apostles' errors and supplied the vital doctrines the apostles had overlooked. They gave us the new, improved, organized religion version of Christianity.

The myth-theology thus hangs a huge question mark over the entire New Testament. That's no accident: the myth-theology's purpose was always to get around, circumvent, nullify, and explain away practically everything Christ's apostles believed, practiced, taught, and documented.

The New Testament is only as trustworthy as the men who wrote it. If we're not completely confident that Christ's apostles are absolutely, unquestionably reliable, then we cannot have complete faith in what they wrote. Even ninety-nine percent confidence is still one percent doubt. And even one percent doubt is more than enough unbelief to keep us trapped in churchianity.

How much did Christ's apostles know about Jesus' Ekklesia? How accurate and reliable were they? Did they know everything there was to know about Christianity? Or did they know only enough to design a temporary, baby church? Did they document everything we need to know, or did they leave out important parts—or maybe even get some things *wrong*?

And today, nearly 2,000 years later, is it even possible to answer these questions?

Of course it's possible. The answers have always been hiding in plain sight. The reason we haven't seen them is because for 1,900 years we've been immersed in the Myth of the Church's Infancy. We've all been taught to view the Bible upside-down. For 1,900 years the Myth has brainwashed us into doubting the New Testament.

The New Testament makes it unmistakably clear that Jesus' apostles are absolutely, unquestionably, one hundred percent accurate and reliable. That's because their reliability is based entirely on Jesus Himself. No Christian would think of accusing Jesus of making errors or misstatements. Yet—as we're about to see—if Jesus' apostles aren't reliable then neither is the Lord Jesus Christ.

Chapter 6

# APOSTLES:
# NEW TESTAMENT DEFINITION

For many years I knew little about apostles. I was told that apostle meant "one who is sent": in other words, a missionary. I was told that the primary qualification for apostleship was to have seen the risen Christ with one's physical eyes (i.e. not in a dream or vision). I learned the names of the Twelve from a Sunday School song.[1] I knew that a few other men were also called apostles, most notably Saul (Paul) of Tarsus. I knew that the apostles had written or approved the twenty-seven books and letters of the New Testament.

Apart from those few details, the only other time I'd ever heard the apostles mentioned was in a standard defense of the gospels' reliability. The defense is valid, but it inadvertently reinforces the Church Infancy Myth. It goes like this:

Critics claim that the New Testament was forged or altered to support the Church's political agenda. But this accusation has a fatal flaw.

The Church always claimed that its bishops derived their authority from Christ's apostles. Apostolic authority was the basis of the church's claim to both political and spiritual control. Yet how are the apostles portrayed in the gospels? Mostly in a bad light:

- They frequently misunderstood Jesus.

- They argued over which one of them was the greatest.

- Their continual lack of faith finally drove Jesus to the point of exasperation.

- On the night before His crucifixion, they slept when Jesus asked them to keep watch.

- Later that night when Jesus was arrested, they deserted Him and fled to save themselves.

- During Jesus' trial, Peter denied three times that he even knew Jesus.

- They didn't believe Mary's report of an empty tomb and an angel's message.

- When Jesus appeared to them after His resurrection, some of them doubted it was really him.

If, as the critics claim, the gospels had been written or changed to promote the Church's political agenda, they would never contain such unflattering accounts of the Church's founders. Thus, the evidence argues that the gospels reliably record eyewitness accounts of actual events.

All of the above is accurate. It really is strong evidence for the gospels' reliability. And in all my years of church attendance, what you've just read was all I ever heard about Jesus' apostles. Unfortunately, it undermined my confidence in them. If they got things wrong that often, maybe they also made mistakes designing Jesus' Ekklesia. Maybe they really *did* neglect to record some vital information in writing.

It turned out that my doubts about the apostles were not due to what I had been taught; the problem was what I had *not* been taught. I and my teachers had overlooked some crucial New Testament facts. I am indebted to Dr. Samuel Waldron for bringing these details to light. Chapter two of his book *To Be Continued?*[2] revolutionized my understanding of the apostles of Christ. Much of what follows is based on the information in that chapter.

### WHAT IS AN APOSTLE?

The definition of apostle as "missionary" is both inadequate and misleading. In first-century Israel nobody had heard of missionaries and apostle had an altogether different meaning. To understand that meaning, we need some grammatical-historical context.

Most Christians have a "Christianized" view of Jesus. That is, we think about Jesus in the context of the New Testament and almost twenty centuries of church history. But to His first-century contemporaries, Jesus was a controversial, miracle-working rabbi. The gospel of John, chapter 3, makes this clear. John 3 begins with Nicodemus, a member of the Sanhedrin, recognizing Jesus as a Jewish rabbi:

> Now a certain man, a Pharisee named Nicodemus, who was a member of the Jewish ruling council, came to Jesus at night and said to him, "*Rabbi*, we know that you are a teacher who has come from God. For no one could perform the miraculous signs that you do unless God is with him." (John 3:1-2, emphasis mine)

So Jesus was a rabbi. But what does this have to do with apostles not being missionaries?

When Jesus appointed His apostles, He was speaking as a Jewish rabbi to a Jewish audience. Almost certainly He was speaking Aramaic,[3] not Greek. The word He would have used was *shaliach*, not *apostolos*.[4] Shaliach (spelled "sjaliach" in the translation from Dutch below) had a precise meaning:

> Recent research has shown that the formal structure of the apostolate is derived from the Jewish legal system in which a person may be given the legal power to represent another. The one who has such power of attorney is called a Sjaliach (apostle). The uniqueness of this relationship is pregnantly expressed by the notion that the Sjaliach (apostle) of a man, is as the man himself.[5]

So a shaliach was not a missionary as we understand the term. Rather, he was a delegate, an envoy, an ambassador: a legal representative who held power of attorney for someone else.

But what if Jesus *was* speaking New Testament Koine Greek instead of Aramaic? Would it make any difference if He called His twelve disciples *apostoloi* instead of *shaliachim*? Not really. The BDAG Lexicon defines apostolos as ". . .predominately in the NT . . . a group of highly honored believers with a special function as God's envoys."

So that Sunday School song "There Were Twelve Disciples" was misleading. It really should have been "There Were Twelve *Apostles*." The terms apostle and disciple are not synonymous. Jesus had many other disciples besides the Twelve. In Luke 10 He sent out seventy-two[6] disciples to proclaim God's kingdom and heal the sick. But He chose only twelve disciples as His apostles.

Both Mark and Luke record that Jesus designated twelve of His disciples as apostles. Luke adds that before doing so, Jesus spent an entire night in prayer—the only time that *all night* prayer is mentioned in the New Testament.[7]

> Now Jesus went up the mountain and called for those he wanted, and they came to him. He appointed twelve (whom he named apostles) . . .
> (Mark 3:13-14)

Now it was during this time that Jesus went out to the mountain to pray,
and he spent all night in prayer to God. When morning came, he called
his disciples and chose twelve of them, whom he also named apostles . . .
(Luke 6:12-13)

Jesus considered His choice of apostles so critically important that He
spent an entire night in prayer beforehand. Obviously the appointment of
apostles was highly significant. Jesus was making an important distinction of
some sort. But what exactly was it? How were Jesus' apostles different from
the rest of His disciples?

When Jesus named twelve of His disciples as apostles, was He using that
term in its formal, legal sense? Did He appoint these men as His personal
ambassadors extraordinary and plenipotentiary[8] with full power of attorney
for the King of Kings? Or were they merely missionaries without a portfolio?
What exactly did Jesus mean?

Here's a clue: the word apostle turns up just once in the book of Hebrews.
It is used precisely in its full formal, legal sense. And it refers to none other
than Jesus Himself.

### GOD THE FATHER'S APOSTLE

According to Hebrews 3:1-2, Jesus is God the Father's apostle: "Jesus, the
apostle and high priest whom we confess, who is faithful to the one who appointed him . . ." God the Father appointed Jesus as His shaliach, His apostle.
As the Father's personal representative, Jesus was fully authorized to speak
and act on His Father's behalf.

For I have not spoken from my own authority, but the Father himself who
sent me has commanded me what I should say and what I should speak.
And I know that his commandment is eternal life. Thus the things I say, I say
just as the Father has told me." (John 12:49-50)

. . . I do nothing on my own initiative, but I speak just what the Father taught
me. And the one who sent me is with me. He has not left me alone, because
I always do those things that please him." (John 8:28-29)

Jesus replied, "I am the way, and the truth, and the life. No one comes to the
Father except through me. If you have known me, you will know my Father
too. And from now on you do know him and have seen him." (John 14:6-7)

Philip said, "Lord, show us the Father, and we will be content." Jesus replied,
"Have I been with you for so long, and you have not known me, Philip? The
person who has seen me has seen the Father! How can you say, 'Show us the
Father'? Do you not believe that I am in the Father, and the Father is in me?

The words that I say to you, I do not speak on my own initiative, but the Father residing in me performs his miraculous deeds…" (John 14:8-10)

"…The Father and I are one." (John 10:30)

Thus whatever Jesus did, the Father did, and whatever Jesus said, the Father said. As His Father's apostle, Jesus was authorized to speak for His Father, forgive sins, perform miracles, even raise the dead. We could say that Jesus had absolute power of attorney for God the Father.

The author of Hebrews obviously understood the legal definition of shaliach or apostle, and so did Jesus. Furthermore, Jesus did not spend an entire night in prayer before sending out the seventy-two disciples in Luke 10. His unique all-night prayer in Luke 6 is strong evidence that He was appointing ambassadors, not missionaries. But we have even stronger evidence: Jesus' own words:

So Jesus said to them again, "Peace be with you. *Just as the Father has sent me*, I also send you." (John 20:21, emphasis mine)

### TWO KINDS OF APOSTLES

Since an apostle is a legal representative who possesses power of attorney for someone else, everything about an apostle depends on who appointed him. So the first thing we need to know about any apostle is: who sent him? Whom does he represent?

In the New Testament, there are two kinds of apostles. At first there were only apostles appointed by Jesus. Later on there were also apostles who were appointed by, and represented, a local Ekklesia. Recognizing this distinction is critically important because not every apostle was Jesus' personal representative. Only a certain few men held power of attorney for the Lord Jesus Christ.

**Apostles of Christ** were appointed by, and represented, the Lord Jesus Christ. Initially there were only twelve such men. In Acts 1:24-26, Matthias was chosen to replace Judas Iscariot. Later on, Saul (Paul) of Tarsus was also recognized as an apostle of Christ.

**Apostles of churches** were appointed by, and represented, a local Ekklesia. Epaphroditus was the messenger of the Ekklesia at Philippi (Phil 2:25). Paul mentions men who were representatives of the churches (2 Cor 8:23). The individuals in this second group were authorized to speak and act on behalf of the congregation that appointed them. They were not, however, legal representatives of the Lord Jesus Christ.

As we continue mythbusting, it's important to keep this distinction in mind. Our purpose in Section 2 is to bust the Myth's accusations against the men who gave us the New Testament—the Apostles of Christ. Jesus made certain statements and promises that apply only to His apostles. If we miss this distinction, we'll misunderstand what Jesus meant.

### WHAT ABOUT MATTHIAS AND PAUL?

God the Father appointed Jesus as His apostle. Only the Father could appoint Jesus as His shaliach or apostle, His personal representative with full power of attorney. In the same way, only Jesus could appoint someone to be His shaliach, His personal representative. No one could appoint himself to be Jesus' apostle. Not even other apostles could appoint someone to this position.

Matthias and Paul appear to be exceptions to this rule. Acts chapter 1 tells how Matthias was chosen to replace Judas Iscariot. If Matthias wasn't appointed directly by Jesus, then he wasn't qualified to be an apostle. If he wasn't qualified, then Peter and the rest of the eleven apostles were mistaken when they accepted him as Judas' replacement. And if they were mistaken, then they aren't reliable.

The eleven apostles weren't mistaken, of course; but we need to understand why. The account of Matthias is simple and straightforward so we'll cover it now. To fully understand Paul's appointment as an apostle of Christ, we'll need the information in the next three chapters. So we'll examine Paul's apostleship at the end of this section.

The eleven apostles didn't appoint Matthias; they selected two men who met the job requirements Jesus had specified (Acts 1:8, 21); but they left the choice up to their Lord:

> Then they prayed, "Lord, you know the hearts of all. *Show us which one of these two you have chosen* to assume the task of this service and apostleship from which Judas turned aside to go to his own place." Then they cast lots for them, and the one chosen was Matthias; so he was counted with the eleven apostles. (Acts 1:24-26, emphasis mine)

Today the idea of discovering God's will by drawing straws or rolling dice seems strange. However, it demonstrates that the apostles understood that only Jesus could appoint someone to be His apostle.

Casting lots had plenty of historical precedent: Numbers 26:55-56, Numbers 33:54, 1 Samuel 14:41, and Jonah 1:7 are just a few examples. And there was the specific promise in Proverbs:

> The dice are thrown into the lap, but their every decision is from the Lord. (Prov 16:33)

# CHAPTER 6

We have now covered the basic information about New Testament apostles:

- An apostle was not a missionary but rather a legal representative with power of attorney;

- There were two kinds of apostles: representatives of Jesus, and representatives of churches;

- Only Jesus could appoint someone to be His apostle;

- All of Jesus' apostles were disciples but not all of His disciples were apostles;

- Initially, only the Twelve apostles were Jesus' personal representatives.

In the rest of Section 2, we're going to find out precisely what Jesus meant in John 20:21 when He told His apostles "Just as the Father has sent me, I also send you."

**Endnotes**

1    "There Were Twelve Disciples" sung to the tune of "Bringing in the Sheaves."

2    Waldron, *To Be Continued?*

3    Mark's Gospel records multiple instances where Jesus spoke Aramaic: "Talitha koum" (5:41); "Ephphatha" (7:34); "Abba" (14:36); "Eloi, Eloi, lema sabachthani?" (15:34). And in Acts 26:14, Paul recounts that on the road to Damascus Jesus spoke to him in Aramaic.

4    "The term used by Jesus, it must be remembered, would be Aramaic, not Greek, and apostolos would be its literal equivalent." (Orr, *International Standard Bible Encyclopedia*, "Apostle")

5    Ridderbos, *Redemptive History and the New Testament Scriptures: 2nd rev. ed.,* 14. (Quoted in Samuel Waldron's *To Be Continued*, 24).

6    Traditionally *seventy*. See the NET Bible's text-critical note at Luke 10:1.

7    NET Bible study note, Luke 6:12

8    *Plenipotentiary*; Merriam-Webster: "a person and especially a diplomatic agent invested with full power to transact business."

Chapter 7

# CHRIST'S APOSTLES: AUTHORITY AND RELIABILITY

According to Hebrews 3:1-2, Jesus is God the Father's apostle. God appointed Jesus as His personal representative with full power of attorney. As His Father's apostle, Jesus was fully authorized to speak and act on God's behalf: to proclaim the Good News of God's Kingdom, forgive sins, perform miracles, even raise the dead. So what exactly did Jesus mean when He told His apostles "Just as the Father has sent me, I also send you"?

> So Jesus said to them again, "Peace be with you. *Just as the Father has sent me*, I also send you." (John 20:21, emphasis mine)

Could Jesus have meant those words literally? Did He really authorize His twelve apostles to speak for him, forgive sins, perform miracles, and even raise the dead? Just what sort of legal and spiritual authority did He give His apostles and how far did that authority extend?

Jesus made certain statements and promises to His apostles that conclusively prove their reliability. These statements and promises make it unmistakably clear that Jesus' apostles are absolutely, unquestionably, one hundred percent accurate and reliable. That's because their reliability is based entirely on Jesus Himself. If Jesus' apostles aren't reliable, then neither is the Lord Jesus Christ.

### RECEIVE HIS APOSTLE = RECEIVE JESUS

Jesus stated that He is the one and only way to the Father:

> Jesus replied, "I am the way, and the truth, and the life. No one comes to the Father except through me." (John 14:6)

In the same way, Jesus made his apostles the way to Himself:

> Whoever receives you receives me, and whoever receives me receives the one who sent me. (Matt 10:40)

> I tell you the solemn truth, whoever accepts the one I send accepts me, and whoever accepts me accepts the one who sent me. (John 13:20)

### REJECT HIS APOSTLE = REJECT JESUS

In Luke 10:10-16 Jesus identified Himself with His apostles in the strongest possible terms. Those who reject the ones He sends, reject both Jesus and God the Father:

> The one who listens to you listens to me, and the one who rejects you rejects me, and the one who rejects me rejects the one who sent me. (Luke 10:16)

This promise applied to seventy-two of Jesus' disciples. Yet only the Twelve were called apostles. Does the New Testament tell us anything more to clarify the authority of the twelve apostles?

### UNIQUE WITNESSES CHOSEN BY GOD

Of course it does! Let's start by considering the significance of the apostles as Jesus' only authorized eyewitnesses. Acts 1:1-9 records Jesus' last meeting with His apostles before He was taken up into heaven. His final words authorized them as His unique witnesses. He promised them supernatural power to carry out this task:

> ...But you will receive power when the Holy Spirit has come upon you, and you will be my witnesses in Jerusalem, and in all Judea and Samaria, and to the farthest parts of the earth. (Acts 1:8)

On multiple occasions (Acts 1:22, 2:32, 3:15, 5:32, 10:39-41) Peter emphasized the significance of the Twelve apostles as Jesus' divinely chosen witnesses:

> We are witnesses of all the things he did both in Judea and in Jerusalem. They killed him by hanging him on a tree, but God raised him up on the third day and caused him to be seen, not by all the people, but by us, the

witnesses God had already chosen, who ate and drank with him after he rose from the dead. (Acts 10:39-41)

So the Twelve apostles were Jesus' unique eyewitnesses, chosen by God and supernaturally empowered. But what does this have to do with their authority as Jesus' personal representatives? John spells it out for us in his first letter. He begins by describing the twelve apostles' firsthand physical knowledge of the Lord Jesus Christ: John and the rest of the Twelve heard, saw, and touched Jesus.

> This is what we proclaim to you: what was from the beginning, what we have heard, what we have seen with our eyes, what we have looked at and our hands have touched (concerning the word of life - and the life was revealed, and we have seen and testify and announce to you the eternal life that was with the Father and was revealed to us). What we have seen and heard we announce to you too, so that you may have fellowship with us (and indeed our fellowship is with the Father and with his Son Jesus Christ). (1 John 1:1-4)

Note that when John says "we," "us," and "our," he is referring to the apostles of Christ: Jesus' unique eyewitnesses. Now consider what he says later in the same letter:

> You are from God, little children, and have conquered them, because the one who is in you is greater than the one who is in the world. They are from the world; therefore they speak from the world's perspective and the world listens to them. *We are from God; the person who knows God listens to us, but whoever is not from God does not listen to us.* By this we know the Spirit of truth and the spirit of deceit. (1 John 4:4-6, emphasis mine)

The pronoun "you" here refers to John's audience. "They" refers to a group that had rejected the apostles' teaching about Jesus. But who does "we" refer to? In context, John is again referring to Jesus' apostles. Seen in this light, 1 John 4:6 is powerful evidence for apostolic authority. A genuine Christian listens to Christ's apostles and submits to their teaching. Anyone who doesn't, doesn't know God.

But this shouldn't come as a surprise; John didn't make this up on his own. He's just restating what Jesus already said in Matthew 10:40, Luke 10:16, and John 13:20.

### ABSOLUTE TEACHING AUTHORITY

1 John 4:6 is strong evidence for the absolute teaching authority of Christ's apostles. But it isn't the only passage that supports the apostles' authority. Paul made the same claim even more explicitly. In his first letter to the Christians

in Corinth he gave detailed instructions about the meetings of the Ekklesia, including spiritual gifts (chapter 12); speaking in tongues (14:27-28); prophets and prophesying (14:29-30); and the role of women (14:33-35). These instructions appear nowhere else in the New Testament. Jesus never mentioned them in the gospels. Yet Paul stated that his instructions are the Lord's command:

> If anyone considers himself a prophet or spiritual person, he should acknowledge that *what I write to you is the Lord's command*. If someone does not recognize this, he is not recognized. (1 Cor 14:37-38, emphasis mine)

That last sentence, "If someone does not recognize this . . ." (14:38), is precisely what John said of himself and the other apostles in 1 John 4:6. A genuine Christian listens to Christ's apostles and submits to their teaching. Anyone who doesn't should consider themselves neither a prophet nor a spiritual person.

### CONCLUSION

The statements that we've reviewed in this chapter—the words of Jesus, John, and Paul—establish certain facts about Christ's apostles:

- Jesus appointed the apostles as His unique, sole, and only eyewitnesses;

- To reject the apostles' teaching is to reject Christ's command;

- To reject Christ's apostle is to reject the Lord Jesus Christ Himself.

All of these statements are strong evidence that when Jesus told His apostles "Just as the Father has sent me, I also send you," He meant it literally. He meant that His apostles were fully authorized to speak for him, forgive sins, perform miracles, and even raise the dead.

However, the New Testament has even more to say about the authority and reliability of Christ's apostles. Jesus made three clear and specific promises to His apostles. These promises explain Paul's teaching authority and constitute conclusive proof of the apostles' reliability.

Because these promises utterly refute churchianity's myth-theology, they have all been misinterpreted. After all, the Myth's purpose is to legitimize church government. Therefore it has to discredit Christ's apostles. It has to get around, circumvent, nullify, and explain away what the apostles of Christ believed, taught, practiced, and documented in the New Testament.

In the next two chapters we will examine Jesus' three promises and show how the Myth has been deceiving us.

Chapter 8

# JESUS' THREE MISUNDERSTOOD PROMISES

How reliable is the New Testament? Does it tell us everything God wants us to know about Christianity, or is it missing vital information about church government and worship? That depends on the New Testament's authors: did they know everything necessary to design and build Jesus' Ekklesia, or did they know only enough to found an infant church? Was their documentation complete and final, or was it partial and temporary?

Churchianity's myth-theology claims that the apostles—Jesus' personal, legal representatives who gave us the New Testament—didn't realize that the Ekklesia would continue past their lifetimes. They designed, built, and documented only a partial and temporary baby version of Christianity:

> . . . the apostles and early Christians . . . were looking for the speedy return of Christ, and consequently *did not organize the church in its infancy*, as it was afterward found necessary to do.[1] (emphasis mine)

So the question for us is: what did Christ's apostles know and when did they know it? It turns out that Jesus made three promises to His apostles that decisively answer this question. Because these promises utterly refute churchianity's myth-theology, they have all been misinterpreted. In this chapter and the next we're going to review Jesus' three promises, expose the misinterpretations, and discover precisely what the New Testament's authors knew and when they knew it.

### EVERY PROMISE IN THE BOOK?

Before we begin, we need to clear up a common misunderstanding about promises in the Bible. Maybe you've heard (or sung) the chorus "Every Promise In The Book Is Mine," but as Bernard Ramm cautions in *Protestant Biblical Interpretation*, this spiritual-sounding but misguided sentiment is one of the overstatements of the century.[2]

The idea that every statement or promise in the Bible applies to every Christian personally at all times is another example of *universalization*, one of myth-interpretation's deceptions. Samuel Waldron points out that it effectively nullifies what the New Testament tells us about Christ's apostles:

> Evangelicals generally do not recognize the prominence and distinctiveness
> of the apostolate in the New Testament. Many passages and promises ad-
> dressed first or even exclusively to the Apostles of Christ are universalized,
> spiritualized and devotionalized and applied to all Christians.[3]

Universalizing, spiritualizing, and devotionalizing, are the three standard methods we covered in chapter 4 that churchianity uses to trick us into reading the Bible upside-down. Every promise in the Bible is most definitely *not* mine, yours, or ours. Dr. Ramm lists four commonsense tests to apply to Bible promises:

1. Is the promise universal in scope? Does it apply to all people everywhere?

2. Is the promise personal? Was the promise made to just one person?

3. Is the promise conditional? Are there conditions which must be met before the promise may be fulfilled?

4. Is the promise for a specific time or for all time?

As we examine Jesus' three misunderstood promises, we're going to apply the principles we've just covered. We *won't* universalize, spiritualize, or devotionalize Jesus' words. But we *will* take them in context, at face value, in their normal sense, and pay close attention to the Six W's[4] - who, what, when, where, why, and how.

And now for the first of the three promises. Jesus promised to give the keys of the Kingdom of Heaven to Peter, and later to the rest of His apostles. But what did Jesus mean?

He meant His own absolute teaching authority, guaranteed personally from heaven.

# CHAPTER 8

## PROMISE #1: ABSOLUTE TEACHING AUTHORITY

> I will give you the keys of the kingdom of heaven. Whatever you bind on
> earth will have been bound in heaven, and whatever you release on earth will
> have been released in heaven. (Matt 16:19)

In all my years of church attendance, I never heard anyone explain this passage—correctly, that is. The common misunderstanding of "the keys of the
kingdom" is that Peter is Heaven's doorward or gatekeeper who admits or re-
fuses admission to departed souls. I even heard one pastor claim that binding
and loosing were weapons of spiritual warfare: demons could be bound and
blessings could be loosed.

After decades of ignorance, I finally learned what Jesus meant by "keys,"
"bind," and "loose." In his book *Velvet Elvis*, Rob Bell explains what translators have known all along about this passage (and also about "yoke" in
Matthew 11:28-30 which we covered in chapter 4 of this book). The section
entitled "Rabbis"[5] is several pages long and full of fascinating background
information. It's very much worth reading but there isn't space for it all here.

In Matthew 16:15-19, Jesus was speaking as a Jewish rabbi and using rabbinical figures of speech. His first-century Jewish audience understood precisely what He meant. A rabbi's "yoke" was his teaching. To "bind" meant to
prohibit something; to "loose" meant to permit it. Wuest's *Expanded Translation* makes this clear:

> I shall give to you the keys of the kingdom of heaven; and whatever you
> bind on earth [forbid to be done], shall have been already bound [forbid-
> den to be done] in heaven; and whatever you loose on earth [permit to be
> done], shall have already been loosed in heaven [permitted to be done].
> (Matt 16:19 WET)

> Assuredly, I am saying to you, Whatever you forbid on earth, shall have
> already been forbidden in heaven. And whatever you permit on earth, shall
> have already been permitted in heaven. (Matt 18:18 WET)

When a rabbi gave his disciple "the keys of the kingdom," he was autho-
rizing that disciple to teach his yoke; conferring upon him the rabbi's own
authority to forbid and permit.[6] Jesus promised Peter, and later the rest of His
apostles (Matthew 18:18), His own absolute teaching authority, guaranteed
from heaven. For Christians, from that point forward, the apostles' decisions
were final, and their word was final!

Now for Jesus' second promise to His apostles: He gave them His own
authority to forgive or retain sin.

61

### PROMISE #2: AUTHORITY TO FORGIVE OR RETAIN SIN

According to John 20:21, Jesus gave His apostles nothing less than the same authority that He had received from the Father:

> So Jesus said to them again, "Peace be with you. *Just as the Father has sent me, I also send you.*" (John 20:21, emphasis mine)

This passage in John is another instance where, as Dr. Waldron observes, Christians fail to recognize the prominence and distinctiveness of the apostles of Christ. What precisely did Jesus mean here? Was He speaking in a general way about Himself and His apostles being "sent ones" without any specific, practical meaning? Or did He intend for His apostles to understand His words in their normal, literal sense? His very next statement makes it clear that He was speaking specifically and literally:

> And after he said this, he breathed on them and said, "Receive the Holy Spirit. If you forgive anyone's sins, they are forgiven; if you retain anyone's sins, they are retained." (John 20:22-23)

Did Jesus have authority to forgive sin or withhold forgiveness? Of course He did! In Matthew 9:2-7 He claimed this authority and then proved His claim by performing a miracle: healing a paralyzed man. In Matthew 12:31-32 He declared a particular sin to be unforgiveable "either in this age or in the age to come."[7] And in John 9:41 He told the Pharisees, the Jewish religious/political leaders *at that time,* that they were not forgiven.

The simplest and most literal interpretation of John 20:22-23 is that Jesus gave His apostles His own authority to forgive sin or withhold forgiveness. But many commentators refuse to take Jesus' statement at face value. They argue that Jesus couldn't actually have meant what he clearly said because "only God can forgive sins"; the same argument the Pharisees made against Jesus in Luke 5:21.

But Jesus' promise in John 20:22-23 is just the practical application of His previous statement: "Just as the Father has sent me, I also send you." Those who deny the normal, literal meaning of this application in John 20:22-23 must also deny the normal, literal meaning of Jesus' previous statement. Thus, once again, the prominence and distinctiveness of the apostles of Christ goes unrecognized by the masses.

The standard Protestant explanation of John 20:21-23 is subtle eisegesis:[8] it adds an unwritten condition to Jesus' promise. It claims that what Jesus *meant* was:

> "Just as the Father has sent me, [except for my authority to forgive or retain sin,] I also send you." (John 20:21-23, emphasis mine, brackets [ ]

62

indicate misquote for emphasis)

It implicitly teaches us to read the Bible with mental reservations: to ignore the Bible's actual words and mentally substitute a different meaning. It implies that the Apostle John did not communicate clearly and that the New Testament is hard to understand. It's like reading the New Testament through churchianity-colored glasses.

If the New Testament didn't record any instances where the apostles of Christ forgave or retained sin, then maybe the standard explanation might be valid. But in Galatians 1:8-9, Paul eternally condemned certain false teachers. In Revelation 22:19, John eternally condemned anyone who "takes away from the words of this book of prophecy." In 1 Corinthians 16:22 Paul stated "Let anyone who has no love for the Lord be accursed." In Acts 5:1-10 Peter regarded Ananias' and Sapphira's lying to the Holy Spirit as a sin worthy of physical death.

### CONCLUSION

We've now examined the first two misunderstood promises that Jesus made to His apostles. If these two promises are taken normally and literally, at face value, they seriously undermine the Myth's accusations that we covered in the previous section. After all, if Jesus delegated to His apostles His own absolute teaching authority backed up personally from heaven; and also delegated to them His own authority to forgive or retain sin; then doubting what the apostles believed, practiced, taught, and documented amounts to doubting Jesus Himself.

But what if, as the Myth claims, the apostles really were so focused on Jesus' speedy return that they simply gave no thought to the long-term design of His Ekklesia? And besides, even with all their delegated authority the apostles were still mere mortals. They weren't omniscient or infallible. How could Jesus entrust such absolute authority to anyone else—even His own apostles? Why, Peter and the others would need to be as infallible as Jesus Himself before they could safely wield such power.

Jesus, the Son of God, the Word (*Logos*) of God in the flesh (John 1:14), was unquestionably infallible, as stated in Colossians 2:3 and most of John's gospel. But what about His apostles? Could anyone other than God Himself claim infallible knowledge? In a word, yes! Jesus promised that His apostles would know *all truth*:

But when he, the Spirit of truth, comes, he will guide you into all truth. (John 16:13)

Did Jesus know all truth? Of course He did! Taken literally, at face value,

63

what Jesus promised His apostles here was that they would know everything He Himself knew about the Kingdom of God, the gospel, and the Ekklesia.

In John 16:13, Jesus promised His apostles qualified infallibility. John 16:13 is monumentally significant. Not only does it reinforce our non-traditional explanation of Jesus' first two promises; it utterly demolishes the Myth, proving it to be a lie.

John 16:13 is our third misunderstood promise. It's the promise Jesus *never* made, but we all think He did! Because this third promise is so critical and so completely misunderstood, we're going to cover it separately in the next chapter.

**Endnotes**

1    Orr, *International Standard Bible Encyclopedia*, "Bishop"

2    Ramm, *Protestant Biblical Interpretation*, 192.

3    Waldron, *To Be Continued,* 22.

4    The Six W's, "who, what, when, where, why, and how," which are commonly used in journalism, whose answers are considered basic in information-gathering.

5    Bell, *Velvet Elvis*, 47-50.

6    Freedman et al, *Anchor Bible Dictionary,* Vol 1, 744; Kittel at al, *Theological Dictionary of the New Testament*, Vol III, 750; Keck, *The New Interpreter's Bible*, Vol VIII, 346.

7    This is also strong evidence that Jesus and His apostles knew there would be an age to come – meaning they were not anticipating the "speedy return of Christ" which is the basis of the Church Infancy Myth.

8    Merriam-Webster: eisegesis is the interpretation of a text (as of the Bible) by reading into it one's own ideas.

Chapter 9

# THE PROMISE
# JESUS *NEVER* MADE

In John 16:13, Jesus clearly promised the Holy Spirit's guidance into all truth: "But when he, the Spirit of truth, comes, he will guide you into all truth." So how can John 16:13 be the promise Jesus *never* made? What was it that Jesus *didn't* promise but we all think He did?

Correctly understood, Jesus' promise in John 16:13 conclusively disproves the Myth's accusations against the apostles. Out of necessity, then, this promise has been misinterpreted by every group that practices church government. The method is simple but subtle: mental misdirection.

In order to expose the trick, we first need to set up the scene. All four gospels contain accounts of the Last Supper[1]—the Passover Seder meal that Jesus and His apostles shared on the evening before the crucifixion. John's gospel, however, recounts in detail the events of that evening and of Jesus' final discourse before His arrest and trial later that night.

What do we know about the Last Supper (besides da Vinci's famous but inaccurate painting)?[2] We know that it took place in an upstairs guest room (Luke 22:11-12; Mark 14:15). We know that only thirteen men were present: Jesus and His twelve apostles (Matthew 26:20; Mark 14:17; Luke 22:14). Finally, we know that Judas Iscariot left the room early. Only John's gospel records this last detail explicitly (John 13:30), but it is implied in the other gospels. At Gethsemane, Judas showed up leading a crowd of armed men (Matthew 26:47; Mark 14:43; Luke 22:47). It seems obvious that he had been gone for some time.

Judas left the upstairs guest room in John 13:30. Later on, in John 16:13, Jesus spoke His third promise to His remaining eleven apostles who were still with Him in the room. Jesus promised that they would know everything He Himself knew about the Kingdom of God, the gospel, and the Ekklesia. Here's the full quote:

> I have many more things to say to you, but you cannot bear them now. *But when he, the Spirit of truth, comes, he will guide you into all truth.* For he will not speak on his own authority, but will speak whatever he hears, and will tell you what is to come. (John 16:12-13, emphasis mine)

Jesus spoke this promise to eleven men in a room. This is all very clear and straightforward. So what is churchianity's simple yet subtle trick that misdirects our minds and misinterprets Jesus' promise? It's this: we've all been told that in John 16:13 Jesus promised the Holy Spirit's guidance to *the Church*. We've been told that when Jesus said "you" to those eleven men, He really meant *other* people who weren't in the room.

### THE PROMISE JESUS NEVER MADE

But is that accurate? Here's a self-test to clarify what Jesus actually promised according to John 16:13:

1.) *Who* would the Holy Spirit guide into all truth?
   A) Every believer
   B) Bishops and pastors
   C) The "church fathers"
   D) None of the above

2.) *What kind of truth* would Jesus' eleven apostles receive?
   A) Initial truth
   B) Partial truth
   C) Temporary truth
   D) None of the above

3.) *How much truth* would the Holy Spirit give Jesus' eleven apostles?
   A) Only enough truth for the first century
   B) Only enough truth for the age of the apostles
   C) Only enough truth for the church's infancy
   D) None of the above

The correct answer to all three questions is D: none of the above. The claim that Jesus' promise in John 16:13 applies to *the Church* is a glaring example of universalizing and thereby nullifying Jesus' words.

Notice what else Jesus *didn't* promise: He didn't promise His apostles sinless perfection, nor that they would, marionette-like, be forced to obey the truth. His promise of infallibility was qualified: it was limited to knowledge. Thus in Galatians 2:11-14, Peter *knew* the truth but chose, wrongly and temporarily, to follow Jewish tradition. This temporary lapse did not invalidate Jesus' promise. Peter still *knew* the truth and repented when confronted by Paul precisely because he knew it.

### ACCUSING JESUS AND THE HOLY SPIRIT

Many Christians believe that in John 16:13, Jesus promised that the Holy Spirit would guide the *Church* into all truth. And if that were the case, it would imply a process of development, change, and growth into maturity. Catholic and Orthodox doctrine claims that God Himself was responsible for second and third century changes that superseded the New Testament's apostolic pattern:

> Still other Christians argue that the Holy Spirit so dwelt in the church and guided its decisions that the developments of the early centuries in doctrine and church structure were the work not of men but of God. They are, therefore, permanently binding for the church.[3]

If this claim is true, then the New Testament—which is silent on the subject of church government—is not God's final and complete revelation and there is in fact other, more recent divine revelation that supersedes and even invalidates the writings of the apostles. And if actions speak louder than words, every Christian who ignores supposedly temporary New Testament instructions agrees with this claim—even Protestant Christians who profess that God's written Sacred Communication is *sola fidei regula*—the only rule of faith.

Then what are we to make of Jesus' promise of the Holy Spirit's guidance? In his booklet *Discovering The Rich Heritage Of Orthodoxy*, Fr. Phillip Bell, Ph.D., quotes that promise and spells out the alarming implications of Jesus' words:

> Jesus said, "I will build my church and the gates of Hades shall not overpower it" (Matt 16:18). Moreover He promised to impart the Holy Spirit to the Church, "the Spirit of truth . . . He will guide you into all the truth . . ." (John 16:13). **Unless we wish to assign failure on the part of Jesus and error on the part of the Holy Spirit**, we must concede that such a thing as '*the true Church*' exists.[4] (boldface mine)

Certainly no Christian would ever intentionally accuse Jesus of failure or the Holy Spirit of error. But by accusing Christ's apostles of ignorance or incompetence, the Myth does both.

John 16:13 makes it impossible to doubt Christ's apostles without accusing the Lord Jesus Christ Himself. Unless we wish to accuse Jesus of error and the Holy Spirit of failure, we must concede that Jesus' eleven apostles—his personal representatives—knew one hundred percent of the truth about the gospel and the Ekklesia when they documented their teaching and practice in the New Testament.

### THE MYTH'S ORIGINAL VERSION:
### THE DIDN'T DILEMMA

Now that we understand what Jesus actually promised in John 16:13, let's take another look at the Myth's accusations. First, the original version:

> . . . the apostles and early Christians . . . were looking for the speedy return of Christ, and consequently *did not organize* the church in its infancy, as it was afterward found necessary to do.[5] (emphasis mine)

The Myth's original version suffers from the Didn't Dilemma: either the apostles *didn't know* that church government was necessary, or else they knew it but *didn't do* it. But if they didn't know it, then they didn't know all truth. That would mean that Jesus erred or else the Holy Spirit failed to fulfill Jesus' promise in John 16:13. Thus the "didn't know it" accusation cannot be valid.

Well then, the apostles must have known that Jesus' Ekklesia needed to be organized. But if they knew it, why didn't they do it? If they knew that Jesus intended for His body to have political government, why didn't they ever mention it? Finally, why did the apostles design Jesus' Ekklesia in a way that made church government impossible?

If Christ's apostles knew that church government was God's will, then they all intentionally practiced, taught, and documented something that God never intended; they all knowingly kept the Holy Spirit's truth secret and took it with them to their graves. Not only that, they all deliberately made organized religion so impossible that their documented design had to be completely scrapped after they died!

### THE MYTH'S STEALTH VERSION:
### THE FLEXIBLE FALLACY

The Myth's stealth version attempts to avoid the Didn't Dilemma by means of the Flexible Fallacy:

> At first, church organization and government in the New Testament was

*flexible* to meet changing needs. But as the church became better established, it gave attention to the right structures and procedures that would help it accomplish its mission . . . Thus, numerous forms of church government are used today to provide order and structure for the work of churches.[6] (emphasis mine)

The Flexible Fallacy claims that Christ's apostles believed in, taught, and practiced church government; they just never settled on one final form. The stealth version even cites a handful of proof texts to support its claims. As you might suspect by now, all of the proof texts have been myth-interpreted - twisted out of context.[7]

But the Flexible Fallacy itself is also a trick. And it's the same one that makes John 16:13 the promise Jesus *never* made: mental misdirection. Our minds, like our eyes, can focus in only one direction at a time; we cannot mentally focus in two directions at once. When our eyes are focused on what's right in front of us, we can't see what's behind our heads. Likewise, when our minds are focused in one direction, things in the opposite direction become invisible. Illusionists exploit this mental blind spot when performing "magic" tricks such as making a quarter disappear and reappear behind someone's ear.

The Flexible Fallacy utilizes our mental blind spot to keep us from seeing what the New Testament actually says. The poem *Antigonish* by William Hughes Mearns illustrates how the myth, though it is an illusion, still occupies space in our minds and appears real:

Yesterday, upon the stair,
I met a man who wasn't there
He wasn't there again today
I wish, I wish he'd go away . . .

By focusing our minds on what isn't there, the Flexible Fallacy makes it *appear* real, so at the same time it keeps us from seeing what would otherwise be clearly visible. The design of Jesus' Ekklesia is clearly documented throughout the New Testament. But by tricking us into focusing on nonexistent "flexible" church government, the Flexible Fallacy effectively makes the apostles' design invisible.

If Jesus didn't err and the Holy Spirit didn't fail, then Christ's apostles knew everything Jesus knew when they designed the Ekklesia and documented their design in the New Testament. And if the truth they knew wasn't partial, temporary, or limited to just the first century, then their design was fixed and permanent, not flexible or temporary.

The problem for organized religion is that the single, fixed, permanent design for Jesus' Ekklesia doesn't have any of the following:

- The office of the bishop or pastor

- Clergy and laity

- Ordination

- Salaried clergy

- Church buildings

- Worship services and the Order of Worship

- Sermons

### CONCLUSION

Churchianity claims that God authorized and approves of church government. And if Jesus really had promised that the Holy Spirit would guide the *Church* into all truth, then this claim might be plausible. But contrary to popular opinion, Jesus did *not* promise that over the next several centuries, the Holy Spirit would slowly guide the "church fathers" into all truth until church government was fully developed. Regardless of any other interpretation that churchianity imposes on His words, Jesus' promise in John 16:13 was made specifically, literally, and solely to His eleven apostles.

According to churchianity, Jesus' promise was not meant for the eleven men to whom He spoke; rather, it was meant for others who were not yet born. But Jesus' actual promise deals a deathblow to churchianity's myth-theology. Since the Holy Spirit guided Jesus' apostles into *all* truth, *how much truth was left* for succeeding generations to discover? (Answer: zip, zero, zilch, nada, none.)

One possible objection to taking John 16:13 at face value could be stated thus: "If the Holy Spirit didn't guide *the Church* into all truth, how would Christians be protected from error and deception?" But this question implicitly assumes churchianity's myth-theology. Christians have always been protected from error and deception. All we have to do is carefully follow the apostles' instructions and examples in the New Testament. But that would require having no one but Jesus as the acting head of His body. And *that* would mean no church government.

And now we're finally ready to answer the question posed at the end of chapter 6: was Paul, the apostle who gave us thirteen of the twenty-seven books of the New Testament, really appointed directly by Jesus as an apostle of Christ?

**Endnotes**

1 Matthew 26:17-30; Mark 14:12-26; Luke 22:7-39; John 13:1-18:1.

2 First-century Jews did not eat the Passover meal, or any other meal, sitting on chairs around a table. (Wight n.d.)

3 Shelley, *Church History In Plain Language: Updated 2nd Edition*, 72.

4 Bell, *Discovering The Rich Heritage Of Orthodoxy*, 10-11.

5 Orr, *International Standard Bible Encyclopedia*, "Bishop"

6 Youngblood, *Nelson's Bible Dictionary*, "Church Government"

7 Editor's Note: Before the author died, he intended to write a second (and third) volume, and wanted to untwist these proof texts in volume 2.

Chapter 10

# SAUL (PAUL) OF TARSUS: APOSTLE OF CHRIST?

Did Jesus personally appoint Saul (Paul) of Tarsus as His apostle? This question is critical because Paul wrote thirteen of the New Testament's twenty-seven books and letters; nearly everything we know about the design and functioning of Jesus' Ekklesia comes from Paul. But if Jesus didn't personally appoint Paul as His apostle, then Paul was never authorized to speak for him.

As we noted previously, only Jesus could appoint someone to be His apostle: His personal legal representative. No one could appoint himself; not even other apostles could appoint him. But Saul of Tarsus appears to be an exception to this rule:

- Jesus didn't appoint Paul along with the Twelve (Mark 3:13-14; Luke 6:12-13).

- Paul wasn't present when Jesus pronounced His three promises to His apostles.

- Paul was an unbeliever even after the day of Pentecost and couldn't meet Peter's conditions in Acts 1:22 (an eyewitness of Jesus "beginning from His baptism by John until the day He was taken up").

If Jesus didn't personally appoint Paul as His apostle, then Paul's teaching about the design and function of the Ekklesia was unauthorized. If Paul was not truly an apostle of Christ, then his thirteen letters aren't reliable. And if his letters aren't reliable, then maybe the Myth of the Church's Infancy isn't a myth after all. If Paul isn't reliable, then for all we know God might actually approve of church government.

So, was Paul really directly appointed by the Lord Jesus Christ—or not?

SINCERE BUT MISTAKEN?

Paul certainly believed that he was a duly appointed apostle of Christ. In nine of his letters, he introduced himself as such.[1] In his letter to the Christians in Galatia, he claimed to have been directly appointed by Jesus:

> From Paul, an apostle (not from men, nor by human agency, but by Jesus Christ and God the Father who raised him from the dead)… (Gal 1:1)

In that same letter, he claimed equal apostolic authority with Peter:

> …(for he who empowered Peter for his apostleship to the circumcised also empowered me for my apostleship to the Gentiles,) (Gal 2:8)

In another letter, Paul claimed to write with Jesus' own authority:

> If anyone considers himself a prophet or spiritual person, he should acknowledge that *what I write to you is the Lord's command.* If someone does not recognize this, he is not recognized. (1 Cor 14:37-38, emphasis mine)

Paul also claimed to be a skilled master builder of Jesus' Ekklesia:

> According to the grace of God given to me, like a skilled master-builder I laid a foundation . . . (1 Cor 3:10)

The problem with all of Paul's claims about his apostleship is that they cannot be independently verified; we must simply take Paul at his word. Certainly Paul's entire life after his conversion demonstrated the sincerity of his belief in Jesus. But sincere belief isn't the same as direct appointment. And only direct appointment by Jesus could qualify Paul as an apostle of Christ with Jesus' own absolute teaching authority.

The three accounts of Paul's conversion on the road to Damascus (Acts 9:1-22; 22:1-21; 26:12-18) are open to the same criticism: they are all Paul's testimony about himself. Yes, there were other men who also saw the light that Paul saw. But according to Paul, they didn't understand the words that he heard (Acts 22:9). So they could not confirm Paul's account.

We know that there were men who falsely claimed to be apostles (2 Cor 11:13; Rev 2:2). What if Paul was sincere but mistaken? Other than Paul's claims about himself, is there any way for us to be certain that Paul really was appointed personally by the Lord Jesus Christ?

As a matter of fact, yes, there is.

## ACTS 15: PAUL'S APOSTLESHIP VALIDATED

As we've seen, the twelve apostles—the men who held power of attorney for the Lord Jesus Christ—were the final authorities on questions regarding the gospel and the Ekklesia. And there was one question that was so important that God wanted it answered once and for all, with the answer recorded in writing for the rest of history. We know this because God arranged for the original apostles of Christ to answer the question while they were all still together in Jerusalem.

The story of that question and its answer is found in Acts chapter 15. Acts 15 is usually subtitled "The Council at Jerusalem." We're generally told that this council determined that Christians are not required to obey Old Covenant Jewish law. However, there's a hugely important aspect of this meeting that seems to get overlooked. God used the council at Jerusalem to clear up any doubt over the reliability of Paul's teaching. At this meeting—with all of Jesus' remaining original apostles present—Paul and Barnabas gave a complete account of their teaching and ministry:

> When they arrived in Jerusalem, they were received by the church and the apostles and the elders, and they reported all the things God had done with them. (Acts 15:4)

All of Jesus' original apostles—the final (and only) authorities on questions regarding the gospel and the Ekklesia—were present except for James, the brother of John, who had been killed by King Herod (Acts 12:1-2). They all heard a complete report of everything Paul and Barnabas taught and practiced. The audience also included men who opposed Paul's understanding of the gospel:

> But some from the religious party of the Pharisees who had believed stood up and said, "It is necessary to circumcise the Gentiles and to order them to observe the law of Moses." (Acts 15:5)

So all the original apostles of Christ had the opportunity to hear every detail of Paul's teaching. They could question or correct anything that varied, however slightly, from the truth that Jesus had promised and that the Holy Spirit had revealed to them. There was certainly the opportunity for Paul and Barnabas to be cross-examined by men who strongly disagreed with them.

The result was that all of Christ's apostles gave Paul's teaching their total, unqualified approval. They recorded their judgment in a letter, and you can read it in Acts 15:23-29. And just for good measure, Peter later documented his personal approval of Paul's letters, recognizing them as inspired by God:

> And regard the patience of our Lord as salvation, just as also our dear broth-
> er Paul wrote to you, according to the wisdom given to him, speaking of
> these things in *all his letters*. Some things in these letters are hard to under-
> stand, things the ignorant and unstable twist to their own destruction, as they
> also do to *the rest of the scriptures*. (2 Peter 3:15-16, emphasis mine)

Since the Lord Jesus Christ, speaking through His authorized apostolic representatives, gave His approval of Paul's teaching and practice, in writing—twice!—we accept Paul's letters as inspired by God, and therefore absolutely, entirely, and unquestionably reliable. We also accept Paul's testimony about being personally appointed as Jesus' apostle.

### CHURCHIANITY'S DIFFERENT JESUS

When second century Christian leaders threw out Paul's design for Jesus' Ekklesia, they brought in a different Jesus—the one Paul warned about in his second letter to the Ekklesia in Corinth:

> For if someone comes and proclaims *another Jesus different from the one we proclaimed*, or if you receive a different spirit than the one you received, or a different gospel than the one you accepted, you put up with it well enough! (2 Cor 11:4, emphasis mine)

How did changing the Ekklesia's design give Christianity a different Jesus? In his first letter to the Corinthians, Paul declared that his teaching about Jesus Christ constituted the permanent and unalterable foundation of the Ekklesia:

> According to the grace of God given to me, like a skilled master-builder *I laid a foundation* but someone else builds on it. And each one must be careful how he builds. For *no one can lay any foundation other than what is being laid*, which is Jesus Christ. (1 Cor 3:10-11, emphasis mine)

In that same letter, Paul gave detailed instructions about the Ekklesia's design and functioning. And elsewhere he also stated that he had declared God's whole purpose:

> For I did not shrink from declaring to you *the whole purpose of God*. (Acts 20:27 NASU, emphasis mine)

The Ekklesia is not an organization, it is an organism. It does not have an org chart - a diagram breaking down the organization's structure and relationships and the relative ranks of its members. According to churchianity's myth-theology, the church is a political organization with an org chart and a visible, acting head; Jesus is just the figurehead. That makes Paul's teaching about Jesus and Paul's design for Jesus' Ekklesia two separate matters; one can be changed without affecting the other. Paul's instructions about the Ekklesia can be thrown out without affecting Paul's teaching about Jesus.

But that isn't possible. Paul's teaching about Jesus and his instructions about the design and functioning of the Ekklesia are one and the same: inseparable. That's because *the Ekklesia is Christ's body*. It isn't possible to change Jesus' body but still proclaim the same Jesus that Paul preached. By nullifying Paul's instructions about Jesus' Ekklesia, the Myth proclaims a different Jesus: a Jesus who changed His mind after AD 100.

The real Lord Jesus Christ has never changed His mind and has never altered or rescinded His apostles' instructions. All of them are still in effect today. We have thirteen letters documenting Paul's teaching, yet not one of those letters mentions the supposedly indispensable matter of church government or even suggests that any of Paul's teaching was temporary. All of this raises additional crucial and controversial questions:

- Since Paul declared God's whole purpose (Acts 20:27), how much of God's purpose remained to be discovered and declared by future generations? (Answer: none.)

- Since Paul never mentioned church government, how much does church government have to do with God's whole purpose? (Answer: none.)

- Since the New Testament gives no indication that any of Paul's teaching is no longer part of God's purpose, on what basis can any part of his teaching be considered temporary? (Answer: on no basis.)

### POSTSCRIPT: PAUL'S "ECCLESIASTICAL NOMENCLATURE"

Technically, the issue we're about to examine has to do with viewing and understanding the Bible upside-down. But since it is mentioned in the next section, we'll cover it only briefly here.

1 Thessalonians 5:12 is one of a handful of proof texts that the Myth's stealth version cites in support of the Flexible Fallacy: the notion that Christ's apostles actually practiced and taught church government; they just did it so flexibly that we can't see it.

Vincent's *Word Studies In The New Testament*, a well-known 19th-century reference work, contains an example of the Flexible Fallacy's faulty logic. The Greek word in question is *proistamenous* (pro-is-TAH-men-os; NT: 4291), translated as "over you" in the KJV:

And we beseech you, brethren, to know them which labour among you, and are *over you* in the Lord, and admonish you; (1 Thess 5:12 KJV, emphasis mine)

Dr. Vincent correctly noted that this word does not refer to any official position. But then he attempted to explain why Paul didn't mention any official titles:

[It does not indicate a particular ecclesiastical office, but is used functionally. *The ecclesiastical nomenclature of the Pauline Epistles is unsettled . . .* (emphasis mine)

In other words, Dr. Vincent is saying that Paul hadn't yet figured out the proper titles for churchianity's political rulers. The logic behind this conclusion is as follows:

- The Church is divided into a ruling clergy and a submitting laity.

- But Paul didn't mention the titles "bishop" or "pastor."

- Therefore, it is obvious that Paul hadn't yet settled on proper titles for church officials.

This is another instance of the Church Infancy Myth showing us things upside-down. Once again we're being tricked into believing the Myth and doubting the New Testament. According to Dr. Vincent, the fact that Paul didn't mention any official titles cannot mean that no such officials existed; rather, the problem is simply that Paul hadn't yet figured out proper titles for the clergy.

But if God authorized church government and yet Paul didn't know the proper titles of the church's officials, then he didn't know all the truth. And if that's the case, then he was mistaken when he stated the following:

Now I want you to know, brothers and sisters, that the gospel I preached is not of human origin. For I did not receive it or learn it from any human source; instead I received it by a revelation of Jesus Christ. (Gal 1:11-12)

. . . that by revelation the divine secret was made known to me, as I wrote before briefly. When reading this, you will be able to understand my insight into this secret of Christ. (Eph 3:3-4)

For I did not hold back from announcing to you the whole purpose of God. (Acts 20:27)

According to the grace of God given to me, like a skilled master-builder I laid a foundation . . . (1 Cor 3:10)

Of course Paul wasn't mistaken and he did know all the truth. Why didn't Paul mention any official titles in 1 Thessalonians 5:12? The correct explanation is:

- As an apostle of Christ, Paul knew all the truth about the gospel and Jesus' Ekklesia.

- Paul never mentioned the office of bishop or pastor.

- Therefore, the Ekklesia has no such office.

The accusation that Paul's ecclesiastical nomenclature was unsettled is just another subtle attempt to discredit Christ's apostles. The Myth has to discredit Paul's teaching. It has to get around, circumvent, nullify, and explain away Christ's commands that Paul documented in his thirteen letters. The reason for this is clear; since it is clearly written, stated, and shown in the New Testament that the true purpose, function, and design of the Ekklesia as documented by Christ's apostles is completely in disagreement with organized religion.

**Endnotes**

1     Rom 1:1, 1 Cor 1:1, 2 Cor 1:1, Gal 1:1, Eph 1:1, Col 1:1, 1 Tim 1:1, 2 Tim 1:1, Titus 1:1

# Section 3:

# BLUEPRINT

The purpose of the Church Infancy Myth is to explain and attempt to legitimize all the differences between New Testament Christianity and churchianity's counterfeit version. That means it has to get around, circumvent, nullify, and explain away virtually all of the New Testament's instructions and examples. It accomplishes its goal by directly and indirectly creating doubt and unbelief about the New Testament.

The Myth's original version creates doubt and unbelief by accusing Christ's apostles of incompetence or error. In Section 2 we unmasked the accusations and exposed them as lies.

The Myth's stealth version creates doubt and unbelief in two ways: by claiming that the New Testament is unreliable, and by effectively blinding us to what it actually says.

The stealth version's Flexible Fallacy claims that church government is right there in the New Testament; it's just so flexible that we can't see it; it's flexibly hiding between the lines. But *if we know what to look for*, then it will magically appear.

The Flexible Fallacy's trick is mental misdirection—getting us to look for something that isn't there. When our minds are focused on what isn't there, what's actually there becomes invisible.

The only way to "find" church government in the New Testament is to view the Bible as a random collection of proof texts: non sequitur numbered sentences that must be yanked out of context and rearranged in order to figure out what God was trying to tell us. It's Hugo of St. Victor's upside-down method of understanding the Bible that we covered in chapter 3: "Learn first what you should believe, and then go to the Bible to find it there." It's like reading the Bible through churchianity-colored glasses.

Churchianity wants us to believe that organized religion is the solution to the problem of false teachers, that organizing under one leader – a visible head – is necessary. But this is false. The Ekklesia was *always* meant to function as an organism, submitting to the invisible head, Jesus.

In section 3 we're going to start looking at what the New Testament actually says. We're going to remove our churchianity-colored glasses, turn the New Testament right-side-up, and see what it clearly tells us about Christianity.

If Jesus and His apostles weren't aware of the future needs of Christians and the problems which may arise from false teachers, then perhaps the organizational solution is the answer. But far from not knowing about this potential problem, the apostles and Jesus clearly defined the problem, and provided a solution – one that makes organized religion *impossible*. The true design of the Ekklesia is God's solution to *everything,* not just false teaching.

When Jesus promised to build His Ekklesia (Matt 16:18), He had a specific design in mind. His apostles knew what His design was and they implemented it perfectly. Not only that: they also documented it thoroughly.

Chapter 11

# THE MAN WHO WAS
# SMARTER THAN JESUS?

In his book *The Divine Conspiracy*, Dallas Willard conclusively declares that Jesus was the smartest man who ever lived.[1] And we who confess Jesus as Lord would certainly agree. Yet if actions speak louder than words, nearly all of us believe that another man was smarter than Jesus. How else can we explain the fact that we ignore what Christ's apostles taught and documented and follow this man's teaching instead? Christians have agreed with him for nearly 1,900 years.

Who am I talking about?

His name was Ignatius, he lived in Antioch (eastern Roman empire), and early in the second century he devised a solution to the Ekklesia's ultimate problem—the problem that, in his opinion, none of Christ's apostles were ever able to solve. The problem of . . . *false doctrine.*

According to Ignatius, Christianity's biggest problem stemmed from a lack of proper organization. The *small change* I mentioned in chapter 1 was Ignatius' way to protect God's flock from false teaching. His plan was to set up a visible head over each local congregation – a practice known as *monepiscopacy* (mahn-uh-PI-skuh-puh-see), which Webster's defines as "Church government by monarchical bishops." In his book, *The Ministry in Historical Perspectives*, H. R. Niebuhr explains:

In a significant article M. H. Shepherd, Jr., argues that Ignatius in urging monepiscopacy was motivated largely by hostility to the gnostic teachers operating among the house churches in various cities. His purpose was to bring all of these house churches in a single city area under a single leader, "who would have complete control and jurisdiction over all liturgical assemblies where baptism and the Eucharist were administered, discipline meted out, and instruction given."[2]

This unique leader was called the bishop (*overseer*) or pastor (*shepherd*). Although both these terms occur in the New Testament, the office of the pastor (or bishop) as the visible head of each Ekklesia does not exist in the New Testament and was invented after the end of the first century:

> . . . monepiscopacy—that is, the pattern of a single bishop, or pastor, at the head of each church . . . does not clearly emerge till the opening years of the second century. The first witness to it is Ignatius, a prophet of the church of Antioch in Syria, who has become the bishop in the sense of the single head, of the church in that city.[3]

The Ekklesia already had official leaders, of course: the elders (or *presbyters*) that Paul and Barnabas had appointed (Acts 14:23); Peter called them "shepherds of God's flock" (1 Peter 5:1-2). But from a natural perspective, the apostolic leadership structure was unwieldy and inefficient. As Thomas Lindsay explains, Ignatius decided that the only way God's flock could be truly protected from error was by having a single, visible head who could exercise authoritative leadership:

> One man can take a firmer grip of things. Divided responsibility continually means varying counsels. What is the business of many is often the work of none. A divided leadership continually brings with it fickle and impotent action. The need for an undivided front in time of danger was what inspired Ignatius, when, with the eye of a statesman and the fire of a prophet, he pleaded for the union of the congregation under one leader.[4]

If Jesus really was the smartest man who ever lived, why didn't He recommend putting one godly man in charge of things? Why didn't He establish a visible head and command his followers to listen to and obey the bishop (or pastor)? Couldn't He think of such a simple and natural solution?

The New Testament has already answered that question. But before we examine that answer there are several issues we need to address first, which will be covered over the next several chapters:

1. Were Jesus and his apostles aware of the problem of false teaching? Because if they weren't, then maybe Ignatius' organizational solution really *was* necessary.

2. But if Jesus and his apostles *were* aware of the problem, then did they

provide a solution? Because if they didn't, then again maybe Ignatius was *right*.

3. But if Jesus and his apostles *did* provide a solution, what was it? Where is it documented? Why haven't we heard about it?

Well, let's tackle one issue at a time. Our first question is: were Jesus and his apostles aware of the problem of false doctrine? What does the New Testament tell us?

### JESUS WARNED OF FALSE PROPHETS

Jesus had, of course, warned about false prophets multiple times. Jesus knew only too well that his Ekklesia would encounter false prophets, and He even gave his followers the "fruit test" to recognize them:

> Watch out for false prophets, who come to you in sheep's clothing but inwardly are voracious wolves. You will recognize them by their fruit. Grapes are not gathered from thorns or figs from thistles, are they? In the same way, every good tree bears good fruit, but the bad tree bears bad fruit. A good tree is not able to bear bad fruit, nor a bad tree to bear good fruit. Every tree that does not bear good fruit is cut down and thrown into the fire. So then, you will recognize them by their fruit. (Matt 7:15-20)

> At that time many will fall away and will betray one another and hate one another. Many false prophets will arise and will mislead many. (Matt 24:10-11 NASU)

> Then if anyone says to you, 'Look, here is the Christ!' or 'There he is!' do not believe him. For false messiahs and false prophets will appear and perform great signs and wonders to deceive, if possible, even the elect. Remember, I have told you ahead of time. (Matt 24:23-25)

But to Ignatius, merely recognizing the problem wasn't the same as solving it. In spite of all of Jesus' warnings, the church still had false prophets and teachers. Ignatius believed that something more effective than mere warnings was obviously required.

### PAUL WARNED OF FALSE APOSTLES AND TEACHERS

Despite his "surpassingly great revelations" (2 Cor 12:7 NIV), the Apostle Paul fared no better when opposing false teachers. Paul and Barnabas confronted a legalist ministry team in Antioch and ended up traveling to Jerusalem in what, to Ignatius, would have seemed a time-consuming and inefficient attempt to solve the problem:

Now some men came down from Judea and began to teach the brothers, "Unless you are circumcised according to the custom of Moses, you cannot be saved." When Paul and Barnabas had a major argument and debate with them, the church appointed Paul and Barnabas and some others from among them to go up to meet with the apostles and elders in Jerusalem about this point of disagreement. (Acts 15:1-2)

Paul even wrote a letter to the Galatian Ekklesia in which he twice pronounced eternal condemnation upon those who proclaimed a different—legalistic—gospel (Gal 1:8-9). In another letter he warned the Corinthians about false apostles:

For such people are false apostles, deceitful workers, disguising themselves as apostles of Christ. And no wonder, for even Satan disguises himself as an angel of light. Therefore it is not surprising his servants also disguise themselves as servants of righteousness, whose end will correspond to their actions. (2 Cor 11:13-15)

There were false teachers in Ephesus as well. Paul could have set up a doctrinal CEO in every congregation to solve this problem—but he didn't. Instead, he asked his coworker[5] Timothy to stay behind and instruct the teachers:

As I urged you when I was leaving for Macedonia, stay on in Ephesus to instruct certain people not to spread false teachings . . . (1 Tim 1:3)

False teachers were damaging people's faith. Paul's solution was for every believer to focus on relationship with Jesus:

. . . and their message will spread its infection like gangrene. Hymenaeus and Philetus are in this group. They have strayed from the truth by saying that the resurrection has already occurred, and they are undermining some people's faith. However, God's solid foundation remains standing, bearing this seal: "The Lord knows those who are his," and "Everyone who confesses the name of the Lord must turn away from evil." (2 Tim 2:17-19)

Paul told Titus that false teachers must be silenced because they were ruining whole household congregations:

For there are many rebellious people, idle talkers, and deceivers, especially those with Jewish connections, who must be silenced because they mislead whole families by teaching for dishonest gain what ought not to be taught. (Titus 1:10-11)

But Paul never proposed an organizational solution. Paul never suggested using political power to enforce his instructions with fines, confiscation, banishment, imprisonment, torture, and death. Churchianity had to wait until the fourth century for that. Ignatius certainly never imagined the horrors his "final solution" would entail. But Ignatius was not an apostle. He didn't know all truth. Jesus' promise in John 16:13 didn't apply to him.

## PETER WARNED OF FALSE PROPHETS AND TEACHERS

The Apostle Peter also warned about false prophets and teachers. He prophesied that many Christians would follow them, bringing the faith into disrepute. But he never suggested a political, organizational solution to solve the problem:

> But false prophets arose among the people, just as there will be false teachers among you. These false teachers will infiltrate your midst with destructive heresies, even to the point of denying the Master who bought them. As a result, they will bring swift destruction on themselves. And many will follow their debauched lifestyles. Because of these false teachers, the way of truth will be slandered. (2 Peter 2:1-2)

## JOHN WARNED OF FALSE PROPHETS

The Apostle John also warned about false prophets. But rather than establish a doctrinal CEO, his solution was for every believer to discern spirits:

> Dear friends, do not believe every spirit, but *test the spirits* to determine if they are from God, because many false prophets have gone out into the world. (1 John 4:1-2, emphasis mine)

> For many deceivers have gone out into the world, people who do not confess Jesus as Christ coming in the flesh. This person is the deceiver and the antichrist! Watch out, so that you do not lose the things we have worked for, but receive a full reward.

> Everyone who goes on ahead and does not remain in the teaching of Christ does not have God. The one who remains in this teaching has both the Father and the Son. If anyone comes to you and does not bring this teaching, do not receive him into your house and do not give him any greeting, because the person who gives him a greeting shares in his evil deeds. (2 John 1:7-11)

Unlike Ignatius—but precisely like Paul—John fully expected ordinary, *unordained* Christians to hear directly from Jesus! Where would he get such a notion? He got it from Jesus, his Master, who declared: "My sheep listen to my voice, and I know them, and they follow me," (John 10:27). Apparently, however, Ignatius thought he knew better than John and Paul.

### JUDE WARNED ABOUT FALSE TEACHERS

Jude also warned his fellow believers about false teachers but never recommended an organizational, political solution:

> Dear friends, although I have been eager to write to you about our common salvation, I now feel compelled instead to write to encourage you to contend earnestly for the faith that was once for all entrusted to the saints. For certain men have secretly slipped in among you - men who long ago were marked out for the condemnation I am about to describe - ungodly men who have turned the grace of our God into a license for evil and who deny our only Master and Lord, Jesus Christ. (Jude 3-4)

### JESUS WARNED US AGAIN, FROM HEAVEN

Around AD 95, near the end of John's life, Jesus gave his last living[6] apostle a *Revelation* which became the final book of the New Testament. In his *Revelation*, Jesus commended the Ephesian Ekklesia for identifying and rejecting false apostles. At this late date, Jesus still endorsed the fruit test:

> ". . . I know your works as well as your labor and steadfast endurance, and that you cannot tolerate evil. You have even *put to the test* those who refer to themselves as apostles (but are not), and have discovered that they are false." (Rev 2:2, emphasis mine)

Pergamum had two sets of false teachers. Jesus commanded them to repent and warned of severe consequences if they didn't:

> "...But I have a few things against you: You have some people there who follow the teaching of Balaam, who instructed Balak to put a stumbling block before the people of Israel so they would eat food sacrificed to idols and commit sexual immorality. In the same way, there are also some among you who follow the teaching of the Nicolaitans. Therefore, repent! If not, I will come against you quickly and make war against those people with the sword of my mouth." (Rev 2:14-16)

Thyatira was absolutely the worst. They tolerated a false prophetess and were even joining the pagans in fertility goddess "worship." Jesus *could have* told John to establish the office of doctrinal CEO in every congregation to solve this problem—but He didn't. Instead, He told his followers in Thyatira to repent. He left it up to them to obey Him voluntarily or suffer the consequences:

> "But I have this against you: You tolerate that woman Jezebel, who calls herself a prophetess, and by her teaching deceives my servants to commit sexual immorality and to eat food sacrificed to idols. I have given her time

to repent, but she is not willing to repent of her sexual immorality. Look! I am throwing her onto a bed of violent illness, and those who commit adultery with her into terrible suffering, unless they repent of her deeds. Furthermore, I will strike her followers with a deadly disease, and then all the churches will know that I am the one who searches minds and hearts. I will repay each one of you what your deeds deserve." (Rev 2:20-23)

The *Revelation* was Jesus' golden opportunity to correct any apostolic errors or omissions (yes, I'm kidding); to let us know which New Testament instructions and examples were about to be rescinded and revoked (there weren't any); and to set up a visible head over each Ekklesia to protect God's flock from false teaching. Yet He did none of these things. Why not? Did it just slip His mind? Was Ignatius smarter than Jesus?

No, Jesus wasn't negligent or forgetful; and no, Ignatius wasn't smarter than Jesus.

### ORGANIZED RELIGION: WRONG SOLUTION TO THE WRONG PROBLEM

We began this chapter with three questions, pertaining to whether Ignatius was correct in implementing a solution to the problem of false prophesy. The first question asks whether the apostles and Jesus were ever aware of the problem in the first place, because if they weren't, then maybe Ignatius was right.

So the answer to our first question is yes: Jesus, Paul, Peter, John and Jude were all fully aware of false apostles, prophets, and teachers. But what about our other questions: did Jesus and His apostles provide a solution to the problem? If they did, what is it? Why haven't we heard about it?

What if the New Testament clearly documents God's solution to the problem of false doctrine? And what if God's solution is drastically different from Ignatius' organizational scheme? In fact, what if God's solution is so radically different that, if we read the New Testament looking for organized religion, God's solution becomes *invisible?*

Or to put it another way: what if 1,900 years of immersion in chuchianity's myth-theology has left us unable to see what the New Testament clearly and plainly says?

By now, you probably wouldn't be surprised to learn that the New Testament clearly presents God's solution to false doctrine. It turns out that false teaching is not the problem: rather, it's a symptom of a different problem. The Apostle Paul documented God's solution to the *real* problem. Ignatius' simple and natural solution was the wrong answer to the wrong problem.

Worse, Ignatius' organizational scheme made it impossible for Christians to implement God's solution to the *real* problem. Which is why, after practicing organized religion for nearly 1,900 years, we still have false doctrine. Ignatius didn't solve the problem: he institutionalized it.

So yes; Jesus and His apostles were aware of the problem of false doctrine. But now we must answer question 2: did they provide a solution?

**Endnotes**

1    Willard, *The Divine Conspiracy*, 95.

2    Niebuhr et al, *The Ministry in Historical Perspectives,* 25.

3    Niebuhr et al, *The Ministry in Historical Perspectives*, 23.

4    Lindsay, *The Church And The Ministry In The Early Centuries*, 206.

5    "Timothy, my fellow worker" (Rom 16:21); "Timothy, our brother and fellow worker" (1 Thes 3:2).

6    i.e., living in His pre-resurrection mortal body. As Samuel Waldron correctly points out, all of the apostles of Christ are alive today in heaven. Waldron also correctly notes that Jesus has never revoked His apostles' authority over His body, the Ekklesia. (Waldron, *To Be Continued*, 37.)

Chapter 12

# GOD'S SOLUTION TO EVERYTHING

In his farewell address to the elders of the Ekklesia in Ephesus, the Apostle Paul made a startling claim:

> For I did not hold back from announcing to you *the whole purpose of God.*
> (Acts 20:27, emphasis mine)

In other words, Paul claimed that there was a "big picture" of God's whole purpose; and that he, Paul, had explained this big picture to the Ephesian elders.

Think about that: if God really has an overarching and unifying purpose, that purpose would have to include God's solution to the problem of false doctrine. It would have to encompass the complete design for Jesus' Ekklesia, right down to the smallest details. It would constitute the blueprint that shows how all twenty-seven New Testament books and letters fit together—no more doctrinal jigsaw puzzle. It would be the key to correctly understanding everything about Christianity.

The big picture of God's whole purpose wouldn't just solve the problem of false doctrine; it would be God's solution to *everything.*

Don't you wish Paul could have shared that big picture with us? Don't you wish you could have been there with the Ephesian elders while Paul was explaining everything to them? Wouldn't it be wonderful to know how to correctly interpret and understand the entire New Testament?

You're in luck! Paul *did* document the big picture. He wrote a short letter that summarized everything he told the elders in Ephesus. We still have his letter. It's part of the New Testament. Can you guess its name?

You guessed it! We call his letter *the book of Ephesians.*

### EPHESIANS—BLUEPRINT FOR THE BODY

God had—and still has—a plan to protect the Ekklesia from false doctrine. God's plan has the added benefit of establishing the Kingdom (reign) of God by destroying the works of the devil. God's plan calls for every believer to actively worship in spirit and truth. And as you might guess, God's plan is the *opposite* of Ignatius' ruling-clergy submitting-laity organizational scheme.

God's plan is called "the body of Christ." The Lord Jesus Christ is the head:

> He did this when he revealed to us the secret of his will . . . *to head up all things in Christ* - the things in heaven and the things on earth. (Eph 1:9-10, emphasis mine)

And the Ekklesia is His body:

> And God put all things under Christ's feet, and he gave him to the church as head over all things. Now *the church is his body*, the fullness of him who fills all in all. (Eph 1:22-23, emphasis mine)

God's plan is well documented in the book of Ephesians. The letter to the Ephesians might as well be called "The Blueprint for the body of Christ." In six short chapters, Paul lays out God's entire purpose for the Ekklesia and describes how Christ's body on earth functions to fulfill that purpose. And what is God's purpose?

> The purpose of this enlightenment is that through the church the multifaceted wisdom of God should now be disclosed to the rulers and the authorities in the heavenly realms. This was according to the eternal purpose that he accomplished in Christ Jesus our Lord . . . (Eph 3:10-11)

In other words, God intends the Ekklesia to be an object lesson revealing His diverse, complex, many-faceted wisdom to Satan, "the ruler of the kingdom of the air, the ruler of the spirit that is now energizing the sons of disobedience" (Eph 2:2).

The first three chapters of Ephesians are strategic: they describe God's overall plan and purpose. The last three chapters are tactical: they spell out the specific steps of action to implement God's plan. Spiritual warfare with its Ephesian armor in chapter six is the final tactical step in the implementation of God's strategic plan. That's why Paul says, "*Finally,* be strong in the Lord and in his mighty power" (Eph 6:10 NIV, emphasis mine).

## GOD'S SOLUTION TO FALSE DOCTRINE

So how *does* God intend to protect the Ekklesia from false doctrine? The answer to that question is found in Ephesians 4:11-16—which also happens to be the description of the *diakonia* (dee-ak-on-EE-ah, NT:1248) service gifts.

Churchianity's myth-theology has caused endless confusion and misunderstanding about New Covenant gifts. We're told, for example, that Paul's letters contain various lists of gifts[1] and that these lists are suggestive rather than exhaustive.[2] In other words, the implication is that Paul's understanding of gifts was just as unsettled as his ecclesiastical nomenclature in 1 Thessalonians 5:12.[3]

The truth is that Paul clearly states that there are three distinct categories of gifts and three different givers. He describes all three kinds of gifts and explains their purpose - but we'll cover this in more detail in the next section.

And now back to the *diakonia* service gifts. These gifts are people whom the Lord Jesus Christ gives to His body:

> It was he who gave some to be apostles, some to be prophets, some to be evangelists, and some to be pastors and teachers, to prepare God's people for works of service . . . (Eph 4:11-12 NIV)

Wait a minute! What's this about "pastors and teachers"? I said that the office of pastor / bishop doesn't exist in the New Testament and was invented after the first century. But here in Ephesians Paul says Jesus gives pastors to His Ekklesia. There had better be a good explanation, right?

There is, and it gets covered in the last section of this book. But right now we're going to focus on Ephesians 4:11-16 and how Jesus' *diakonia* gifts protect His Ekklesia from false teaching.

The purpose of the *diakonia* gifts is to prepare the body parts of Christ's body for works of service. The job of apostles, prophets, evangelists, and shepherd-teachers is to prepare the rest of us to function as Christ's body on earth. When Jesus' body parts function as intended, the body of Christ grows up and becomes mature:

> . . . so that the body of Christ may be built up until we all reach unity in the faith and in the knowledge of the Son of God and become mature, attaining to the whole measure of the fullness of Christ. (Eph 4:12-13 NIV)

False doctrine is just a symptom. The real problem is spiritual immaturity:

> So we are no longer to be *children*, tossed back and forth by waves and *carried about by every wind of teaching* by the trickery of people who craftily carry out

their deceitful schemes. (Eph 4:14 NIV, emphasis mine)

The Ephesian *diakonia* service gifts are the means God has ordained to bring the body of Christ to maturity. Spiritual maturity produces unity in the faith and solves the problem of false doctrine.

. . . Instead, speaking the truth in love, *we will in all things grow up* into him who is the Head, that is, Christ. (Eph 4:15 NIV, emphasis mine)

But Christ's body grows up into maturity when each part functions according to its *gifts*:

From him the whole body, joined and held together by every support-ing ligament, grows and builds itself up in love, *as each part does its work.*
(Eph 4:16 NIV, emphasis mine)

And what is it that we are to do when we become mature in Christ? God intends that we—mere mortals in the visible realm, but the glorious, resur-rected, immortal, supernaturally empowered body of Christ in the unseen realm—should implement His strategic purpose by standing in both spiritual and physical victory over the wicked spiritual powers that rule the world:

Finally, be strengthened in the Lord and in the strength of his power. Clothe yourselves with the full armor of God so that you may be able to stand against the schemes of the devil. For our struggle is not against flesh and blood, but against the rulers, against the powers, against the world rulers of this darkness, against the spiritual forces of evil in the heavens. For this reason, take up the full armor of God so that you may be able to stand your ground on the evil day, and having done everything, to stand. (Eph 6:10-13)

That last phrase, "to stand," according to Robertson's *Word Pictures in the New Testament*, means to stand in victory over a defeated foe.[4]

### DID GOD RESCIND APOSTLES AND PROPHETS?

According to Ephesians 4:11-16, spiritual maturity is the result of the follow-ing two-step process:

1. Apostles, prophets, evangelists, and shepherd-teachers prepare God's people for works of service;

2. Every body part of Christ's body does the work he or she has been gifted and prepared for.

Apostles and prophets are the two highest-ranking *diakonia* gifts. The Apostle Paul tells us:

And God has placed in the church *first* apostles, *second* prophets, third teachers, then miracles, gifts of healing, helps, gifts of leadership, different kinds of tongues. (1 Cor 12:28, emphasis mine)

If maturity was God's solution, and the Ephesians gifts were how God planned to bring Jesus' Ekklesia *into* maturity, and if apostles and prophets are the most important in that plan, then in order to answer whether Jesus and His apostles provided a solution to our problem, we need to know something important. The question for us now is: does Jesus still give apostles and prophets to His Ekklesia? Or did He stop after the first century? If the top two *diakonia* service gifts became extinct after AD 100, then maybe Ephesians 4:11-16 is no longer in effect. Maybe God now has a different plan for bringing Christ's body to maturity. If so, then maybe other parts of Paul's Ephesian letter have also passed their "use by" date and are now of historical interest only. And if that's the case, what about the rest of Paul's letters and the rest of the New Testament?

On the other hand, if all of Paul's Ephesian letter is still valid—if Jesus never rescinded or revoked the *diakonia* service gifts of apostles and prophets—then why don't we see any of them today? What became of them? Where did they go?

In the case of apostles, we've already answered that question. Today we still have just as much apostolic ministry as Christians had in the middle of the first century. That's because Christ's apostles knew *all truth* and they documented that truth in the New Testament's twenty-seven books and letters. Jesus delegated His own teaching authority to them and He didn't revoke that authority when they died. Jesus' apostles are alive with Him in heaven and they still exercise the same authority today as they did in the first century. As Samuel Waldron explains:

> ...the apostles continue to be the foundation of the church and continue under Christ to rule over the church from heaven through their teaching. Their teaching is the living Word of God, and it continues to have a mighty power over the church by the ongoing activity of the Spirit of Christ.[5]

But what about prophets? Does Jesus still give prophets and prophecy to His Ekklesia today? In my parents' church we were taught that God rescinded those gifts after the first century. Prophecy, we were told, was temporary: God spoke through prophets to reveal New Covenant truth only until the New Testament was completed. Once John penned the final "Amen" in the Revelation, the written Bible became God's complete and final communication. From then on, anyone who claimed to have new revelation from God was either deceived or lying (or both). After AD 95, prophets and prophecy were not just unnecessary, we believed they were enemies of the truth.

We had the best of intentions. We were defending the inspiration and inerrancy of the Bible "unto which nothing at any time is to be added, whether by new revelations of the Spirit, or traditions of men."[6] In our minds, the choice was either *Sola Scriptura* with no possibility of further divine revelation or else *Prima Scriptura* with its unwritten Holy Tradition, church fathers, and papal infallibility.

The *camel's nose metaphor* says that if you let the camel get its nose under the tent, this small, seemingly innocuous step will open the door for a very undesirable outcome – the whole camel will end up in the tent with you. Prophetic ministry was the camel's nose, the first false step down a slippery slope. If we ever allowed the Catholic camel to get its nose inside our Protestant tent, the rest was sure to follow.

But blaming God for the disappearance of prophetic ministry created more problems than it solved. It unavoidably nullified a number of clear New Testament instructions. We were caught in an impossible contradiction. If God *didn't* cancel prophets and prophecy after AD 95, then the written Bible wasn't God's complete and final Word. But if He *did* cancel prophetic ministry, then large portions of the New Testament were now invalid, misleading, and dangerous. Or as we preferred to say, "not for today"—of historical interest only.

Our dilemma was only apparent, not real—the result of myth-understanding the Bible. We could see just two alternatives: the Myth's original version (the Bible is temporary, partial, and incomplete) or the stealth version (the Bible is confusing, obscure, and hard to understand). We opposed the Myth's original version so we were forced to side with the stealth version.

In Homer's Greek myth, Odysseus' maritime path was blocked by Scylla, a six headed monster that lived on a rock on one side of a narrow strait, and by a large whirlpool called Charybdis on the other side. Trying to avoid one meant the other would take you.

The Myth's lose-lose logic trapped us between *Sola's* Scylla and *Prima's* Charybdis. And like Odysseus we chose the lesser of evils. Better to lose prophets to *Sola* than to lose the entire Bible to *Prima*. Like Peter Arnett's famous misquoted statement about the Viet Nam war, we had to destroy the Bible in order to save it.

There was a third alternative, but myth-interpretation made it invisible. There's a problem with prophets and prophecy all right, but it isn't what we thought. It's true that after the first century prophetic ministry declined and seemed to disappear. But that wasn't because God changed His design for the body of Christ or because the Lord Jesus revoked one of His Ephesian *diakonia* gifts. There's no conflict between New Covenant prophetic ministry and the principle of *Sola Scriptura*. The conflict is between prophetic ministry and organized religion.

Previously, we asked three questions and have now answered two: first, we now know that the problem of false doctrine was known and well-documented. Second, we covered that God *did* provide a solution to the problem. Finally, in the next section, we will answer the question of *what* that solution is and what it entails. Before we go into detail about that, let's first examine the consequences of Ignatius' natural solution.

**Endnotes**

1   Orr, *ISBE (original)*, "Spiritual Gifts"

2   Orr, *ISBE (Revised Edition)*, "Spiritual Gifts"

3   Vincent, *Word Studies In The New Testament*, "1 Thess 5:12"

4   And having done all to stand (kai hapanta katergasamenoi steenai). After the fight (wrestle) is over to stand (steenai) as victor in the contest. Effective aorist here (Robertson, *Word Pictures in the New Testament*, "Ephesians 6:13").

5   Waldron, *To Be Continued*, 17.

6   Westminster Assembly, 1646.

## Chapter 13

# WHAT BECAME OF
# PROPHETS?

History records that after the first century prophetic ministry declined and seemed to disappear. The official explanation is that prophecy was temporary. This explanation holds that once the New Testament was completed—once John penned the final "amen" in the Revelation in AD 95—the written Bible became God's complete and final communication. From then on, anyone claiming to have new revelation from God was either deceived or lying (or both). With the stroke of a pen, prophets stopped being Jesus' second most important *diakonia* gift and became enemies of the truth.

That's the official explanation. Trouble is, it's mythology, not history. And it creates more problems than it solves. If Jesus rescinded the *diakonia* gift of prophets, then Ephesians 4:11 is no longer valid. If Ephesians 4:11 is no longer valid, then a number of clear apostolic instructions about prophets and prophecy are of historical interest only. And the New Testament is confusing, obscure, and hard to understand.

There is, however, an unofficial explanation for the disappearance of prophetic ministry. It has several advantages over the official version. For one thing, it's historically verifiable: it's history, not mythology. For another, it doesn't blame God or accuse the New Testament of being confusing or misleading. It doesn't require Jesus to rescind any of His Ephesians 4:11 gifts. It doesn't nullify any clear apostolic instructions. It doesn't need a higher authority to tell us which New Testament instructions and examples to follow and which to ignore because they're "not for today."

What is this unofficial but historically accurate explanation? If it's true, then Ephesians 4:11 is still in effect. If it's true, then Jesus has never rescinded His second most important *diakonia* gift. But if Jesus still gives prophets to His *Ekklesia* today, why don't we see any of them? What became of them? Where did they go?

We're about to find out. We'll begin by reviewing those New Testament instructions that organized religion claims are no longer valid. Then we'll turn to history to learn the real reason that prophets and prophecy disappeared.

### NEW COVENANT PROPHETIC MINISTRY

Our review starts in Acts chapter 2 on the morning of the day of Pentecost. As you'll recall, all of Jesus' believers were together in one place:

> Now when the day of Pentecost had come, they were all together in one place. Suddenly a sound like a violent wind blowing came from heaven and filled the entire house where they were sitting. And tongues spreading out like a fire appeared to them and came to rest on each one of them. All of them were filled with the Holy Spirit, and they began to speak in other languages as the Spirit enabled them. (Acts 2:1-4)

Pentecost was a feast day (described in Leviticus 23:15-21). Pentecost means "fiftieth" and took place on the 50th day after Passover.[1] Jews from all over the Roman empire had traveled to Jerusalem to participate:

> Now there were devout Jews from every nation under heaven residing in Jerusalem. (Acts 2:5)

The roaring noise of wind was so loud that it drew a crowd. The visiting Jews were amazed to hear local people speaking their own (foreign) languages:

> When this sound occurred, a crowd gathered and was in confusion, because each one heard them speaking in his own language. (Acts 2:6)

These Jews from all over the empire couldn't understand how a group of locals from Galilee had suddenly become fluent in so many foreign languages:

> Completely baffled, they said, "Aren't all these who are speaking Galileans? And how is it that each one of us hears them in our own native language? Parthians, Medes, Elamites, and residents of Mesopotamia, Judea and Cappadocia, Pontus and the province of Asia, Phrygia and Pamphylia, Egypt and the parts of Libya near Cyrene, and visitors from Rome, both Jews and proselytes, Cretans and Arabs - we hear them speaking in our own languages about the great deeds God has done!" (Acts 2:7-11)

The crowd was dumbfounded, discombobulated, confusticated, bebothered, gobsmacked. What in heaven's name was going on? But some of the onlookers jumped to a cynical conclusion and accused Jesus' followers of being drunk:

> All were astounded and greatly confused, saying to one another, "What does this mean?" But others jeered at the speakers, saying, "They are drunk on new wine!" (Acts 2:12-13)

There were several problems with this accusation. For one thing, it didn't explain the mysterious roar of wind coming from the house. For another, although wine has been known to cause slurred speech, when has it ever conferred the ability to fluently speak a foreign language? But most importantly, Pentecost was a feast day and observant Jews didn't eat or drink before 9:00 A.M. on feast days.[2]

At this point Peter stood up to set the record straight. There was a valid explanation for both the noise and the languages. But it had nothing to do with drunkenness. Rather, it was the supernatural fulfillment of God's promise.

Let's review Peter's explanation and find out what he said about prophecy.

### PETER'S UNLIMITED PROMISE

Peter began by quoting the Old Testament book of Joel. God promised to pour out His Spirit on all people. As evidence of that outpouring, men and women would prophesy:

> But Peter stood up with the eleven, raised his voice, and addressed them: "You men of Judea and all you who live in Jerusalem, know this and listen carefully to what I say. In spite of what you think, these men are not drunk, for it is only nine o'clock in the morning. But this is what was spoken about through the prophet Joel:
>
> 'And in the last days it will be,' God says,
>
> 'that I will pour out my Spirit on all people,
>
> and your sons and your daughters will prophesy,
>
> and your young men will see visions,
>
> and your old men will dream dreams.
>
> Even on my servants, both men and women,
>
> I will pour out my Spirit in those days, and they will prophesy.'
> (Acts 2:14-18)

Peter explained that what his audience saw and heard (the men from Galilee speaking foreign languages that they had never learned) was the fulfillment of Joel's prophecy:

> This Jesus God raised up, and we are all witnesses of it. So then, exalted to
> the right hand of God, and having received the promise of the Holy Spirit
> from the Father, he has poured out what you both see and hear. (Acts 2:32-
> 33)

Peter declared that God's promise was not limited or restricted. It was
unlimited, open-ended, ongoing, and continual:

> Peter said to them, "Repent, and each one of you be baptized in the name
> of Jesus Christ for the forgiveness of your sins, and you will receive the
> gift of the Holy Spirit. For the promise is for you and your children, and
> for all who are far away, as many as the Lord our God will call to himself."
> (Acts 2:38-39)

I was taught that the gift Peter promised was the Holy Spirit Himself. That
part of the promise was "for today"—ongoing and continual. But the result
or evidence of that gift—prophesying—was limited, temporary, and "not for
today"—no longer in effect.

But Peter made no such distinction. Breaking Peter's promise in half and
then claiming that one half is still in effect but the other half is not for today
is myth-interpretation. It adds a qualification that Peter never stated. It imposes a foreign meaning on Peter's words. It accuses Peter, and God, of not
communicating clearly.

Does the rest of the New Testament offer any clues to what Peter meant?
Of course it does! In his first letter, Peter says that both speaking and serving
are expressions of God's gift:

> Just as each one has received a gift, use it to serve one another as good stew-
> ards of the varied grace of God. Whoever speaks, let it be with God's words.
> Whoever serves, do so with the strength that God supplies . . . (1 Peter 4:10-
> 11)

But what gift was Peter referring to? Was it the supernatural gift of Acts 2,
or did he simply mean the natural gifts that we're all born with?

The Apostle Paul has already answered this question.

### PAUL'S INSTRUCTIONS

In Romans 12:6-8 Paul lists the seven *energema* (en-ERG-ay-mah, NT:1755)
motivational gifts. We'll take a closer look at them later in this book. But right
now our focus is Paul's instructions about prophecy.

Like Peter, Paul says that both speaking and serving are God's gifts:

> And we have different gifts according to the grace given to us. If the gift is

prophecy, that individual must use it in proportion to his faith. If it is service, he must serve; if it is teaching, he must teach; (Rom 12:6-7)

Paul distinguishes prophecy from teaching, so they're not identical. If God rescinded the gift of prophecy after the first century, did He also rescind the gifts of serving and teaching? Paul's instruction about prophecy is clear: "that individual must use it." Paul limited this instruction with a single qualification: "in proportion to his faith." Did Paul intend to add a second qualification—"until John finishes the *Revelation*"—but somehow neglected to do so?

In his first letter to the Ekklesia in Corinth, Paul mentions prayer and prophecy together in the same sentence:

Any man who prays or prophesies with his head covered disgraces his head. (1 Cor 11:4)

Obviously God has not rescinded prayer. But if He rescinded prophecy then half of Paul's instruction is no longer in effect. Yet Paul didn't qualify this instruction. There's no warning that the first part is permanent but the second part is temporary.

In the same letter, Paul lists the nine *charisma* (KHAR-is-ma, NT: 5486) gifts of the Holy Spirit and states their purpose:

To each person the manifestation of the Spirit is given for the benefit of all. For one person is given through the Spirit the message of wisdom, and another the message of knowledge according to the same Spirit, to another faith by the same Spirit, and to another gifts of healing by the one Spirit, to another performance of miracles, to another prophecy, and to another discernment of spirits, to another different kinds of tongues, and to another the interpretation of tongues. (1 Cor 12:7-10)

Paul wrote this letter between AD 53 and 57.[3] If God rescinded prophecy in AD 95, then many of Paul's instructions were valid only for about forty years. Paul clearly states that the purpose of these gifts is for the benefit of all (or in the NIV "for the common good"). Did the common good stop being good when John finished the *Revelation*? Did the Holy Spirit's nine supernatural gifts suddenly stop being beneficial and become inimical or damaging?

And if God rescinded the *charisma* gift of prophecy, did He also revoke the gift of faith? Is God still allowed to give Christians supernatural faith today? But if He is, what about the other eight gifts?

Paul mentions love, spiritual gifts, and prophecy in the same sentence. He even emphasizes prophecy:

Pursue love and be eager for the spiritual gifts, especially that you may prophesy. (1 Cor 14:1)

Obviously God has not rescinded love. But if He rescinded spiritual gifts and especially prophecy, then the rest of Paul's instruction is no longer valid and must now be ignored and disobeyed.

Paul explains that the purpose of prophecy is to strengthen, encourage, and comfort God's people:

> But the one who prophesies speaks to people for their strengthening, encouragement, and consolation. (1 Cor 14:3)

Paul wished that all the believers in Corinth spoke in tongues but he wished even more that all of them would prophesy. He explained that in combination, the gifts of speaking in tongues and interpreting tongues are both the equivalent of prophecy:

> I wish you all spoke in tongues, but even more that you would prophesy. The one who prophesies is greater than the one who speaks in tongues, *unless he interprets* so that the church may be strengthened. (1 Cor 14:5, emphasis mine)

Peter said the same thing in Acts 2. On the morning of Pentecost the believers were speaking in tongues and Peter said they were prophesying. On that occasion no interpretation was necessary because the foreign-speaking Jews already understood what was being said.

Paul says that both prophecy and teaching build up the Ekklesia.

> Now, brothers and sisters, if I come to you speaking in tongues, how will I help you unless I speak to you with a revelation or with knowledge or prophecy or teaching? (1 Cor 14:6)

According to Paul, one function of prophecy is to reveal the secrets of people's hearts. This supernaturally disclosed information is convincing proof of God's presence:

> But if all prophesy, and an unbeliever or uninformed person enters, he will be convicted by all, he will be called to account by all. The secrets of his heart are disclosed, and in this way he will fall down with his face to the ground and worship God, declaring, "God is really among you." (1 Cor 14:24-25)

Paul gives clear instructions about prophecy in the meetings of the Ekklesia:

> Two or three prophets should speak and the others should evaluate what is said. And if someone sitting down receives a revelation, the person who is speaking should conclude. (1 Cor 14:29-30)

Paul again states prophecy's purpose and says that all can prophesy:

For you can all prophesy one after another, so all can learn and be encouraged. (1 Cor 14:31)

Paul wraps up his teaching about spiritual gifts and the meetings of the Ekklesia with two clear instructions:

So then, brothers and sisters, be eager to prophesy, and do not forbid anyone from speaking in tongues. (1 Cor 14:39)

He gives similar instructions in his letter to the Ekklesia in Thessalonica:

Do not put out the Spirit's fire; do not treat prophecies with contempt.
(1 Thess 5:19-20 NIV)

Yet if Jesus rescinded the *diakonia* gift of prophet and the *charisma* gift of prophecy, then today we must ignore and disobey Paul's instructions. We must prohibit prophecy and forbid speaking in tongues.

### THE NEW TESTAMENT'S MISSING "USE BY" DATE

As we've just seen, the New Testament contains a number of clear instructions about prophecy. But organized religion claims that all those instructions were temporary and were rescinded after AD 95.

In order to get around Peter's unlimited promise in Acts 2:39, organized religion has to break the promise in half and claim that Peter was really talking about two different things—and that one of them had a "use by" date but the other didn't. As for all of Paul's instructions, we're told that because Paul's teaching about spiritual gifts is found in just one of his thirteen letters—and an early letter at that—those instructions were not only temporary, they applied only to Corinth and nowhere else. (Spoiler alert: this accusation is transparently false. It's clearly refuted multiple times in the rest of the letter itself.)

The problem with all of churchianity's explanations is, once again, the New Testament's silence. There's no slightest hint that half of Peter's promise, all of Paul's instructions, and Jesus' second most important Ephesians 4:11 *diakonia* gift had a time limit or "use by" date. The whole "not for today" accusation is a subterfuge. It's one more way organized religion contradicts the New Testament without appearing to do so. And any explanation, interpretation, or teaching that contradicts clear New Testament instructions is a lie.

Now we're ready to hear from history and learn the real reason that prophets and prophecy disappeared.

**Endnotes**

1    Orr, *International Standard Bible Encyclopedia,* "Pentecost"

2    Wiersbe, *Wiersbe's Expository Outlines on the New Testament,* "Acts 2:15"

3    Orr, *International Standard Bible Encyclopedia,*" "First Epistle To The Corinthians"

Chapter 14

# CHRISTIANITY'S
# CAGE MATCH

Prophets and prophecy virtually disappeared after the first century. But that wasn't because God changed His documented design for the body of Christ or because Jesus rescinded His second most important *diakonia* gift. Rather, prophets disappeared because gifts and organized religion cannot exist together in one place. Ignatius' ruling clergy / submitting laity scheme created a cage match between the bishop and the Holy Spirit: two would enter but only one would leave.

Ignatius' plan required a single, visible head who ruled through political power. Therefore, all rivals to the bishop's power had to be subjugated or eliminated. And what was it that rivaled the bishop's power and prestige? Quite simply, any manifestation of the Holy Spirit in *anyone else*. Prophetic ministry was intrinsically authoritative and could not be subjugated; therefore it was eliminated.

This was the inevitable result of replacing the invisible headship of the Lord Jesus Christ with a visible, human headship. "No one can serve two masters" (Matt 6:24), no organization can serve two CEOs, and no kingdom can serve two kings.

Chapter VI of Thomas Lindsay's *The Church and the Ministry in the Early Centuries* chronicles the overthrow of prophetic ministry. The following quotations highlight the process:

It is evident that this new official task of guaranteeing the true apostolic teaching, which is laid upon the office-bearers in general, and on the pastors or bishops in particular, must have had a very restraining effect upon the prophetic ministry.[1]

The office-bearers who were in the succession were now made the judges of what ought to be taught…they were therefore set in the position of judging all who undertook the function which was the peculiar work of the prophetic ministry.[2]

The office-bearers, and especially the bishops, would inevitably become the instructors as well as the judges of the instruction that was given.[3]

The need for some authority to express the dogmatic unity of the Church, and the idea that this authority lay in the office-bearers of the churches, must have placed the prophetic ministry in an inferior position and tended to destroy it altogether.[4]

In this changed organization of the second and third centuries the old prophetic ministry was completely abandoned, and the local or congregational ministry now had no superiors to interfere with them and to supersede them in exhortation, in the dispensing of the Holy Supper, and in prescribing how Christians ought to live in the fear of God.[5]

We're now going to hear from Ignatius and see how his solution violated and nullified God's design for Christianity. English translations of Ignatius' letters are widely available, but here's what he said about church government.

(Note: the quotations below are from the American edition of the Ante-Nicene Fathers. This translation retains the Greek sentence structure, making it awkward and difficult to follow.)

### IGNATIUS

**To the Smyrneans, 55-56:** Let no man do anything connected with the Church without the bishop. Let that be deemed a proper Eucharist, which is [administered] either by the bishop, or by one to whom he has entrusted it. Wherever the bishop shall appear, there let the multitude [of the people] also be; even as, wherever Jesus Christ is, there is the Catholic [universal] Church. *It is not lawful without the bishop* either to baptize or to celebrate a love-feast; but whatsoever he shall approve of, that is also pleasing to God, so that everything that is done may be secure and valid. (emphasis mine)

"It is not lawful without the bishop." But this "law" cannot be found in the New Testament. So where did it come from? As we saw previously, only Christ's apostles were authorized to bind (forbid) and loose (permit). Ignatius testified that he was not an apostle.[6] He had no authority to add to or change what was commanded by Jesus and His apostles.

But Ignatius had the best of intentions: he wanted everything to be secure and valid. And in his view the obvious way to achieve that worthy goal was to enforce unquestioning obedience to a visible human authority. So he invented a "law" that added to God's Word. To Ignatius, the end justified the means.

\* \* \*

**To the Philadelphians, 23-24:** Take ye heed, then, to have but one Eucharist. For there is one flesh of our Lord Jesus Christ, and one cup to [show forth] the unity of His blood; one altar; as there is one bishop, along with the presbytery and deacons, my fellow-servants: that so, whatsoever ye do, ye may do it according to [the will of] God.

Since the Day of Pentecost, believers had been celebrating the Eucharist (also called the Lord's Supper) in their house churches, as Thomas Lindsay points out:

We are told that in the primitive church at Jerusalem the Lord's Supper was dispensed in the houses, (Acts 2:46) and that the brethren met in the house of Mary the mother of John Mark, (Acts 12:12), in the house of James the brother of our Lord, (Acts 21:18, 12:17) and probably elsewhere. At the close of the Epistle to the Romans, St. Paul sends greetings to three, perhaps five, groups of brethren gathered round clusters of distinguished Christians whom he names. One of these groups he calls a "church," and the others were presumably so also. (Romans 16:3-5; 10-11, 14-15)[7]

Ignatius' demand for one Eucharist meant that individual house churches could no longer celebrate the Lord's Supper.

(Ignatius') purpose was to bring all of these house churches in a single city area under a single leader, "who would have complete control and jurisdiction over all liturgical assemblies where baptism and the Eucharist were administered, discipline meted out, and instruction given."[8]

The Apostle Paul documented God's instructions concerning the Lord's Supper in 1 Corinthians 11:20-34. The Lord Jesus Christ, speaking through His Apostle Paul, placed two restrictions on His Supper: the first one general, the second one conditional:

So then, my brothers and sisters, when you come together to eat, *wait for one another. If* anyone is hungry, *let him eat at home,* (1 Cor 11:33-34)

In Ephesians 4:4-6, Paul lists seven unities that all believers share:

There is one body and one Spirit, just as you too were called to the one hope of your calling, one Lord, one faith, one baptism, one God and Father of all, who is over all and through all and in all. (Ephesians 4:4-6)

But Ignatius thought he had a better plan than Jesus.

\* \* \*

**To the Smyrneans, 60-61:** It is well to reverence both God and the bishop. He who honours the bishop has been honoured by God; he who does anything without the knowledge of the bishop, does [in reality] serve the devil.

When Ignatius' bishop became the acting head of Jesus' Ekklesia, Jesus became merely the figurehead. From then on, if Jesus wanted His body to function He would first have to obtain permission from the bishop. And anyone who dared to obey Jesus without the bishop's permission was accused of serving the devil.

\* \* \*

**To the Trallians, 9-10:** In like manner, let all reverence the deacons as an appointment of Jesus Christ, and the bishop as Jesus Christ, who is the Son of the Father, and the presbyters as the sanhedrin[9] of God, and assembly of the apostles. *Apart from these, there is no Church.* (emphasis mine)

Did you catch that? Ignatius asserts that Jesus' body consists solely of church officials. Everybody else is excluded. But Jesus stated that "where two or three are assembled in my name, I am there among them," (Matt 18:20). According to Ignatius, Jesus neglected to mention that the two or three had to be a deacon, presbyter, or bishop.

\* \* \*

**To the Trallians, 39-41:** He that is within the altar is pure, but he that is without is not pure; that is, he who does anything apart from the bishop, and presbytery, and deacons, such a man is not pure in his conscience.

**To the Magnesians, 31:** . . . as some indeed give one the title of bishop, but do all things without him. Now such persons seem to me to be not possessed of a good conscience, seeing they are not steadfastly gathered together according to the commandment.

To summarize, Ignatius is saying that there is a commandment that one must do all things with, or in accordance with, the bishop; that anyone who doesn't follow this *commandment* is devoid of moral character.

As we'll see, the entire book of Acts refutes this claim. Neither Jesus nor

His apostles made any such claim anywhere in the New Testament. Ignatius implicitly claims to have divine revelation that is different from, more recent than, and superior to, the New Testament. But Ignatius is just getting started.

\* \* \*

**To the Ephesians, 30:** Wherefore it is fitting that ye should run together in accordance with the will of your bishop, which thing also ye do. For your justly renowned presbytery, worthy of God, is fitted as exactly to the bishop as the strings are to the harp.

**To the Magnesians, 14-15:** . . . submitting to him [your bishop], or rather not to him, but to the Father of Jesus Christ, the bishop of us all. It is therefore fitting that you should, after no hypocritical fashion, obey [your bishop], in honour of Him who has willed us [so to do], since he that does not so deceives not [by such conduct] the bishop that is visible, but seeks to mock Him that is invisible.

**To the Trallians, 13:** Fare ye well in Jesus Christ, while ye continue subject to the bishop, as to the command [of God], and in like manner to the presbytery.

**To the Magnesians, 36:** . . . while your bishop presides in the place of God, and your presbyters in the place of the assembly of the apostles . . .

**To the Ephesians, 21:** . . . and that, being subject to the bishop and the presbytery, ye may in all respects be sanctified.

**To the Ephesians, 36:** Let us be careful, then, not to set ourselves in opposition to the bishop, in order that we may be subject to God.

In these passages, Ignatius equates obedience to the bishop with obedience to God. The bishop and the presbytery (elders) effectively control access to God. Ignatius thus denies the priesthood of all believers (1 Peter 2:5, 9; Rev 1:6, 5:10) and lays the foundation for the doctrines of apostolic succession, which refers to the uninterrupted transmission of authority from the apostles of Christ to today's bishops, and papal infallibility; the notion that the Pope cannot err when teaching in matters of faith and morality.

\* \* \*

**To Polycarp, 32:** If he [a celibate man] begins to boast, he is undone; and if he reckon himself greater than the bishop, he is ruined. But it becomes both men and women who marry, to form their union with the approval of the bishop, that their marriage may be according to God, and not after their own lust.

The Apostle Paul recorded God's revelation on the subject of marriage in 1 Corinthians 7. Yet Paul never mentioned a bishop nor did he instruct believers to obtain approval from any ecclesiastical authority. Paul got his teaching directly from Jesus.[10] But Ignatius' teaching is different than Paul's. So either Jesus changed His mind, or else Ignatius got his teaching from someone other than Jesus. (Spoiler alert: Jesus didn't change His mind.)

\* \* \*

**To Polycarp, 36-37:** Give ye heed to the bishop, that God also may give heed to you.

The Lord's prayer—the model prayer that Jesus gave His disciples—is found both in Matthew 6 and Luke 11. Neither passage mentions any condition that must be met in order for God to hear our prayers. But according to Ignatius, Jesus neglected to add: "And give heed to our prayer as we also give heed to the bishop."

\* \* \*

**To the Philadelphians, 12:** For as many as are of God and of Jesus Christ are also with the bishop.

According to the Apostle John, the presence of the Holy Spirit was the evidence that "we reside in God and he in us" (1 John 4:13). Paul agreed: "Now if anyone does not have the Spirit of Christ, this person does not belong to him" (Rom 8:9).

By whose authority does Ignatius nullify the teaching of the Apostles Paul and John, replacing the Holy Spirit with the bishop?

\* \* \*

**To the Magnesians, 39:** As therefore the Lord did nothing without the Father, being united to Him, neither by Himself nor by the apostles, so neither do ye anything without the bishop and presbyters.

**To the Philadelphians, 61:** . . . Do nothing without the bishop . . .

Ignatius, by requiring that believers gain approval from the bishop before directly and personally serving God, put the bishop between us and direct relationship and communion with our Lord. But no such condition can be found in the New Testament, in fact, Paul instructs all believers to function by *using their gifts*:

> And we have different gifts according to the grace given to us. If the gift
> is prophecy, that individual must use it in proportion to his faith. If it is
> service, he must serve; if it is teaching, he must teach; if it is exhortation, he
> must exhort; if it is contributing, he must do so with sincerity; if it is leader-
> ship, he must do so with diligence; if it is showing mercy, he must do so with
> cheerfulness. (Rom 12:6-8)

Not surprisingly, Peter says the same thing:

> Just as each one has received a gift, use it to serve one another as good
> stewards of the varied grace of God. Whoever speaks, let it be with God's
> words. Whoever serves, do so with the strength that God supplies, so that in
> everything God will be glorified through Jesus Christ. (1 Peter 4:10-11)

In addition, the book of Acts chronicles about thirty years of church history during which believers did *everything* without the bishop. By whose authority does Ignatius nullify the direct commands of Paul and Peter and the
examples in Acts?

* * *

**To the Ephesians, 43-44:** For we ought to receive every one whom the
Master of the house sends to be over His household, as we would do Him
that sent him. It is manifest, therefore, that we should look upon the bishop
even as we would upon the Lord Himself.

This is a partial quotation of Matthew 24:45. What Jesus actually said was:

> Who then is the faithful and wise slave, whom the master has put in charge
> of his household, to *give the other slaves their food* at the proper time? (empha-
> sis mine)

So the Lord Jesus Christ puts some of His servants in charge of *feeding*
the rest of us. He also warns those entrusted with this responsibility neither
to overstep their delegated authority, nor to beat those they are commanded
to *serve*:

> Blessed is that slave whom the master finds at work when he comes. I tell
> you the truth, the master will put him in charge of all his possessions. But if
> that evil slave should say to himself, 'My master is staying away a long time,'
> and he begins to beat his fellow slaves and to eat and drink with drunkards,
> then the master of that slave will come on a day when he does not expect
> him and at an hour he does not foresee, and will cut him in two, and assign
> him a place with the hypocrites, where there will be weeping and gnashing of
> teeth. (Matt 24:46-51)

### CONCLUSION

Ignatius focused on a symptom—false doctrine—instead of the cause—immaturity. He didn't trust Jesus to properly care for His own body, and he didn't trust Christians to hear directly from Jesus and be led by the Holy Spirit. His wrong solution was to replace Jesus as the acting head of His body and to replace the Holy Spirit's guidance with human political control.

Ignatius' wrong solution nullified God's plan for spiritual maturity and paralyzed Christ's body. When second century churches made the pastor/bishop solely responsible for "anything connected with the church," they abandoned the Ephesian gift-ministry of prophet. But preparing God's people for works of service requires all of the *diakonia* ministries functioning together. God neither authorizes nor equips any one person to do the whole job alone.

Instead of apostles, prophets, evangelists, and shepherd-teachers preparing God's people for works of service, church officials quit preparing and started performing meaningless Old Covenant-style "worship" rituals. The practical result of doing nothing without the bishop was that the body parts of Christ's body did nothing at all. Instead of every part of Christ's body working, Christians quit functioning and became a passive audience.

> The early freedom of worship no longer existed. The reading, prayers, and exhortations were all in the hands of the clergy. The people shared in the singing only.[11]

By making one elder the visible head over everyone else, Ignatius instituted the very thing Paul had warned the Ephesian elders against:

> Even from among your own group men will arise, teaching perversions of the truth to draw the disciples away after them. (Acts 20:30)

When second-century Christians abandoned God's plan for the body of Christ, spiritual immaturity and false doctrine became inevitable. And something else became inevitable as well. As we'll see when we look at the Corinthian *charisma* gifts, no individual ever has all the truth; or stated another way: no mortal human being is infallible—not even *ordained* human beings. The multiple Ephesian gift-ministries were God's checks and balances to protect the *Ekklesia* from human fallibility. When second-century Christians rejected God's design by putting one man in charge of all works of service, they brought the doctrine of human infallibility in through the back door and guaranteed that from then on only partial truth would be taught.

**Endnotes**

1   Lindsay, *The Church And The Ministry In The Early Centuries*, 228-229.

2   Lindsay, *The Church And The Ministry In The Early Centuries*, 229.

3   Lindsay, *The Church And The Ministry In The Early Centuries*, 228.

4   Lindsay, *The Church And The Ministry In The Early Centuries*, 229.

5   Lindsay, *The Church And The Ministry In The Early Centuries*, 244.

6   Ignatius, to the Trallians, III; to the Romans, IV; to the Ephesians, IV.

7   Lindsay, *The Church And The Ministry In The Early Centuries*, 41-42.

8   Niebuhr et al, *The Ministry in Historical Perspectives*, 25.

9   Merriam-Webster: Sanhedrin: the supreme council and tribunal of the Jews during postexilic times headed by a High Priest and having religious, civil, and criminal jurisdiction.

10   Covered in chapter 8 of this book. Found in Acts 20:27; Gal 1:1, 11-12; 2:8; 1 Cor 3:10; 14:37; Eph 3:3-4.

11   Lindsay, *The Church And The Ministry In The Early Centuries*, 251.

Chapter 15

# How Christianity Was Counterfeited

"Form," declared American architect and father of skyscrapers Louis Sullivan, "ever follows function. It is the law."[1] In other words, a building's function dictates its form, and a change of function necessitates a corresponding change of form. The apostles of Christ were the architects of Jesus' Ekklesia—the *only authorized* architects, as we have seen—commissioned to build God's spiritual house (1 Pet 2:5). They designed the Ekklesia to function, quite literally, as the body of Christ - a concept that has been so utterly lost that the phrase "body of Christ" no longer conveys any practical meaning - and *they designed the form to support the functioning.* Then to top things off, they documented *both* form and function in the twenty-seven books and letters of the New Testament.

Ignatius' plan for church government consisted of giving Christ's body a different, visible, *acting* head:

> During the 2nd century the ministry was subject to a change. The ruling body of office-bearers in every congregation received a permanent president, who was called the pastor or bishop, the latter term being the commoner.[2]

Elevating one elder to the position of president (or *prima inter pares*—"first among equals"—or "senior pastor/elder") and putting him in charge of "anything connected with the church"[3] meant everything from the head down had to change accordingly. Once the bishop (or pastor) replaced Jesus as the acting head of each local Ekklesia, a whole series of subsequent changes became necessary and inevitable. These changes were both outward and inward—seen and unseen. Ignatius and the Christian leaders who implemented his plan never imagined the drastic consequences of their seemingly slight change.

Church government was implemented by changing the structure (or *form*) and functioning of Jesus' Ekklesia:

> These *changes in the structure and functioning* of the church, especially the role of bishops, raise crucial and controversial questions. Christians of nearly every denomination admit that these changes took place.[4] (emphasis mine)

We're going to examine four changes to the apostolic design of the church. These changes logically had to occur in order to implement church government:

1. Jesus could no longer be the acting head of his body, the Ekklesia;

2. Therefore Christians could no longer hear and obey Jesus directly;

3. Therefore Christians could no longer function as body parts of Christ's body;

4. Therefore Christian meetings had to be radically redesigned.

To understand the changes and their significance we will answer the following questions about each one:

- What had to change?

- Why did it have to change?

- What did it change from?

- What did it change to?

- When did the change occur?

- What was the significance of the change?

Let's expound on these; we'll start with the initial, top-level, most obvious change of all.

### CHANGE #1:
#### JESUS COULD NO LONGER BE THE ACTING HEAD OF HIS EKKLESIA

**What had to change:** Jesus could no longer be the acting head of his body, the Ekklesia.

**Why it had to change:** No man can serve two masters and no body can serve two heads. In the apostolic design of the church the elders (plural) in each Ekklesia (singular)[5] had no visible head because Jesus was the invisible head of his body. But human government requires a hierarchical chain of command and a visible, acting CEO or Commander in Chief.

**What it changed from:** The account of Saul's conversion on the road to Damascus provides what is probably *the* classic example of how the Ekklesia was designed to function as Christ's body:

> Now there was a disciple in Damascus named Ananias. The Lord said to him in a vision, "Ananias," and he replied, "Here I am, Lord." Then the Lord told him, "Get up and go to the street called 'Straight,' and at Judas' house look for a man from Tarsus named Saul. For he is praying, and he has seen in a vision a man named Ananias come in and place his hands on him so that he may see again." (Acts 9:10-12)

Ananias is about to do something that will change the course of history, under the impression that he is obeying the direct command of the risen and ascended Lord Jesus Christ. Ananias is not going to consult with a bishop or obtain anyone's permission before obeying his Lord. What would Ignatius of Antioch have to say about all this? Would he tell Ananias, "Let no man do anything connected with the Church without the bishop"?[6] Would he warn Ananias, "he who does anything without the knowledge of the bishop, does [in reality] serve the devil"?[7]

But Ignatius of Antioch had not yet appeared on the scene, and so Ananias was free to obey his Lord and King with a clear conscience. Ananias could function as a body part of Christ's body without obtaining any additional permission or authorization:

> So Ananias departed and entered the house, placed his hands on Saul and said, "Brother Saul, the Lord Jesus, who appeared to you on the road as you came here, has sent me so that you may see again and be filled with the Holy Spirit." (Acts 9:17)

**What it changed to:** The outward, visible change was that the Bishop (or Pastor) became the acting head of each congregation. Once this change was accepted, Christians could no longer be allowed to receive instructions directly from Jesus and act on them. They could still *hear* from their Lord and King, but they couldn't *obey* Him without the Bishop's permission and authorization.

By the early third century, when ". . . the Christian churches, together with their bishops and clergy, were no longer what they had been,"[8] Ananias would have been guilty of insubordination by neglecting to obtain the Bishop's permission. Worse, he would have usurped the Bishop's prerogative by laying hands on Saul! Ananias was a mere disciple, a member of the *laity* - he was not *ordained!* How *dare* he presume to lay hands on anyone!

**When it changed:** During the second century (101-200 AD).

> One further stage in the development of the early ministry needs to be traced. This is the rise of monepiscopacy – that is, the pattern of a single bishop, or pastor, at the head of each church. We are so accustomed to this pattern – despite our controversies about episcopacy – that we may not realize that it does not clearly emerge till the opening years of the second century.[9]

> After the turn of the century Ignatius, the pastor of the church at Antioch, wrote a series of letters. In these he speaks habitually of a single bishop (or pastor) in each church, a body of presbyters, and a company of deacons. *God's grace and the Spirit's power, he teaches, flow to the flock through* this united ministry.[10] (emphasis mine)

> Episcopacy, the power and prestige of the bishops, developed slowly . . . We know, for example, that Alexandria had no single bishop until about A.D. 180.[11]

> By the late second century, however, the unchallenged leader in church affairs was the bishop.[12]

**The significance of the change:** The inward, unseen change was that the Ekklesia ceased to function as Christ's body on earth. The apostles of Christ designed Jesus' Ekklesia as an Organism. The Ekklesia is Christ's body only when Jesus is in direct control, making the decisions and giving the orders. When Christians are required to obtain anyone else's permission or authorization before obeying Jesus, Jesus is no longer the head. Once the bishop became the acting head, the Ekklesia ceased to function as Christ's body. Jesus became the symbolic head or *figurehead* and the Ekklesia changed from an organism to an organization.

Today we are so accustomed to this subverted status quo that the New Testament phrase "body of Christ" conveys no real, practical, physical meaning to our minds, and most understand the word *members* in Romans 12:5, 1 Corinthians 6:14, 1 Corinthians 12, and Ephesians 5:20 to mean "those who belong to the organization" instead of parts of a *body*.

CHANGE #2:

**CHRISTIANS COULD NO LONGER HEAR AND OBEY JESUS DIRECTLY**

**What had to change:** As noted above, the immediate logical consequence of making the Bishop the acting head of each congregation was that Christians could no longer be allowed to receive instructions directly from Jesus and act on them.

**Why it had to change:** If Christians could hear from Jesus and obey Him without permission or authorization, Jesus would be the acting head and the Bishop would be out of a job. To put it bluntly, which part of "do nothing without the bishop" don't you understand?

**What it changed from:** In the documented design of Jesus' Ekklesia, every believer is a priest,[13] with immediate, direct access to God through Jesus Christ.[14] Believers are related horizontally as body parts of Christ's body,[15] not vertically as rulers and subjects of a political organization.[16] Submission is mutual[17] and voluntary,[18] based on functioning, not on an org chart or special title.

**What it changed to:** The outward, visible change was that Christ's body was divided into rulers (clergy) and subjects (laity). The Priesthood of All Believers[19] then became the Priesthood of Some (ordained) Believers. The focus of the Christian life was no longer relationship with the Lord Jesus Christ or *walking in the Spirit*; the focus was now obedience to the clergy and lists of rules.

> The Church, which was in earlier days a "brotherhood of saints," became a community over whom a bishop presided. It was defined, not so much by the manner of life led by its members, as by the government which ruled over them . . . It was no longer—people worshipping and some of them leading the common devotions, saints believing and some among them instructing and admonishing; it became—teachers who imparted and pupils who received, priests who interceded and sinners who were pardoned through the intercession, *rulers who commanded and subjects who were bound to obey*.[20] (emphasis mine)

> The community was sharply divided into clergy and laity . . . The division of the congregation into clergy and laity and the common mode of making the difference apparent in daily ecclesiastical life were both borrowed from the usages of the civil society round them. The laity were called *plebs* and the clergy the *ordo*—the names applied to the commons and the senate of the Italian and provincial towns. As the members of the senate or the ordo had a special bench called the *concessus*, in the basilica or court-house, so the clergy had special seats in church. "It is the authority of the Church," says Tertullian, "that makes the difference between the ordo and the plebs—this and the honour consecrated by the special bench of the ordo."[21]

> . . . the conception began to grow that the one duty of the laity in the presence of the clergy was that of simple obedience."[22]

**When it changed:** During the second and early third centuries (120-220 AD).

Pictures of this ministry which ruled in the *end of the second and in the earlier part of the third century*, have been preserved for us in early ecclesiastical manuals.[23] (emphasis mine)

. . . we do not find a common term in general use . . . until the *beginning of the 3rd century*. In the west the word was ordo, and in the east clerus, from which come our "orders" and "clergy."[24] (emphasis mine)

**The significance of the change:** The inward, unseen change was that the Holy Spirit's power, both moral and miraculous, was turned off. By the early third century the moral influence of the Holy Spirit had declined noticeably. As church historian Bruce Shelley describes it:

At the beginning of the third century, however, something significant happened. The extraordinary moral fiber in the church weakened . . . By the year 220 it was evident that the Christian churches, together with their bishops and clergy, were no longer what they had been.[25]

Thomas Lindsay thought the decline in moral standards was due to political calculation:

. . . the Church wished to keep hold on crowds of adherents, who in the years of peace from persecution were flocking to join it, and who could not be retained if the old hard conditions or, perhaps one ought to say, the earlier high standard of Christian life, were insisted upon.[26]

But Lindsay's explanation reverses cause and effect. First-century Christians lived holy lives not because they strictly and sternly obeyed lists of rules, but because they were filled and empowered by the Holy Spirit – i.e. they each had a *personal* relationship with Jesus.

The extraordinary moral fiber of first-century Christians was the visible evidence of an inward relationship. Because of that relationship, the power of the Spirit of *Holiness* flowed out through believers' lives. The Holy Spirit was the source of both moral power and miraculous power. Once Christians were no longer allowed to hear and obey Jesus directly—that is, to walk in the Spirit—the power was turned off.

CHANGE #3:

**CHRISTIANS COULD NO LONGER FUNCTION AS PARTS OF CHRIST'S BODY**

**What had to change:** Most Christians could no longer be allowed to function as parts of the body of Christ. This third change is simply the logical result of the first two changes. With the bishop as the visible and acting head and only some Christians—the clergy—allowed to hear directly from God, ordinary (i.e. unordained) Christians could no longer function as body parts of Christ's body on earth. In practice this meant they could no longer function at all.

**Why it had to change:** Functioning as a part of Christ's body would require allegiance to and direct control by the Lord Jesus Christ instead of the bishop. This would constitute rebellion against the bishop which would be considered by the ordo to be rebellion against God.

**What it changed from:** In Jesus' very first mention of the Kingdom of God He explained that entrance into God's kingdom requires a new, spiritual birth that makes people like the wind—uncontrollable by human political power:

> The wind blows wherever it will, and you hear the sound it makes, but do not know where it comes from and where it is going. So it is with everyone who is born of the Spirit. (John 3:8)

Jesus also promised to build his Ekklesia:

> And I tell you that you are Peter, and on this rock I will build my church, and the gates of Hades will not overpower it. (Matt 16:18)

He also declared that He was present in even the smallest gatherings of his people:

> For where two or three are assembled in my name, I am there among them. (Matt 18:20)

He also promised that his followers would do the same miraculous works He Himself did:

> I tell you the solemn truth, the person who believes in me will perform the miraculous deeds that I am doing, and will perform greater deeds than these, because I am going to the Father. (John 14:12)

Because some of us have been immersed in churchianity all our lives, we fail to connect the dots and realize that these statements and promises all fit together into a practical picture of the Christian life. Jesus is literally present in the meetings of his people and He purposes to continue doing the same miraculous deeds through his body, the Ekklesia, that He performed in person during his ministry on earth. That's the practical, literal meaning of the phrase "the body of Christ."

**What it changed to:** The outward, visible change was that Christ's body parts stopped functioning and became a passive audience. Paul's instructions about all body parts being necessary (1 Corinthians 12:12-27) and each part functioning (Ephesians 4:11-16) were scrapped and replaced with an "order of worship" that cannot be found anywhere in the New Testament.[27]

**When it changed:** During the second and early third centuries (120-220 AD).

> The beginnings of the change date from the early decades of the second

century; by the end of the century it was almost complete . . . the "prophet-ic" ministry passed away, its functions being appropriated by the permanent office-bearers of the local churches . . .[28]

During the last decades of the second and throughout the entire third century . . . every Christian community had at its head a single president who is almost always called the bishop . . . The whole Christian activity of the community found its centre in him . . .[29]

The early freedom of worship no longer existed. The reading, prayers, and exhortations were all in the hands of the clergy. The people shared in the singing only.[30]

**The significance of the change:** The inward, unseen change was that Christ's body could no longer function as designed and was effectively paralyzed.

### MEETINGS REDESIGNED = WORSHIP REDEFINED

The three changes we just reviewed might seem mostly theoretical, but they all led inevitably to our modern worship service. Once Christians could no longer function as parts of Christ's body, their meetings had to be radically redesigned. The change in design meant that worship had to be radically re-defined.

The redesign of meetings and the corresponding redefinition of worship constitute the fourth and final change that church government required. To understand the significance of this change, we first need to do some myth-busting.

Churchianity claims that the New Testament is silent about worship. But that's more mental misdirection. Once again we're being tricked into looking in the wrong direction, reading the Bible upside-down. Turn it right-side-up and the entire New Testament becomes a worship manual. In the next section we'll learn what the New Testament tells us about true worship, Christian meetings, and examine organized religion's redesign.

## Endnotes

1    Sullivan 1896, "The Tall Office Building Artistically Considered." *Lippincott's Magazine*, 403–409.

2    Orr, *International Standard Bible Encyclopedia*, "Ministry"

3    Ignatius, to the Smyrneans, 55-56.

4    Shelley, *Church History In Plain Language: Updated 2nd Edition*, 71.

5    Acts 14:23, 20:17; Titus 1:5; James 5:14.

6    Ignatius, to the Smyrneans, 55-56.

7    Ignatius, to the Smyrneans, 60-61.

8    Shelley, *Church History In Plain Language: Updated 2nd Edition*, 74.

9    Niebuhr et al, *The Ministry in Historical Perspectives*, 23.

10    Shelley, *Church History In Plain Language: Updated 2nd Edition*, 70.

11    Shelley, *Church History In Plain Language: Updated 2nd Edition*, 70.

12    Shelley, *Church History In Plain Language: Updated 2nd Edition*, 71.

13    1 Peter 1:5, 9; Revelation 1:6, 5:10

14    1 Timothy 2:5

15    1 Corinthians 12:12-27

16    Matthew 20:25-28, Mark 10:42-45, Luke 22:25-27

17    1 Peter 5:3-5

18    1 Corinthians 16:15,16

19    1 Peter 2:5,9; Rev 1:6; Rev 5:10

20    Lindsay, *The Church And The Ministry In The Early Centuries*, 266.

21    Lindsay, *The Church And The Ministry In The Early Centuries*, 245-6.

22    Lindsay, *The Church And The Ministry In The Early Centuries*, 276.

23    Lindsay, *The Church And The Ministry In The Early Centuries*, 245.

24    Orr, *International Standard Bible Encyclopedia*, "Ministry"

25    Shelley, *Church History In Plain Language: Updated 2nd Edition*, 74.

26    Lindsay, *The Church And The Ministry In The Early Centuries*, 273.

27    ". . . the New Testament does not instruct worshipers in a specific procedure to follow in their services . . ." (Youngblood, *Nelson's Illustrated Bible Dictionary*, "Worship").

28    Lindsay, *The Church And The Ministry In The Early Centuries*, 169.

29    Lindsay, *The Church And The Ministry In The Early Centuries*, 204-205.

30    Lindsay, *The Church And The Ministry In The Early Centuries*, 251.

# Section 4:

# WORSHIP

The advent of a single, visible head over the church meant that Jesus became merely the *figurehead*. This change, though seemingly small at first
when it was introduced by Ignatius, meant that worship had to be radically
redefined and the church to be radically redesigned in order to make churchianity's new *organizational* version of Jesus' Ekklesia possible. The Ekklesia,
also called *the church*, or *the body of Christ*, was always meant to operate as an
organism, *not* as an organization. In the true design, each part of the body
submits to the head, operating together horizontally, not hierarchically. They
do not worship in buildings or temples, and do not have rituals, or costumes.
They worship God the same way Jesus did – He is always our perfect example.

How *did* Jesus worship God the Father? According to churchianity, and
*Nelson's Bible Dictionary*, the Bible is silent about a "specific procedure to follow" in worship services. But if we look at what Jesus *did*, instead of what
churchianity tells us He *should* have done, we find that His whole life *was* worship. "Worship" services are not found in the New Testament. Rather, we are
given example after example of a very special kind of worship.

The church, or *body of Christ*, is an organism, and must function as such.
Furthermore, Jesus is the head, and the body was meant to function supernaturally with each part serving and directly relating to Jesus *personally*. There
is no proxy; no visible head.

However, we ourselves cannot build the Ekklesia, nor can we change it.
Only Jesus can build it; we are responsible only for how we relate to Jesus
*personally*. A body can only function when each part listens to the *head*. Neither
can any part act without the head. The body grows into maturity *as each part*

*functions* according to Ephesians 4:16. Paul lists various gifts, whose function is meant to *prepare* the rest of the body to perform works of service. Each person is responsible for their own gifts and how to use them, and as each part functions, the body grows up into maturity.

What does this mean? How are we to serve and worship? For 1,800 years, the only game in town has been organized religion with its Old Covenant temple-style rituals. But the New Testament does not instruct believers to hold worship services at all – there are no special buildings, costumes, orders of worship, priests, or anything else *anywhere* in the New Testament. Organized religion accounts for this silence by claiming it's up to us, namely the *church fathers* to define worship - but that's upside down. As such, we miss what's right before us when we look for what organized religion tells us *should* be there in the Bible.

What does the New Testament say about worship? What changed? In this section we will cover how it changed, why it changed, what it changed to, and what it changed *from*. Far from being silent about worship, the entire New Testament is a worship manual.

Chapter 16

# WORSHIP IN SPIRIT AND TRUTH

Church government isn't the only Sacred Tradition that suffers from divine silence. Nelson's Bible Dictionary candidly admits that ". . . the New Testament does not instruct worshipers in a specific procedure to follow in their services . . ."[1] That carefully worded statement conceals two implicit assumptions: (1) Christians are supposed to hold worship services, and (2) the New Testament is missing important information. But the inconvenient truth is that the New Testament isn't simply silent about "a specific procedure to follow"; it doesn't instruct believers to hold worship services at all!

Why is it that in the entire New Testament there isn't even one example of a worship service? Jesus had three years to train His disciples. Shouldn't at least one of the gospels recount some sort of instructions regarding worship? Perhaps like this grossly misquoted version of Jesus' words in Matthew 10:

Jesus sent out these twelve, instructing them as follows:

["As you go, preach this message: 'The kingdom of Heaven is found in ritual and ceremony.' Ceremonially enact the drama of the gospel. Take no extra tunic, or sandals, or a staff, but rather take along some richly brocaded sacerdotal vestments. And whatever town or village you enter, inquire who in it has a house with a tall thin spire and gray stone arches that seem to bespeak centuries of august tradition, and there abide. And if the house have religious light from stained glass laying dimly on things, creating a kind of holy dusk, let your peace come upon it; but if it be bare and spare, devoid of most Christian symbolism, let your peace return to you."][2] (brackets [ ] indicate misquotation for emphasis)

Here is what He actually said:

"… As you go, preach this message: 'The kingdom of heaven is near!' Heal the sick, raise the dead, cleanse lepers, cast out demons. Freely you received, freely give. Do not take gold, silver, or copper in your belts, no bag for the journey, or an extra tunic, or sandals or staff, for the worker deserves his provisions. Whenever you enter a town or village, find out who is worthy there and stay with them until you leave. As you enter the house, greet those within it. And if the house is worthy, let your peace come on it, but if it is not worthy, let your peace return to you. And if anyone will not welcome you or listen to your message, shake the dust off your feet as you leave that house or that town…" (Matthew 10:7-14)

It's true that our modern worship service and order of worship cannot be found anywhere in the New Testament. But that's not because God left out important information. The New Testament actually *does* provide specific instructions about worship, but myth-interpretation makes them invisible. Once again, the problem is not that God is silent, but that we've been tricked into looking in the wrong direction.

When Christian meetings were redesigned to fit the requirements of church government, the definition of worship also had to change. The reason we can't find instructions about worship is because we're looking for the new, wrong definition.

We can't find our traditional Sunday morning worship service because New Covenant worship in spirit and truth has nothing to do with special buildings, clergy, ceremonies, costumes, or rituals. The same org chart thinking that causes us to look for church government in the New Testament and be baffled by God's silence also causes us to look for a Christian version of Old Covenant temple worship.

### OLD COVENANT VERSUS NEW COVENANT WORSHIP

The Bible describes two different kinds of worship, and the one we're all familiar with is the Old Covenant kind. In the first century, God already had an organized religion with rules (the Law of Moses), a temple, priests, vestments, liturgy, tradition, ceremonies, rituals, praise, worship, incense, an altar, sacrifices, a "church" calendar—everything a religious human being could wish for. But God had something different in mind. Jesus declared God's intention to the woman at the well:

Jesus said to her, "Believe me, woman, a time is coming when you will worship the Father neither on this mountain nor in Jerusalem . . . a time is coming - and now is here - when the true worshipers will worship the Father in spirit and truth, for the Father seeks such people to be his worshipers. God is spirit, and the people who worship him must worship in spirit and truth." (John 4:21; 23-24)

Notice what Jesus did *not* say: ["For God is spirit, and those who worship Him must worship in ornate, beautiful buildings with ritual and ceremony,"] (brackets [ ] indicate misquotation for emphasis). Jesus did not become the "son of man" in order to exchange an old religious organization for a new one. The *Logos* of God did not 'become flesh and dwell among us' in order to replace the temple in Jerusalem with the Sistine Chapel—or a church building for that matter. In fact, "church" buildings would not be invented until the third century[3]—the same time that the moral and miraculous power of the Holy Spirit was in obvious decline.[4]

Unless Jesus was making a distinction without a difference, there must be something noticeably, obviously, qualitatively different between Old Covenant temple worship and New Covenant spiritual worship. But what could it be? Does the New Testament give us any clue?

Of course it does! Jesus is always our perfect example of any and every aspect of the Christian life. So . . . how did Jesus worship God? If we look for organized religion's definition of worship, we find that the New Testament is unaccountably silent. But if we look at what Jesus *did*, instead of looking for what churchianity tells us He *should have done*, we find that Jesus' entire life was a worship service:

Therefore, when Christ came into the world, he said:

"Sacrifice and offering you did not desire,

but a body you prepared for me;

with burnt offerings and sin offerings you were not pleased.

Then I said, 'Here I am—it is written about me in the scroll—

I have come to do your will, O God.'" (Heb 10:5-7 NIV)

Jesus worshiped the Father by doing the Father's will. And what *was* God's will? Here it is, in Jesus' own words:

"The Spirit of the Lord is upon me,

because he has anointed me to proclaim good news to the poor.

He has sent me to proclaim release to the captives

and the regaining of sight to the blind,

> to set free those who are oppressed,
>
> to proclaim the year of the Lord's favor."

> Then he rolled up the scroll, gave it back to the attendant, and sat down . . .
> (and) he began to tell them, "Today this scripture has been fulfilled even as
> you heard it being read." (Luke 4:18-21)

In Matthew 10, Jesus instructed the Twelve to proclaim the good news of
the Kingdom of Heaven the same way He did:

> Jesus sent out these twelve, instructing them as follows: . . ."As you go,
> preach this message: 'The kingdom of heaven is near!' Heal the sick, raise
> the dead, cleanse lepers, cast out demons. Freely you received, freely give…"
> (Matt 10:5, 7-8)

Peter tells us that Jesus healed all who were oppressed by the devil:

> . . . God anointed him with the Holy Spirit and with power. He went around
> doing good and healing all who were oppressed by the devil, because God
> was with him. (Acts 10:38)

John gave us another one-sentence summary of Jesus' ministry:

> . . . The Son of God appeared for this purpose, to destroy the works of the
> devil. (1 John 3:8 NASU)

Based on these scriptures, we could reasonably infer that New Covenant
spiritual worship involves healing people and setting Satan's prisoners free.
And Jesus did make an unlimited and unequivocal promise to that effect:

> I tell you the solemn truth, the person who believes in me will perform the
> miraculous deeds that I am doing, and will perform greater deeds than these,
> because I am going to the Father. (John 14:12)

So yes, we could infer that New Covenant spiritual worship has nothing to
do with special buildings, costumes, rituals, and ceremonies, but rather is all
about functioning as Jesus' body, doing God's will the same way that Jesus did.
But we don't have to infer it. The Apostle Paul, who declared God's whole
purpose, tells us clearly and precisely how to worship God in spirit and truth.

### NEW COVENANT SPIRITUAL WORSHIP

In Romans chapter 12, Paul defines New Covenant spiritual worship. But
because his definition utterly refutes organized religion's Old Covenant-style
ritual worship, we're never told what Paul was talking about. Have you ever
wondered just *how* you're supposed to offer your body as a living sacrifice?

> Therefore I urge you, brethren, by the mercies of God, to present your bodies a living and holy sacrifice, acceptable to God, which is your *spiritual service of worship*. (Rom 12:1 NASU, emphasis mine)

The reason this instruction is confusing is because it's never accurately explained. And many Bible translations render the final phrase as "your reasonable service." That's even less clear because today reasonable means "fair," or "equitable," or "not excessive" (as in: "Considering all that God has done for you, it's reasonable to offer Him your body as a living sacrifice in return.") But that's not what Paul said or meant.

The Greek words are *logikeen latreian: logikos* (log-ik-OS, NT:3050) means "logical" or "rational"; *latreia* (lat-RI-ah, NT:2999) means "to worship by means of service." Wuest's *Expanded Translation* explains it this way: ". . . your rational, sacred service, (rational, in that this service is performed by the exercise of the mind.)"

What Paul is saying is that we offer our bodies to God the same way Jesus did. The *Ekklesia* is Christ's body and we worship God by doing the works Jesus did. We are all body parts of the body of Christ (1 Cor 12:27): we are Jesus' eyes and ears and nose and mouth, His arms and legs, hands and feet. If Jesus is going to fulfill God's whole purpose on earth today, He needs our bodies to do it!

But what do our logical, rational minds have to do with worshiping God in spirit and truth? Paul explains all this in the next seven verses. Virtually every teaching I've ever heard treats verses 1, 2 and 3 as separate, unconnected sermonettes or devotions and then ignores verses 4 through 8 as though they didn't exist. But Romans 12:1-8 is all one thought and loses its meaning when broken apart. The context of Romans 12:1-8 is the organismic functioning of the body of Christ by means of *gifts*.

### SPIRITUAL WORSHIP AND GIFTS

For some odd reason, whenever the Apostle Paul writes about the design and functioning of Jesus' Ekklesia, he invariably brings up the subject of gifts. In Ephesians, where he explains the Ekklesia's purpose, he lists Jesus' diakonia service gifts. In Romans, where he defines the Ekklesia's worship, he gives instructions about God's *energema* (en-ERG-ay-mah, NT:1755) motivational gifts. And in 1 Corinthians, where he gives instructions about the Ekklesia's meetings, he goes into exhaustive detail about the Holy Spirit's *charisma* (KHAR-is-mah, NT:5486) spiritual gifts.

Why does he keep doing that? It's as if he thought that Christ's body was designed to function supernaturally. Where would he get such an idea? Certainly not from Ignatius of Antioch!

We'll explore the connection between gifts and the design and functioning of Jesus' Ekklesia in the next chapter. But right now our focus is New Covenant spiritual worship: why does it require our logical, rational minds, and what does it have to do with God's *energema* motivational gifts?

And what are *diakonia, energema,* and *charisma* gifts anyway?

Those three Greek words are technical terms that Paul uses to distinguish three different kinds of gifts. In 1 Cor 12:4-6 Paul explains that there are three distinct categories of gifts and three different givers. This isn't readily apparent in most translations, but Wuest's Expanded Translation makes it clear:

> Now, there are different distributions of **spiritual gifts** (*charisma*), these gifts being diverse from one another, but there is the same (Holy) **Spirit**. And there are different distributions of various kinds of **ministries** (*diakonia*, works of service), but the same **Lord** (Jesus). And there are different distributions of **divine energy** (*energema*) motivating these gifts in their operation, but the same (Father) **God** who by His divine energy operates them all in their sphere. (1 Cor 12:4-6 WET, emphasis and parenthetical material mine)

When studying gifts, we need to pay attention to three things: (1) who is the giver; (2) who is the recipient; and (3) what is the gift, as in what is its purpose and how is it used? The subject of gifts goes beyond the scope of this book and needs an entire section to do it justice.[5]

Now back to spiritual worship. In the case of the Romans 12 gifts, God the Father is the giver, all believers are the recipients, and the gift is intrinsic to our personalities and is motivated through relationship with God.

### ROMANS 12:1

> Therefore I urge you, brethren, by the mercies of God, to present your bodies a living and holy sacrifice, acceptable to God, which is your spiritual service of worship. (Rom 12:1 NASU)

Offering our bodies means exercising our gift to serve God and our fellow believers. But what do our logical, rational minds have to do with worshiping God in spirit and truth? Simply this: that's the only way to exercise our Romans 12 gift. It's a gift that is deeply connected to our personality, and we must choose how to use it.

### ROMANS 12:2

> Do not be conformed to this present world, but be transformed by the renewing of your mind, so that you may test and approve what is the will of God - what is good and well-pleasing and perfect.

This present world (or "age") was designed by the god of this age who has blinded the minds of unbelievers (2 Cor 4:4). Satan desires worship as he defines it: perched at the apex of the org chart with the power to make everybody below him miserable or dead. That's why every organization in the world, whether business, political, military, religious, or what have you, has to have two things: (1) an org chart, and (2) excrement that rolls downhill.[6]

God's Kingdom has neither. The wrong, world system use of our gift is to worship and serve ourselves, and make certain that everybody below us on the org chart knows we're above them. The Romans 12 gift of leadership can command an enviable position in a religious organization. Other gifts such as serving, giving, and showing mercy earn neither money nor respect.

Our minds need to be renewed so that we can use our Romans 12 gift to serve our fellow believers, not lord it over them.

### ROMANS 12:3

> For by the grace given to me I say to every one of you not to think more highly of yourself than you ought to think, but to think with sober discernment, as God has distributed to each of you a measure of faith.

Paul was under no illusions about the potential for abuse of the Romans 12 gifts. Diotrephes, in 3 John, may very well have had a gift of leadership, but he also loved to be first. He thought so highly of himself that he ordered his fellow believers around and even kicked them out of his house church for insubordination. John said that Diotrephes didn't know God.

The Romans 12 gift of leadership does not legitimize the division of Christ's body into a ruling clergy and a submitting laity. Such World System, org chart thinking proceeds from minds that are still conformed to the pattern of this world.

### ROMANS 12:4-5

> For just as in one body we have many members, and not all the members serve the same function, so we who are many are one body in Christ, and individually we are members who belong to one another.

Paul states this again in 1 Corinthians:

The body is a unit, though it is made up of many parts; and though all its parts are many, they form one body. So it is with Christ . . . Now you are the body of Christ, and each of you is a part of it. (1 Cor 12:12, 27 NIV)

In other words, Christ's Body doesn't have an org chart. We are body parts—eyes, mouths, ears, noses, arms, legs, hands, feet—of the Body of Christ. We have different functions, but each of us belongs to all the others. Every body part is necessary to the proper functioning of Christ's Body.

When we impose an org chart, and some parts take over functions they're not gifted for, and other parts stop functioning because they're not *ordained*, Christ's Body is impaired—paralyzed—and can no longer worship in spirit and truth.

### ROMANS 12:6-8

> Since we have gifts that differ according to the grace given to us, each of us is to exercise them accordingly: if prophecy, according to the proportion of his faith; if service, in his serving; or he who teaches, in his teaching; or he who exhorts, in his exhortation; he who gives, with liberality; he who leads, with diligence; he who shows mercy, with cheerfulness. (NASU)

In other words, every believer is supposed to worship God through the exercise of his or her gift. Don't bother trying to picture the Romans 12 gifts operating in a typical Sunday morning "worship" service. God's *energema* gifts were never intended for Old Covenant temple worship. They are designed for a radically different type of wineskin.[7]

God's gift is also God's authorization to exercise that gift. No additional permission or ceremony is required.

### CONCLUSION

God does not dwell in temples made with hands[8] and He isn't interested in the rituals and ceremonies that take place in temples, cathedrals and/or church buildings. The Father desires worship in spirit and in truth. To that end, He gives each of us one (or more) of the Romans 12 gifts. New Covenant spiritual worship is all about functioning as parts of Christ's body by using our God-given gifts.

**Endnotes**

1    Youngblood, *Nelson's Illustrated Bible Dictionary*, "Worship"

2    Portions of this paraphrase were adapted from Thomas Howard's *Evangelical Is Not Enough:* "The liturgy of the Church is made up of two elements, ritual and ceremony" (p. 96). "The Drama of the Gospel" (p. 100). "These were neither the richly brocaded sacerdotal vestments that I was to encounter much later . . ." (p. 59). "The tall thin spire and the gray stone of the arches seemed to bespeak centuries of august tradition . . ." (p. 21). "Religious light from the stained glass lay dimly on things, creating a kind of holy dusk" (p. 21). "Its bare, spare churches, devoid of most Christian symbolism . . ." (p. 35).

3    "The earliest trace we find of buildings set apart exclusively for Christian worship dates from the beginning of the third century (202-210): Clement of Alexandria, *Stromata*, vii. 5" (Lindsay, *The Church And The Ministry In The Early Centuries*, 43, (footnote 3).

4    Shelley, *Church History In Plain Language: Updated 2nd Edition*, 74.

5    Editor's Note: before the author of this book died, he intended to write a second volume which would have such a section going into detail about Paul's teaching about gifts.

6    "Excrement" is a euphemism. The actual phrase is common in the military. It means that whenever things go wrong, blame passes *down* the org chart to subordinates; never *up* to those in charge.

7    Matt 9:17; Mark 2:22; Luke 5:37-39.

8    Acts 17:24.

Chapter 17

# THE EKKLESIA'S
# DESIGN AND FUNCTIONING

Throughout this book I have repeatedly stated that the design of Jesus' Ekklesia makes organized religion—or church government—impossible. Now we're ready to prove it.

We've reviewed several New Testament passages that describe the purpose, design, and functioning of the Ekklesia—Christ's body on earth:

- The Ekklesia's purpose—Ephesians 3:10-11.

- The Ekklesia's design—Ephesians 4:11-16 (the *diakonia* gifts).

- The Ekklesia's functioning—Romans 12:1-8 (the *energema* gifts).

Now we're going to connect the dots and see why authentic Christianity and churchianity's counterfeit are so absolutely, utterly, and totally opposed. We're going to consider the questions: why does Jesus need a body on earth? What exactly does He want His body to do? Does the New Testament tell us anything, or do we have to fill in the blanks?

(Spoiler alert: no, we don't have to guess. The New Testament both shows us and tells us why Jesus needs a body on earth and what He wants His body to do.)

### SHOW AND TELL

For over 1,800 years, organized religion has kept us convinced that Jesus wants His body on earth to don costumes (our "Sunday best"), meet in temples, and perform Old Covenant-style worship rituals. The problem is that the New Testament is silent about all this. It contains neither instructions for, nor examples of, any "order of worship." It neither tells us nor shows us that He wants His body to meet in temples on Sunday and: sing; listen to a prayer; sing; put money in a plate; listen to another prayer; listen to a choir or soloist; listen to a sermon or homily by an ordained clergy-person; listen to a benediction. Instead, it *does* show and tell us that He wants His body to continue doing the works that He did in His pre-resurrection body on earth.

Consider this radical possibility: since the Ekklesia is Jesus' body on earth, could Jesus have intended for His body to continue doing the same works He did? And if He did, might the apostles of Christ have intentionally designed the Ekklesia to fulfill this purpose?

And could it be possible that this purpose was put into action especially when Christians met together? And what if the form of meeting documented in Paul's first letter to the Corinthians was precisely the way all of this design and functioning was meant to work?

To answer those questions, we'd have to start with the purpose of the Ekklesia. Jesus revealed that purpose in the very first mention of His Ekklesia in Matthew 16:18:

> . . . I will build my church, *and the gates of Hades will not overpower it.*
> (Matt 16:18, emphasis mine)

Right from the start, Jesus envisioned His Ekklesia involved in some sort of conflict with the "gates of Hades," but what did He mean by that? Let's begin by considering what Jesus did *not* say:

> [I will build my physical, visible, political-religious Organization whose essential identity consists of its quasi-World-System dynastic form of government, with its legitimacy flowing from the unbroken line of its bishop-monarchs beginning with my disciple, Simon Peter, and when the forces of Hell attack my Organization with *gates*, they will not prevail, thus ensuring that my Organization will have continuous physical, visible existence throughout history.] (brackets [ ] indicate misquotation for emphasis)

Even after Jesus' resurrection, the Twelve supposed that Jesus intended to set up an earthly, political kingdom:

> So when they had gathered together, they began to ask him, "Lord, is this the time when you are restoring the kingdom to Israel?" (Acts 1:6)

But Jesus had already explained that a world-system-style political organization was not His purpose:

> Jesus replied, "My kingdom is not from this world. If my kingdom were from this world, my servants would be fighting to keep me from being handed over to the Jewish authorities. But as it is, my kingdom is not from here." (John 18:36)

Then what *are* the gates of Hades, and what do they have to do with Jesus' Ekklesia? The context gives us a clue: Jesus spoke these words near Caesarea Philippi (Matthew 16:13) where there was a cliff and cave called the Gates of Hades. The local pagans believed this was the entrance to the spiritual underworld.

Caesarea Philippi was also the site of a temple dedicated to the goat god Pan. Christians have speculated that Jesus meant that His Ekklesia would include even the pagans of Caesarea Philippi whose depraved worship involved sex with goats, or else that not even the pagan Roman Empire would be able to stop His Ekklesia.[1]

While I think both those explanations are valid, there's a third explanation that I prefer. Jesus obviously did not mean that a literal cliff and cave near Caesarea Philippi would not overcome His Ekklesia. Therefore He was speaking figuratively.

Hades was the prison house of the dead. The NET's textual note suggests that Jesus was employing metonymy: using the name of one thing for something else associated with it, such as saying "the Kremlin" to refer to the government of Russia.[2] In this case, "the gates of Hades" would refer to the power of death.

That makes sense, because we're also told that Satan held the power of death:

> . . . he likewise shared in their humanity, so that through death he could destroy *the one who holds the power of death (that is, the devil)*, and set free those who were held in slavery all their lives by their fear of death. (Heb 2:14-15, emphasis mine)

In John 10:10 Jesus gave us a one-sentence summary of His purpose and once again alluded to conflict with an enemy:

> The thief comes only to steal and kill and destroy; I have come so that they may have life, and may have it abundantly. (John 10:10)

Peter tells us that Jesus healed all who were oppressed by the devil:

> You know the message he sent to the people of Israel, proclaiming the good news of peace through Jesus Christ (he is Lord of all) - you know what hap-

pened throughout Judea, beginning from Galilee after the baptism that John announced: with respect to Jesus from Nazareth, that God anointed him with the Holy Spirit and with power. He went around doing good and *healing all who were oppressed by the devil*, because God was with him. (Acts 10:36-38, emphasis mine)

John gave us another one-sentence summary of Jesus' ministry:

. . . The Son of God appeared for this purpose, to destroy the works of the devil. (1 John 3:8 NASU)

And if all that isn't clear enough, we have Jesus' own words from Luke 4:18-21: "The Spirit of the Lord is upon me . . ." But Jesus not only told us, He also showed us:

Now he was teaching in one of the synagogues on the Sabbath, and a woman was there who had been disabled by a spirit for eighteen years. She was bent over and could not straighten herself up completely. When Jesus saw her, he called her to him and said, "Woman, you are freed from your infirmity." Then he placed his hands on her, and immediately she straightened up and praised God. But the president of the synagogue, indignant because Jesus had healed on the Sabbath, said to the crowd, "There are six days on which work should be done! So come and be healed on those days, and not on the Sabbath day." Then the Lord answered him, "You hypocrites! Does not each of you on the Sabbath untie his ox or his donkey from its stall, and lead it to water? Then shouldn't this woman, a daughter of Abraham whom Satan bound for eighteen long years, be released from this imprisonment on the Sabbath day?" (Luke 13:10-16)

Jesus also stated unequivocally that whoever believed on Him would do the same miraculous works He Himself did:

I tell you the solemn truth, the person who believes in me will perform the miraculous deeds that I am doing, and will perform greater deeds than these, because I am going to the Father. (John 14:12)

God's purpose is to replace the existing world order—the reign of Satan—with God's order—the reign of God. Satan's reign is expressed in physical reality: human lives. God's own image and likeness are marred by physical and psychological disease and suffering; human relationships are marred by selfishness and cruelty; relationship with God is twisted into rituals, ceremonies and lists of rules. The purpose of the reign of God is to destroy all these expressions of Satan's reign: "to destroy the works of the devil," as John put it.

Satan's reign is not something that will happen after we die; it's going on right here and now. God's Kingdom—the reign of God—is also meant to happen right here and now. Jesus did *not* teach us to pray "Thy kingdom come, thy will be done, *[but not until the millennium,]*" (brackets [ ] indicate mis-quotation for emphasis).

Instead, He teaches us to pray "may your kingdom come. May your will be done, *on earth as it is in heaven*" (Matt 6:10, emphasis mine).

Hades is a prison and its gates (the power of death) are there to prevent the prisoners from escaping. Gates are strictly *defensive*; they are not weapons. Their purpose is for defense, not offense. When Jesus said that the gates of Hades would not prevail against His church, He wasn't picturing Satan coming and attacking His Ekklesia with *gates*! Rather, I personally believe that He was picturing His Holy Spirit-empowered believers *attacking Satan's fortress, storming the gates, TEARING THEM DOWN and setting Satan's prisoners free*!

Jesus healed all who were under the power of the devil (Acts 10:38); He commanded His disciples to heal the sick, raise the dead, cleanse the lepers and cast out demons (Matt 10:8); His purpose was to destroy the devil's work (John 3:8); and He stated unequivocally that whoever believed on Him would do not only the same works He Himself did, but would do even greater works! (John 14:12). The New Testament is the record of the first-century church following Jesus' example by putting God's purpose into action.

And during the first century Christians *did* destroy the devil's works when they met together. How does everything we've covered fit into Ephesian's big picture of God's whole purpose? Does the New Testament tell us anything, or must we fill in the blanks?

There are two possible answers:

1. He wants His body to meet in temples on Sunday and: sing; listen to a prayer; sing; put money in a plate; listen to another prayer; listen to a choir or soloist; listen to a sermon or homily by an ordained clergy-person; listen to a benediction.

2. He wants His body to continue doing the works that He did in His pre-resurrection body on earth.

**Answer Number 1** is what organized religion has been telling us for about 1,900 years. The problem with Answer Number 1 is that it cannot be found anywhere in the New Testament.

> The early freedom of worship no longer existed. The reading, prayers, and exhortations were all in the hands of the clergy. The people shared in the singing only.[3]

**Answer Number 2** is clearly documented throughout the New Testament. The problem with Answer Number 2 is that it makes church government impossible.

But if answer 2 *is* correct, how do we continue doing His works? How did the first-century Christians destroy the devil's works? What is the purpose of the Ekklesia?

Paul's letter to the Ephesians describes how Christ's body on earth functions to fulfill that purpose. And what is God's purpose?

> The purpose of this enlightenment is that through the church the multifaceted wisdom of God should now be disclosed to the rulers and the authorities in the heavenly realms. This was according to the eternal purpose that he accomplished in Christ Jesus our Lord . . . (Eph 3:10-11)

In other words, God intends the Ekklesia to be an object lesson revealing His diverse, complex, many-faceted wisdom to Satan, "the ruler of the kingdom of the air, the ruler of the spirit that is now energizing the sons of disobedience" (Eph 2:2), and his government in the unseen realm.

Jesus told the woman at the well (and us) that God is seeking worshippers. But churchianity tells us that the New Testament is silent about worship. Since the Ekklesia is Christ's body, why does Jesus need a body on earth? What is it that He wants His body to do?

The body of Christ was designed to function supernaturally—in the power of the Holy Spirit. Of course the entire New Testament fits together perfectly. There was only ever one design for Jesus' Ekklesia. The Holy Spirit didn't lead Christ's apostles in different directions. There was only ever one Truth.

Let's summarize what New Covenant worship is according to the Bible, not according to churchianity: it is an organism, it functions as a *body,* and it does not meet in temples. Each part is related horizontally – no part being less important and no part being excluded from the body's *function.*

The Apostle Paul tells us fourteen times in his thirteen letters that the Ekklesia is Christ's body:

> Now the church is his body, the fullness of him who fills all in all. (Eph 1:23)

According to Ephesians 4:16, Christ's body grows up into maturity when each part functions:

> From him the whole body, joined and held together by every supporting ligament, grows and builds itself up in love, *as each part does its work.* (Eph 4:16 NIV, emphasis mine)

What does it mean for each *part* to *do its work?* What this requires is that each part relates to the *head,* directly and personally, and like Ananias (Acts 9:10-12) we must be free to follow Jesus' commands. What this means is that *relation-*

*ship*, personal and deep connection with the head, is fundamental. We cannot *build* the Ekklesia, nor can we redesign it. We are parts, and relationship is the only way a body can function.

> He is the head of the body, the church, as well as the beginning, the first-born from the dead, so that he himself may become first in all things. (Col 1:18)

> far above every rule and authority and power and dominion and every name that is named, not only in this age but also in the one to come. And God *put all things under* Christ's *feet*, and gave him to the church as head over all things. Now the church is his body, the fullness of him who fills all in all. (Eph 1:21-23)

Finally, I want to reiterate what Jesus told the woman at the well; that God is seeking worshipers:

> Jesus said to her, "But a time is coming - and now is here - when the true worshipers will worship the Father in spirit and truth, for the Father seeks such people to be his worshipers. God is spirit, and the people who worship him must worship in spirit and truth." (John 4:23-24)

Meetings today look nothing like what we find in the New Testament. Clearly something changed, but why? How did it change, what exactly did change, and *when?*

**Endnotes**

1    Bell, *Velvet Elvis*, 132.

2    Merriam-Webster: "the citadel of a Russian city…the *Kremlin*, citadel of Moscow and seat of government of Russia and formerly of the Soviet Union."

3    Lindsay, *The Church And The Ministry In The Early Centuries*, 251.

Chapter 18

# COUNTERFEIT MEETINGS,
# MEANINGLESS WORSHIP

The redesign of Christian meetings was the fourth and final change required to implement church government. As soon as ordinary, *unordained*
believers could no longer function as body parts of Christ's body—meaning
they could no longer worship God *in spirit and truth*—meetings had to be
radically redesigned and worship had to be radically redefined. The result was
our traditional worship service and order of worship.

In Matthew 15 and Mark 7, Jesus characterizes worship based on human
"sacred" tradition as vain—in other words, meaningless or purposeless:

> He replied, "Isaiah was right when he prophesied about you hypocrites; as it
> is written:
>
> > 'These people honor me with their lips,
> >
> > but their hearts are far from me.
> >
> > *They worship me in vain;*
> >
> > their teachings are but rules taught by men.'
>
> You have let go of the commands of God and are holding on to the traditions
> of men." (Mark 7:6-8 NIV, emphasis mine)

By the early third century, organized religion had let go of God's commands regarding meetings and was holding on to Old-Covenant-style ritual worship.

This is now a good time to explain the difference between the Old and New Covenants. Frequently you've heard me mention that they are not the same, but what exactly is different about the New Testament versus the Old?

## OLD VERSUS NEW COVENANT – WHY ARE THEY DIFFERENT?

To explain the difference, I'm going to quote Andrew Farley, particularly his book *God Without Religion*. In fact, I recommend this and his book *The Naked Gospel*[1] if you're on your journey – out of religion and *into* relationship. But to summarize what would take an entire book to do it justice, here is the difference:

Before Jesus died for our sins, we were bound by the law. The law of Moses, the ten commandments – these were, with a few possible exceptions such as the story of Job, impossible to follow. We tried for millennia, and even Job did not understand God as well as he came to by the end of the book of Job.

He followed the law, even going so far as to atone for sins his children *hadn't yet committed*. But after everything he went through, he was an object lesson for us to better understand that God isn't interested in the law, thinking we have God in a bag and that if we do X, God does Y. But relationship is key, and Jesus paved the way for us to have relationship with Him *without* the law getting its hands on us. We are dead to the law (Romans 7:4). We have *no use for it as believers*. There is no payment for sin, not even a list of rules, or the ten commandments – we are free from *all of it*. As far as the law is concerned, we are dead and it cannot touch us, simply because we believe in the one who died and was risen – Jesus. Anyone who hands you rules is still living under the Old Covenant, which no longer has any hold over our lives as believers. So, why do we have the Old Testament if the covenant no longer applies to us? As Andrew Farley illustrates:

> The law tutors us as unbelievers, showing us our sin. But once we come to faith in Jesus, we no longer have use for the law. Christians are not under the law and not to be supervised by the law after salvation (Gal. 3:25; 5:18; Rom. 6:14). The Ten Commandments and other moral laws, even as understood intuitively by our consciences, are essential to nonbelievers. These standards point out how every one of us is born with an addiction to sin: "The requirements of the law are written on their hearts, their consciences also bearing witness, and their thoughts now accusing, now even defending them" (Rom. 2:15). The law accuses us, and we attempt to defend ourselves. We live the best we can. But once we admit our guilt and cross over into new life in Jesus, our relationship with the law is over. We enter into that new contract with God. We're ready for the new way of the Spirit.[2]

New Covenant spiritual worship consists of Christ's body parts functioning via the seven Romans 12 gifts. Spiritual worship and God's supernatural power are a single reality, one and the same, inseparable. When Christian meetings changed to resemble Old Covenant-style worship, spiritual worship and spiritual power were both lost. Since the early third century, churchianity's gospel has been powerless and its worship has been meaningless.

### CHRISTIAN MEETINGS HAD TO BE RADICALLY REDESIGNED

**What had to change:** The vast majority of Christians (the *laity*) could no longer function as the parts of Christ's body when they met together.

**Why it had to change:** Once the pastor / bishop became the acting head of each local *Ekklesia*, anything not under his control had to be eliminated. God's supernatural power is not subject to human control. Therefore it was eliminated.

**When it changed:** During the second and early third centuries (AD 120-220).

**What it changed from:** First-century Christian meetings were held in private homes, not in special buildings; there was no pastor, sermon, or order of worship; and everyone actively participated. It should be noted that;

1. First-century Christians had no church buildings – as Thomas Lindsey points out:

    The earliest trace we find of buildings set apart exclusively for Christian worship dates from the beginning of the third century (202-210) . . .[3]

In one instance, Paul held meetings in a lecture hall (Acts 19:9-10), but the fact that this circumstance merited special mention testifies to its unusual quality.[4]

2. Meetings were held in private homes.

    . . . as the number of believers grew, more than one house must have been placed at the service of the brethren for their meetings for public worship and for the transaction of the necessary business of the congregation. We are told that in the primitive church at Jerusalem the Lord's Supper was dispensed in the houses, (Acts 2:46) and that the brethren met in the house of Mary the mother of John Mark, (Acts 12:12), in the house of James the brother of our Lord (Acts 21:18, 12:17), and probably elsewhere. At the close of the Epistle to the Romans, St. Paul sends greetings to three, perhaps five, groups of brethren gathered round clusters of distinguished Christians whom he names. One of these groups he calls a "church," and the others were presumably so also. (Romans 16:3-5; 10-11, 14-15)[5]

It becomes evident too as we study these early records that when it was possible, that is, when any member had a sufficiently large abode and was willing to open his house to the brethren, comparatively large assemblies, including all the Christians of the town or neighbourhood, met together at stated times and especially on the Lord's Day, for the service of thanksgiving. Gaius was able to accommodate all his fellow Christians, and was the "host of the whole Church." (Romans 16:23)[6]

St. Paul sends salutations to other house-churches; to that meeting in the house of Philemon at Colossae (Philemon 2), to that meeting in the house of Nymphas in Laodicea (Colossians 4:15), and to that meeting in the house of Stephanus. (1 Corinthians 16:15)[7]

3. First-century Christian churches had no pastor as we understand that term today:

There is no trace of one man, one pastor, at the head of any community. The ruling body was a senate, without a president . . . The organization of the Primitive Christian Church in the last decades of the first century without one president in the community, and with the anomalous prophetic ministry, has no resemblance to any modern ecclesiastical organization . . .[8]

One further stage in the development of the early ministry needs to be traced. This is the rise of monepiscopacy—that is, the pattern of a single bishop, or pastor, at the head of each church. We are so accustomed to this pattern—despite our controversies about episcopacy—that we may not realize that it does not clearly emerge till the opening years of the second century. The first witness to it is Ignatius, a prophet of the church of Antioch in Syria, who has become the bishop in the sense of the single head, of the church in that city.[9]

4. First-century Christian meetings had no "order of worship" as we understand that term today:

. . . The New Testament does not instruct worshipers in a specific procedure to follow in their services . . .[10]

5. First-century Christian meetings had no sermons as we understand that term today. Although some elders were teachers (1 Timothy 5:17), all the men[11] participated in various ways, including teaching:

What then shall we say, brothers? When you come together, everyone has a hymn, or a *word of instruction*, a revelation, a tongue or an interpretation. All of these must be done for the strengthening of the church. (1 Cor 14:26 NIV, emphasis mine)

The only New Testament example of a first-century Christian meeting is found in Paul's first letter to the Corinthians but is representative of all the churches he founded:

> It is St. Paul, in his First Epistle to the Corinthians, who gives us the most distinct picture of the meetings of the earliest Christian communities.[12]

> The meeting described by the apostle is not to be taken as something which might be seen in Corinth but was peculiar to that city; it may be taken as a type of the Christian meeting throughout the Gentile Christian Churches; for the Apostle, in his suggestions and criticisms, continually speaks of what took place throughout all the churches.[13]

> Such is the picture of a Christian church in the Apostolic age, as it appears in the pages of the Epistles of St. Paul to the Corinthians, and, although no such clear outline is given us of any other Christian community, still we are warranted, as we shall see, in assuming that the Church in Corinth did not differ much from the other churches . . .[14]

**What it changed to:** The visible changes were that house-church meetings were consolidated into special buildings (temples) where the pastor / bishop could exercise sole control; active participation was restricted to the clergy; meeting format was formalized and fixed as the "order of worship" no longer subject to the control of the Holy Spirit (the "wind" of John 3:5-8); and revelation (prophecy), tongues, and interpretation were replaced with an oration (sermon) by the bishop.

> The early freedom of worship no longer existed. The reading, prayers, and exhortations were all in the hands of the clergy. The people shared in the singing only.[15]

Sound familiar?

**The significance of the change:** The inward, unseen change was that the Ephesian blueprint for the Body of Christ was thrown out and replaced with a counterfeit modeled after Rome's state religion—the "great prostitute" of Revelation 17.

> The first temple actually built to the godhead of the emperor was built in 29 B.C. at Pergamum in Asia Minor.[16]

> To the angel of the church in Pergamum write the following: . . .

> I know where you live - where Satan's throne is. Yet you continue to cling to my name and you have not denied your faith in me, even in the days of Antipas, my faithful witness, who was killed in your city where Satan lives. (Rev 2:12-13)

155

John traces the oppression of believers to the devil himself, to the great red dragon, who wages war against the saints through two agents—the beasts of Revelation 13. The first is the beast from the sea (or abyss), the imperial power. The second is the beast from the land (the false prophet), or the imperial worship.[17]

... the Christian churches did copy the great pagan hierarchy ... in the distinction introduced into the ranks of bishops by the institution of metropolitans and grades of bishops, and ... also in the multiplication of the lower orders of clergy on the model of the organization of the state temple service.[18]

When the Bishop of Rome claimed to be the *Pontifex Maximus* and to rule the Christian metropolitans, and when the metropolitans claimed rights over the bishops of their provinces, and when these claims were largely acceded to, then the pagan hierarchy of the imperial pagan worship was christened and became the framework of the visible unity of the Church of Christ.[19]

... Christian bishops of important centres demanded and obtained from Christian emperors the same places of civil precedence which belonged to the provincial priests of the *Divi Imperatores* ... The vestments of the clergy, unknown in these early centuries—dalmatic, chasuble, stole and maniple—were all taken over by the Christian clergy from the Roman magistracy ...[20]

### EPHESIANS—BLUEPRINT, NOT RFP

Churchianity regards Paul's letter to the Ephesians not as a blueprint, but merely as an RFP – a Request For Proposal; a public document describing a project, soliciting bids from contractors to complete it. For example, my 1967 Scofield Reference Bible states that the letter to the Ephesians ". . . contains the highest Church truth, but has nothing about church order."[21] In other words, Ephesians details God's whole purpose for the body of Christ but is strangely silent about how to implement that purpose via church government.

Vincent's New Testament Word Studies takes a similar view: "The ecclesiastical nomenclature of the Pauline Epistles is unsettled . . ."[22] In other words, Paul's church government org chart was never clear; he never managed to connect his job descriptions with correct titles for the clergy.

Churchianity thus claims the ability to recognize and correct apostolic "errors and omissions." It's as if there's some secret, extra-biblical source of divine revelation that tells us what Paul *meant* to say or *should have* said.

Churchianity has agreed with Ignatius and followed his plan for almost 1,800 years. We've all been taught that Ignatius' plan is right there in the pages of the New Testament. We're sure that we see church government every time we read the New Testament. Thus far, all of our attempts to recover the power of the Holy Spirit and the experience of New Testament body life begin by assuming some version of Ignatius' plan.

We were all born with churchianity-colored glasses. Organized religion has been putting them on everybody for nearly eighteen centuries.

God had—and has—a plan to bring the *Ekklesia* to maturity, but God's plan was—and is—a mortal offense to minds that are conformed to the pattern of this world. That's because God's design for the body of Christ puts everyone on an equal basis. There's no possibility of some Christians having pre-eminence over other Christians. No believer has status or rank higher than any other believer. The body parts of Christ's body are related mutually, not hierarchically; horizontally, not vertically. There are no titles of honor – no "Father," "Reverend," or "Canon" – and no one gets to lord it over anyone else.

In other words, no one gets to serve as Satan's human proxy by receiving the supremacy and worship that the World System is designed to provide (if this isn't clear, don't worry, we cover it in detail in a later chapter). Christ's body doesn't have an org chart.

Christians were prohibited from growing up in all things and becoming "mature, attaining to the whole measure of the fullness of Christ." The unity of all believers that Jesus prayed for became impossible. Organized religion became the only way Christians could relate to Jesus.

**Endnotes**

1    Zondervan Publishing was at some point giving away free PDF copies of Andrew Farley's *The Naked Gospel* on the web. It is still circulating at the time of this publication and can be found with a quick search.

2    Farley, *God Without Religion,* 46-47.

3    Lindsay, *The Church And The Ministry In The Early Centuries,* 43, (footnote 3).

4    Lindsay, *The Church And The Ministry In The Early Centuries,* 41, (footnote 1).

5    Lindsay, *The Church And The Ministry In The Early Centuries,* 41-42.

6    Lindsay, *The Church And The Ministry In The Early Centuries,* 42.

7    Lindsay, *The Church And The Ministry In The Early Centuries,* 42, (footnote 2).

8    Lindsay, *The Church And The Ministry In The Early Centuries,* 155.

9    Niebuhr et al, The Ministry in Historical Perspectives, 23.

10    Youngblood, *Nelson's Illustrated Bible Dictionary,* "Worship"

11    That only believing *men* participated in the meetings of the first-century *Ekklesia* is not obvious from the NET's *gender-accurate* translation of "adelphoi" as "brothers *and sisters*" (14:26) because the pronoun "you" must refer back to the preceding subject: "What should you do then, *brothers and sisters*? When *you* come together . . ."

12    Lindsay, *The Church And The Ministry In The Early Centuries,* 43.

13    Lindsay, *The Church And The Ministry In The Early Centuries,* 48.

14    Lindsay, *The Church And The Ministry In The Early Centuries,* 57.

15    Lindsay, *The Church And The Ministry In The Early Centuries,* 251.

16    Shelley, *Church History In Plain Language: Updated 2nd Edition,* 43.

17    Shelley, *Church History In Plain Language: Updated 2nd Edition,* 45.

18    Lindsay, *The Church And The Ministry In The Early Centuries,* 350.

19    Lindsay, *The Church And The Ministry In The Early Centuries,* 351.

20    Lindsay, *The Church And The Ministry In The Early Centuries,* 352-353.

21    Scofield, *The New Scofield Reference Bible,* 1272.

22    Vincent, *Word Studies in the New Testament,* "1 Thessalonians 5:12"

Chapter 19

# No Maturity,
# No Unity

John's gospel records Jesus' final discourse before His crucifixion. Jesus prayed that those who believe in Him would have complete unity:

> I pray also for those who will believe in me through their message, that *all of them may be one*, Father, just as you are in me and I am in you. May they also be in us so that the world may believe that you have sent me. I have given them the glory that you gave me, *that they may be one as we are one*: I in them and you in me. *May they be brought to complete unity* to let the world know that you sent me and have loved them even as you have loved me. (John 17:20-23 NIV, emphasis mine)

Today, nearly 2,000 years later, Christians still don't have the unity that Jesus prayed for.

Why not?

The answer to that question is found in the book of Ephesians—the big picture of God's whole purpose—the blueprint for the Body of Christ. Ephesians chapter 4 begins by describing the unity that God desires:

> I, therefore, the prisoner for the Lord, urge you to live worthily of the calling with which you have been called, with all humility and gentleness, with patience, bearing with one another in love, making every effort to keep *the unity of the Spirit in the bond of peace*. (Eph 4:1-3, emphasis mine)

God's unity is the unity of the Spirit. It is spiritual, not natural. It is maintained in the bond of peace, not imposed by force. God's unity comes through humility, gentleness, patience and love—the fruit of the Spirit:

> But the fruit of the Spirit is love, joy, peace, patience, kindness, goodness, faithfulness, gentleness, and self-control. Against such things there is no law. Now those who belong to Christ have crucified the flesh with its passions and desires. If we live by the Spirit, let us also behave in accordance with the Spirit. Let us not become conceited, provoking one another, being jealous of one another. (Gal 5:22-26)

Paul continues by naming seven unities that the parts of Jesus' body all share:

> There is one body and one Spirit, just as you too were called to the one hope of your calling, one Lord, one faith, one baptism, one God and Father of all, who is over all and through all and in all. (Eph 4:4-6)

Since Jesus prayed for us to have complete unity, and since we already share these seven unities, how is it possible that after nearly twenty centuries we're more divided than ever? The reason we still don't have unity is because back during the second century, Christian leaders chose the wrong kind of unity. And today we still agree with their wrong choice.

### THE WRONG KIND OF UNITY

God's unity is spiritual and is maintained in the bond of peace. But Ignatius' plan required a different kind of unity—the natural, World System kind. Church government unity is visible and physical, imposed and enforced by human political power: a ruling clergy exercising authority over a submitting laity.

Jesus warned His disciples not to practice World System authority:

> But Jesus called them and said, "You know that the rulers of the Gentiles lord it over them, and those in high positions use their authority over them. It must not be this way among you! Instead whoever wants to be great among you must be your servant, and whoever wants to be first among you must be your slave - just as the Son of Man did not come to be served but to serve, and to give his life as a ransom for many." (Matt 20:25-28)

> So Jesus said to them, "The kings of the Gentiles lord it over them, and those in authority over them are called 'benefactors.' Not so with you; instead the one who is greatest among you must become like the youngest, and the leader like the one who serves…" (Luke 22:24-26)

If God had intended to answer Jesus' prayer by having believers submit to a ruling clergy, Ephesians chapter 4 was a golden opportunity to say so. The

Greek word for submission (*hupotasso*, hoop-ot-AS-so, NT:5293) is a military term meaning to serve in the ranks under someone. It is defined as follows:

> "hupotasso," primarily a military term, "to rank under" (hupo, "under," tasso, "to arrange"), denotes (a) "to put in subjection, to subject,"…(b) in the middle or passive voice, to subject oneself, to obey, be subject to…[1]

*Hupotasso* occurs forty times in the New Testament and three of those instances are in Ephesians.[2] Clearly, God considers submission important. And if He wanted believers to submit to a ruling clergy, He had forty opportunities to tell us so. So where in the New Testament are we instructed to submit to church officials? Well, the New Testament has some bad news and some worse news for organized religion:

**The bad news:** none of the three instances of *hupotasso* in Ephesians so much as hint at submission to church officials.

**The worse news:** neither do any of the other thirty-seven references in the rest of the New Testament.

In the entire book of Ephesians, church government and church authorities are not even mentioned. Implementing God's strategic plan has *nothing* to do with *any* form of organization.

The Apostle Paul had multiple opportunities to cite obedience to church officials as the basis of Christian unity but never did so. That was not due to oversight or error. Paul understood that true unity is organic and spiritual; not organizational and political. That's because Paul got *his* revelation from the Lord Jesus Christ.

Church government—making one man the visible, acting head of the organization—dividing the body of Christ into a ruling clergy and a submitting laity—violates God's plan for unity. The only unity that can accomplish God's strategic plan is unity of the Spirit. Unity of Spirit cannot be imposed from the outside; it must come from within—from the Spirit, through *relationship* with Jesus. But political unity could be, and was, imposed by force. Nonconformists could be, and were, persecuted, imprisoned, tortured, and murdered.

Like the Galatians of the previous century, second-century Christian leaders imagined that God's purpose could be accomplished by natural means, foolishly attempting to achieve a spiritual goal through human effort. They should have known better. We were warned:

> Are you so foolish? Although you began with the Spirit, are you now trying to finish by human effort? (Gal 3:3)

The unity that God wants His children to have—the unity that Jesus prayed for—is spiritual, not natural. It cannot be produced or imposed through natural means. Then how are we supposed to obtain it? Paul answers that question in Ephesians 4:7-16. We covered his answer briefly in chapter 12. Now we're going to unpack the details.

### GOD'S PLAN FOR UNITY

Paul follows up his call for unity by describing God's supernatural plan for the unity of all believers. God's plan begins with the *diakonia* service gifts: apostles, prophets, evangelists, and shepherd/teachers.

> But to each one of us grace was given according to the measure of the gift of Christ. Therefore it says, "When he ascended on high he captured captives; he gave gifts to men." Now what is the meaning of "he ascended," except that he also descended to the lower regions, namely, the earth? He, the very one who descended, is also the one who ascended above all the heavens, in order to fill all things. It was he who gave some as apostles, some as prophets, some as evangelists, and some as pastors and teachers . . . (Eph 4:7-11)

Jesus gives the *diakonia* gift-ministries of apostles, prophets, evangelists, and shepherd-teachers to prepare the rest of us—the parts of Christ's body— for works of service:

> . . . to prepare God's people for works of service, that is, to build up the body of Christ. . . (Eph 4:12 NIV)

The job of these gifted individuals is to *prepare* the body to perform the works, through *relationship* with Jesus. And that is just as true for shepherd/ teachers as it is for the other three gifts. When the *diakonia* gift-ministries do their jobs as intended, we all attain unity and grow up in Christ:

> . . . until we all attain to the unity of the faith and of the knowledge of the Son of God - a mature person, attaining to the measure of Christ's full stature. (Eph 4:13)

Spiritual maturity, not church government, is God's plan to protect us from false doctrine:

> So we are no longer to be *children*, tossed back and forth by waves and *carried about by every wind of teaching* by the trickery of people who craftily carry out their deceitful schemes. (Eph 4:14, emphasis mine)

When Jesus' body parts perform the works of service for which they have been prepared, the body of Christ grows up and becomes mature.

**Endnotes**

1   Vine, *Vine's Complete Expository*
2   Eph 1:22, Eph 5:21, Eph 5:24

# *Section 5:*

# BUSTED!

We're now ready to answer the question: what does God think about organized religion? To answer this question once and for all, we will need
to examine the New Testament for clues about *how* the apostles of Christ
continued to live after Jesus' death and resurrection, and what they continued
to teach. The apostles were given *all truth* about the Ekklesia (John 16:13).
Paul stated that he declared the *whole purpose of God* (Acts 20:27). Therefore,
if organized religion was approved of by God, we will surely find some clue
in the New Testament. We have the foundation now, so in this section, we are
going to find out: is the book of Acts a book of history, or an example we are
to follow? What can we learn from the *Acts of the Apostles*?

In order to find church government in the New Testament, as we've seen
so far, we would have to read the New Testament with churchianity-colored
glasses – we would have to read the Bible upside-down. We won't do that. Instead, we will read the Bible right-side-up, normally, and we will see what the
apostles *did,* and what they *did not* do. The New Testament does not mention
church buildings, costumes, rituals, or orders of worship.

What it *does* have is a written account of what the apostles actually did
during the first century. Acts is our best clue as to how the apostles lived and
worshiped Jesus after His ascension, so we will examine this account closely.
We will answer the question of whether the book of Acts is *pre*scriptive, or
merely *de*scriptive. We will then examine every instance of the three words
commonly translated as "bishop," and the only word that is sometimes translated as "pastor." Finally, we will examine four possible answers to our primary question - only one of which can be true - to find out if God does, in fact,

approve of organized religion.

The New Testament, correctly understood, makes organized religion impossible. Not only that, we can be certain that it was actually written during the first century and not changed afterwards. The New Testament itself contains the strongest possible evidence for its own reliability, but the information has been suppressed. Until now.

To finish what we started, we must disprove the accusation that some or all of the New Testament's twenty-seven books and letters either were forgeries, or else were altered in later centuries. Bible scholars have published abundant evidence that refute these claims, but few people have the time and inclination to study all their research. So we will discuss the strongest evidence for the New Testament's reliability that you've *never* heard.

In section 5, the final section, we will once and for all *bust* the myth.

Chapter 20

# ACTS:

# THE EKKLESIA IN ACTION

# PART 1

The book of Acts portrays Jesus' Ekklesia—the body of Christ—in action. Luke's gospel ends when Jesus ascends into heaven, but Acts reveals that Jesus is still on earth and He hasn't changed His mind or His methods. Jesus did not change His purpose following His resurrection and ascension: He intended to continue implementing the reign of God by destroying the devil's works through His body on earth, the Ekklesia.

Luke, a physician and companion of the Apostle Paul, wrote more of the New Testament than any other author. *The Acts of the Apostles* chronicles the original "Jesus movement" during the middle decades of the first century. God gave us an entire book to reveal the nature of Jesus' Ekklesia and show us how Christ's corporate body is intended to function.

If churchianity's traditions were valid, the book of Acts should depict the apostles erecting temples, donning priestly costumes, and leading the faithful in liturgically proper "worship" rituals. At the very least, we should find the members of Christ's body divided into clergy ("those who are to be obeyed") and laity ("those who are to obey").[1]

What we find instead is a divinely-inspired record of organic functioning over a period of some thirty years. The Holy Spirit is mentioned more than fifty times. The entire New Testament contains only twenty-two references to church officials: "elders" are mentioned seventeen times; "bishops" four times; "pastors" just once; and "priests" not at all. In contrast, excluding the gospels, there are nearly three hundred references to Christian "brothers," "disciples," and "saints," and over a fifth of these are found in Acts.

The title *The Acts of the Apostles* implies that Luke's narrative is a book of history—that it records what the apostles did—that it is *de*scriptive, not *pre*-scriptive. But Luke didn't name his book "Acts"—that title was invented much later. So is Acts a book of history only, or is it an example that we should follow? If Jesus wanted His body on earth to be ruled by "those who must be obeyed," why can't we find any hint of it in Luke's divinely inspired record of apostolic teaching and practice?

### SIMON (PETER) SAYS: WE'RE ALL BROTHERS

> In those days Peter stood up among the *believers* (a gathering of about one hundred and twenty people) and said, "*Brothers*, the scripture had to be fulfilled that the Holy Spirit foretold through David concerning Judas - who became the guide for those who arrested Jesus . . . (Acts 1:15-16, emphasis mine)

Peter addressed all the believers in the world as "brothers" without using any titles or giving any special recognition. If Matthew 16:18 (". . . you are Peter, and on this rock I will build my church . . .") proves apostolic succession and the primacy of the bishop of Rome, then doesn't Acts 1:15-16 similarly prove that all believers are brothers without titles or org chart relationships?

Who decided that Matthew 16:18 is doctrine while Acts 1:15-16 is merely history, or that Matthew proves that the body of Christ has a ruling class but Acts *doesn't* prove the opposite? How do we know that Peter wasn't setting an example for all believers to follow? If Peter had used a title or given anyone special recognition, this passage would now be a proof text for church government. But since Peter failed to divide believers into "those who must be obeyed" and "those who are to obey," his words here are viewed merely as history. This is another example of how churchianity dupes us into viewing the Bible upside-down.

### THE TWELVE SAID WE'RE ALL BROTHERS

> So the twelve called the *whole group of the disciples* together and said, "It is not right for us to neglect the word of God to wait on tables. But carefully select from among you, *brothers*, seven men who are well-attested, full of the Spirit and of wisdom, whom we may put in charge of this necessary task. (Acts 6:2-3, emphasis mine)

"Brothers" again! All the disciples are called brothers and Jesus' apostles all agree that the brothers are fully capable of recognizing and selecting those among themselves who are full of the Spirit and wisdom. But churchianity tells us that Acts is what the apostles *did*, not what believers today are supposed to *do*—that Acts is a closed history, not an example to follow.

### ANANIAS' UNAUTHORIZED OBEDIENCE

Now there was a disciple in Damascus named Ananias. *The Lord said to him* in a vision, "Ananias," and he replied, "Here I am, Lord." Then the Lord told him, "Get up and go to the street called 'Straight,' and at Judas' house look for a man from Tarsus named Saul. For he is praying, and he has seen in a vision a man named Ananias come in and place his hands on him so that he may see again." (Acts 9:10-12, emphasis mine)

So Ananias departed and entered the house, placed his hands on Saul and said, "Brother Saul, *the Lord Jesus*, who appeared to you on the road as you came here, *has sent me* so that you may see again and be filled with the Holy Spirit." (Acts 9:17, emphasis mine)

By the early third century, when ". . . the Christian churches, together with their bishops and clergy, were no longer what they had been,"[2] Ananias would have been guilty of insubordination by neglecting to consult a bishop. Worse, he would have usurped the bishop's prerogative by laying hands on Saul! Ananias was a mere disciple! How *dare* he presume to lay hands on anyone!

Even without the rest of the book of Acts, the example of Ananias alone should be enough to refute Ignatius' notions of clergy and laity. But today we've all been taught to regard the account of Ananias and Saul as history only. After all, this incident took place during the "age of the apostles" when it was still permissible for mere brothers and disciples to hear directly from Jesus. The Ekklesia still needed flexibility to meet changing needs. The apostles were preoccupied with more important matters, so necessary organization had to wait until Christ's body became better established. At least, that's churchianity's myth-theological explanation.[3]

### FUNCTIONING WITHOUT AN ORG CHART

If Ananias' example is shocking from churchianity's perspective, the rest of Acts is positively scandalous! To highlight churchianity's categorical incompatibility with Jesus' design for His Ekklesia, we're going to look at every instance of "elder," "bishop," "disciple," "brother," and "saint"[4] in Acts (no pastors or priests are ever mentioned). The thing to notice here is *who* is doing *what*. The Lord Jesus Christ—risen, ascended, and seated at the right hand of the Father—is about to walk the earth again in His corporate body, the Ekklesia.

### ACTS 9:19-20

*Saul spent several days with the disciples* in Damascus. At once he began to preach in the synagogues that Jesus is the Son of God. (Acts 9:19-20 NIV, emphasis mine)

Damascus had disciples, but no pastors, priests or bishops are mentioned. And no one authorized Saul to preach: no one other than Jesus, that is.

### ACTS 9:26-27

When he arrived in Jerusalem, he attempted to associate with the *disciples*, and they were all afraid of him, because they did not believe that he was a disciple. But Barnabas took Saul, brought him to the *apostles*, and related to them how he had seen the Lord on the road, that the Lord had spoken to him, and how in Damascus he had spoken out boldly in the name of Jesus. (Acts 9:26-27, emphasis mine)

First Damascus and now Jerusalem: once again there's no mention of pastors, priests or bishops. And Barnabas brought Saul to the twelve apostles, not to any clergy-person.

### ACTS 9:30

When the *brothers* found out about this, they brought him down to Caesarea and sent him away to Tarsus. (Acts 9:30, emphasis mine)

The brothers acted on their own without seeking any prior permission or authorization. No clergy are mentioned.

### ACTS 9:38

Because Lydda was near Joppa, when the *disciples* heard that Peter was there, they sent two men to him and urged him, "Come to us without delay." (Acts 9:38, emphasis mine)

Joppa, like Damascus and Jerusalem, had disciples but no clergy.
(Note that Tabitha, the woman Peter raised from the dead, is called a disciple in Acts 9:36. So the term disciple refers to both men and women. Disciples are also called brothers and sisters.)

### ACTS 10:23

So Peter invited them in and entertained them as guests.

On the next day he got up and set out with them, and some of the *brothers* from Joppa accompanied him. (Acts 10:23, emphasis mine)

The Apostle Peter was accompanied by brothers, i.e. male disciples. Again, no clergy are mentioned.

## ACTS 11:1

Now the *apostles and the brothers* who were throughout Judea heard that the Gentiles too had accepted the word of God. (Acts 11:1, emphasis mine)

As we saw in the account of Saul's arrival in Jerusalem, Jesus' Ekklesia had apostles and disciples who were called brothers and sisters. This passage shows that the same pattern extended throughout Judea. And no clergy are mentioned anywhere.

## ACTS 11:12

The Spirit told me to accompany them without hesitation. These six *brothers* also went with me, and we entered the man's house. (Acts 11:12, emphasis mine)

Peter referred to the six men who accompanied him from Joppa as brothers and didn't mention any official titles. Paul likewise neglected to mention any clerical titles in 1 Thes 5:12. Vincent's New Testament Word Studies surmises that this was because Paul's ecclesiastical nomenclature was unsettled.[5] But that's upside-down. As apostles of Christ, Peter and Paul knew all the truth about the gospel and Jesus' Ekklesia (John 16:13). The right-side-up explanation is that the Ekklesia has no clergy and no laity, just disciples who are brothers and sisters in Jesus Christ.

## ACTS 11:29-30

So the *disciples*, each in accordance with his financial ability, decided to send relief to the *brothers* living in Judea. They did so, sending their financial aid to the *elders* by Barnabas and Saul. (Acts 11:29-30, emphasis mine)

This charitable gift was given in response to a prophecy warning of a coming famine. But who decided to provide financial aid? Who exercised *leadership*? Also, Barnabas and Saul delivered the funds to the elders (plural) in Judea, not to any pastor, priest, bishop, or apostle. The elders were the official and only representatives of the Ekklesia in Judea.

### ACTS **12:17**

Peter motioned with his hand for them to be quiet and described how the Lord had brought him out of prison. "Tell James and the *brothers* about this," he said, and then he left for another place. (Acts 12:17 NIV, emphasis mine)

Some commentators hold that the "brothers" mentioned here were elders and that James was the bishop. But if that's the case, then this prayer meeting was unsupervised because the men to whom Peter refers are not present. And if it was unsupervised, who organized it?

### ACTS **13:1-3**

Now there were these *prophets and teachers* in the church at Antioch: Barnabas, Simeon called Niger, Lucius the Cyrenian, Manaen (a close friend of Herod the tetrarch from childhood) and Saul. While they were serving the Lord and fasting, the Holy Spirit said, "Set apart for me Barnabas and Saul for the work to which I have called them." Then, after they had fasted and prayed and *placed their hands on them*, they sent them off. (Acts 13:1-3, emphasis mine)

In obedience to a prophecy, a group of prophets (plural) and teachers (plural) placed their hands on Barnabas and Saul. The Holy Spirit did not require the sanction or even the presence of any pastor, priest, bishop, or apostle for this act of consecration.

### ACTS **13:52**

And the *disciples* were filled with joy and with the Holy Spirit. (Acts 13:52, emphasis mine)

The disciples were filled with the Holy Spirit without the authorization of any pastor or bishop. What would Ignatius say?

### ACTS **14:2**

But the Jews who refused to believe stirred up the Gentiles and poisoned their minds against the *brothers*. (Acts 14:2, emphasis mine)

Once again, no mention of pastors, priests, or bishops.

### ACTS **14:19-20**

But Jews came from Antioch and Iconium, and after winning the crowds over, they stoned Paul and dragged him out of the city, presuming him to be dead. But after the *disciples* had surrounded him, he got up and went back into the city. On the next day he left with Barnabas for Derbe. (Acts 14:19-20, emphasis mine)

If Lystra had pastors, priests, or bishops, why did only disciples show up when the apostle Paul was left for dead?

## ACTS 14:23

Paul and Barnabas appointed *elders* for them in each *church* and, with prayer and fasting, committed them to the Lord, in whom they had put their trust. (Acts 14:23 NIV, emphasis mine)

Here we find elders (plural) in each Ekklesia (singular). No pastors, priests, or bishops; just multiple elders. Ignatius thought that only a single, visible head could make everything connected with the church secure and valid. Yet Paul and Barnabas appointed multiple elders with no president or "head" elder.

## ACTS 14:26-28

From there they sailed back to Antioch, where they had been commended to the grace of God for the work they had now completed. When they arrived and gathered *the church* together, they reported all the things God had done with them, and that he had opened a door of faith for the Gentiles. So they spent considerable time with *the disciples*. (Acts 14:26-28, emphasis mine)

Barnabas and Saul returned to Antioch, reported to the church, and stayed with the disciples. Luke never mentions a pastor, priest, or bishop. Organized religion in Antioch had to wait another generation or so until Ignatius arrived on the scene.

We can see by what the apostles *did* and *did not* do, as well as what they *said* and *wrote,* that a single, visible head did not exist and was not intended to exist. When the apostles and elders and the Ekklesia met together, it was as *brothers and sisters,* not as *clergy and laity.* But bear with me, there's still more to cover as we go through the rest of the book of Acts in the next chapter.

**Endnotes**

1    "Pictures of this ministry which ruled in the end of the second and in the earlier part of the third century, have been preserved for us in early ecclesiastical manuals... The community was sharply divided into clergy and laity..." (Lindsay, *The Church And The Ministry In The Early Centuries*, 245-6.)

"Although we find the distinction between those who are to be obeyed and those who are to obey clearly laid down in the Epistles of Paul, we do not find a common term in general use to denote the former class until the beginning of the 3rd century" (Orr, *International Standard Bible Encyclopedia*, "Ministry").

2    Shelley, *Church History In Plain Language: Updated 2nd Edition*, 74.

3    "At first, church organization and government in the New Testament was flexible to meet changing needs. But as the church became better established, it gave attention to the right structures and procedures that would help it accomplish its mission…Thus, numerous forms of church government are used today to provide order and structure for the work of churches" (Youngblood, *Nelson's Bible Dictionary*, "Church Government").

4    Except for four instances of "saints" which are not applicable to our inquiry: Acts 9:13, 9:32, 9:41, and 26:10.

5    "The ecclesiastical nomenclature of the Pauline Epistles is unsettled..." (Vincent, *Vincent's New Testament Word Studies*, "1 Thessalonians 5:12").

Chapter 21

# ACTS:
# THE EKKLESIA IN ACTION
# PART 2

Let's continue through acts to find out what the apostles, whom Jesus appointed as His personal representatives, did after Jesus' ascension. In the last chapter, we made our way through the first fourteen chapters of Acts to examine more closely any mention of "brothers," "elders," "apostles," and "disciples." So far we've seen no mention of any one visible head; no bishops, pastors, or priests. What we see are *brothers (and sisters,) elders (plural),* and the *apostles.* Let's keep reading starting with Acts chapter 15.

## ACTS 15:1

Now some men came down from Judea and began to teach the *brothers,*
"Unless you are circumcised according to the custom of Moses, you cannot
be saved." (Acts 15:1, emphasis mine)

This is the beginning of Acts chapter 15, "The Council at Jerusalem." A legalist ministry team, supposedly with the approval of the elders in Judea, arrived in Antioch and began proclaiming a false gospel. Paul and Barnabas opposed them, but there's no mention of any pastor, priest, bishop, or even elders; just brothers. Acts 11:19-26 tells how the gospel came to Antioch. Apparently, up to this time, Antioch had never had any official leaders.

## ACTS **15:2**

When Paul and Barnabas had a major argument and debate with them, *the church appointed* Paul and Barnabas and some others from among them to go up to meet with the apostles and elders in Jerusalem about this point of disagreement. (Acts 15:2, emphasis mine)

In chapter 10 we briefly reviewed Acts 15 as it related to Paul's apostleship. But now notice two things: first, who appointed Paul and Barnabas as representatives? Second, if there were any official church leaders in Antioch, why aren't they mentioned? Luke records that the entire Ekklesia, without any official leadership, appointed representatives.

## ACTS **15:3**

So they were sent on their way by *the church*, and as they passed through both Phoenicia and Samaria, they were relating at length the conversion of the Gentiles and bringing great joy to all the *brothers*. (Acts 15:3, emphasis mine)

The entire Ekklesia appointed representatives and sent them out, presumably with provisions for their journey. And on that journey they met with brothers, but no pastors, priests, or bishops.

## ACTS **15:4**

When they arrived in Jerusalem, they were received by *the church* and *the apostles* and *the elders*, and they reported all the things God had done with them. (Acts 15:4, emphasis mine)

"The church and the apostles and the elders" . . . Hmmm, who's missing here? (Nobody's missing—that's the point!)

## ACTS **15:6**

Both *the apostles* and *the elders* met together to deliberate about this matter. (Acts 15:6, emphasis mine)

The apostles were involved because they were the only ones Jesus had commissioned to define and proclaim the good news about the Kingdom of God. The elders were involved because they would have been responsible for sending out any ministry teams. No other officials are mentioned because during the first century there weren't any others.

## ACTS 15:7

> After there had been much debate, Peter stood up and said to them, "*Broth-ers*, you know that some time ago God chose me to preach to the Gentiles so they would hear the message of the gospel and believe…" (Acts 15:7, emphasis mine)

Just as he did before in Acts 1:16, once again Peter calls everybody "brothers." Either his ecclesiastical nomenclature hadn't yet settled down, or else Peter knew something that Dr. Vincent didn't know when he stated "the ecclesiastical nomenclature of the Pauline Epistles is unsettled…" In case you aren't aware, the Pauline Epistles are the thirteen letters of the New Testament attributed to Paul.

## ACTS 15:13

> After they stopped speaking, James replied, "*Brothers*, listen to me…"
> (Acts 15:13, emphasis mine)

Uh-oh! James doesn't use any titles either! So that's three apostles—Paul, Peter, and James—all of whom were New Testament authors—whose ecclesiastical nomenclature is unsettled according to Dr. Vincent? What about Jesus' promise in John 16:13 that His apostles would know all truth? Did Jesus err or the Holy Spirit somehow fail?

## ACTS 15:22

> Then the apostles and elders, with the whole church, decided to send men chosen from among them, Judas called Barsabbas and Silas, *leaders among the brothers*, to Antioch with Paul and Barnabas. (Acts 15:22, emphasis mine)

Here the entire Ekklesia takes part in a matter that, according to Ignatius, was the sole responsibility of the bishop. Barsabbas and Silas were neither apostles nor elders, but are called leaders and act as official representatives of the Jerusalem Ekklesia. This is how Christ's body on earth is meant to function.

## ACTS 15:23

> They sent this letter with them:
>
> From the apostles and elders, *your brothers*, to the Gentile *brothers and sisters* in Antioch, Syria, and Cilicia, greetings! (Acts 15:23, emphasis mine)

The apostles and elders refer to themselves as brothers with no official titles, and they send a letter addressed to brothers and sisters but do not mention pastors, priests, or bishops.

### ACTS **15:32**

Both Judas and Silas, *who were prophets themselves*, encouraged and strengthened the *brothers* with a long speech. (Acts 15:32, emphasis mine)

Now we learn that Judas and Silas were prophets with no office or title. Beginning in the second century, churchianity rejected prophetic ministry and consolidated all leadership in the office of the pastor / bishop. Also during this time, manifestations of the Holy Spirit's miraculous power began to decline.

### ACTS **15:33**

After they had spent some time there, they were sent off in peace by *the brothers* to those who had sent them. (Acts 15:33, emphasis mine)

Who sent Judas and Silas back to Jerusalem? And who is conspicuously absent here?

### ACTS **15:36**

After some days Paul said to Barnabas, "Let's return and visit the *brothers* in every town where we proclaimed the word of the Lord to see how they are doing." (Acts 15:36, emphasis mine)

Whom did Paul and Barnabas visit?

### ACTS **15:40**

but Paul chose Silas and left, commended by the *brothers* to the grace of the Lord. (Acts 15:40 NIV, emphasis mine)

Who commended Paul and Silas?

### ACTS **16:2**

The *brothers* at Lystra and Iconium spoke well of him. (Acts 16:2, emphasis mine)

Lystra and Iconium had brothers but there's no mention of pastors, priests, or bishops. That's not because Luke negligently ignored them. It's because there weren't any.

## ACTS 16:4

As they went through the towns, they passed on the decrees that had been decided on by the *apostles and elders* in Jerusalem for the Gentile *believers* to obey. (Acts 16:4, emphasis mine)

If James was the pastor or bishop of the Jerusalem Ekklesia, why isn't any such title mentioned here? The way Luke puts it you'd think James was just a fellow elder. That's hardly surprising: Peter said the same thing:

So as *your fellow elder* and a witness of Christ's sufferings and as one who shares in the glory that will be revealed, I urge the *elders* among you . . . (1 Peter 5:1, emphasis mine)

## ACTS 16:40

After Paul and Silas came out of the prison, they went to Lydia's house, where they met with the *brothers* and encouraged them. Then they left. (Acts 16:40 NIV, emphasis mine)

Paul and Silas met with the brothers but not with any pastors, priests, or bishops.

## ACTS 17:6-7

When they did not find them, they dragged Jason and some of the *brothers* before the city officials, screaming, "These people who have stirred up trouble throughout the world have come here too, and Jason has welcomed them as guests!..." (Acts 17:6-7, emphasis mine)

Jason's name is mentioned because the mob attacked his house, where Paul and Silas were staying. But Jason is not called a pastor, priest, or bishop. The only descriptive title given in this account is brothers.

## ACTS 17:9-10

After the city officials had received bail from Jason and the others, they released them.

The *brothers* sent Paul and Silas off to Berea at once, during the night. When they arrived, they went to the Jewish synagogue. (Acts 17:9-10, emphasis mine)

Who sent Paul and Silas away?

### ACTS **17:14**

Then the *brothers* sent Paul away to the coast at once, but Silas and Timothy remained in Berea. (Acts 17:14, emphasis mine)

Who sent Paul to the coast?

### ACTS **18:18**

Paul, after staying many more days in Corinth, said farewell to the *brothers* and sailed away to Syria accompanied by Priscilla and Aquila. (Acts 18:18, emphasis mine)

To whom did Paul say farewell?

### ACTS **18:27**

When Apollos wanted to cross over to Achaia, the *brothers* encouraged him and wrote to the *disciples* to welcome him. (Acts 18:27, emphasis mine)

The brothers encouraged Apollos and wrote a letter of introduction to the disciples. No pastors, priests, or bishops are mentioned.

### ACTS **19:30**

But when Paul wanted to enter the public assembly, the *disciples* would not let him. (Acts 19:30, emphasis mine)

Who wouldn't let Paul appear before the crowd?

### ACTS **20:1**

After the disturbance had ended, Paul sent for the *disciples*, and after encouraging them and saying farewell, he left to go to Macedonia. (Acts 20:1, emphasis mine)

Whom did Paul send for?

### ACTS **20:17**

From Miletus he sent a message to Ephesus, telling the *elders* of the *church* to come to him. (Acts 20:17, emphasis mine)

Ephesus has elders (plural) of the church (singular) and there's no mention of a pastor, priest, or bishop.

## ACTS **20:28**

Watch out for yourselves and for all the flock of which the Holy Spirit has made you *overseers*, to *shepherd* the church of God that he obtained with the blood of his own Son. (Acts 20:28, emphasis mine)

Paul addresses the elders (plural) of the church (singular) in Ephesus and calls them overseers (bishops) who shepherd (pastor) God's flock. Peter says the same thing using the same words:

. . . I urge the *elders* among you: Give a *shepherd's* care to God's flock among you, exercising *oversight* . . . (1 Peter 5:1-2, emphasis mine)

## ACTS **21:3-5**

We landed at Tyre, where our ship was to unload its cargo. Finding the *disciples* there, we stayed with them seven days. Through the Spirit they urged Paul not to go on to Jerusalem. But when our time was up, we left and continued on our way. All the *disciples* and their wives and children accompanied us out of the city, and there on the beach we knelt to pray. (Acts 21:3-5 NIV, emphasis mine)

Tyre had disciples but no pastors, priests, or bishops.

## ACTS **21:7**

We continued the voyage from Tyre and arrived at Ptolemais, and when we had greeted the *brothers*, we stayed with them for one day. (Acts 21:7, emphasis mine)

Ptolemais had brothers but no pastors, priests, or bishops.

## ACTS **21:15-18**

After these days we got ready and started up to Jerusalem. Some of the *disciples* from Caesarea came along with us too, and brought us to the house of Mnason of Cyprus, a *disciple* from the earliest times, with whom we were to stay. When we arrived in Jerusalem, the *brothers* welcomed us gladly. The next day Paul went in with us to see James, and all the *elders* were there. (Acts 21:15-18, emphasis mine)

Some commentators take "brothers" in Acts 12:17 to mean "elders." But here we have brothers distinguished from elders. Maybe the brothers in Acts 12:17 were just brothers in Christ? Also, James is mentioned separately from elders.

Does that mean James was a pastor or bishop? If so, why does he receive no special mention in Acts 15:4, 6, and 23, where only apostles and elders are mentioned?

James was the brother (Mark 6:3, Gal 1:9), or technically the half-brother (Luke 3:23) of the Lord Jesus. After His resurrection, Jesus appeared to James, and subsequently James is called an apostle (1 Cor 15:3-7; Gal 1:18-19). So James was an apostle who functioned as a fellow elder in the church in Jerusalem.

### ACTS 28:14-15

> There we found some *brothers* and were invited to stay with them seven days. And in this way we came to Rome. The *brothers* from there, when they heard about us, came as far as the Forum of Appius and Three Taverns to meet us. (Acts 28:14-15, emphasis mine)

Rome has brothers but no pastors, priests, or bishop.

### CONCLUSION

This concludes our review of three decades of Christian life recorded in the book of Acts. We find apostles; we find multiple elders who are overseers (bishops) in each local Ekklesia; we find leaders who have no office or title; but mostly we find "brothers" who function as body parts of the body of Christ without the authorization of any clergy-person.

Leadership is *divided* among *brothers,* but why? Consolidating leadership is the *opposite* of the design for Jesus' Ekklesia.

> Where no counsel is, the people fall: but in the multitude of counsellors there is safety. (Prov 11:4 KJV)

But more importantly, one person can easily fall into corruption, and consolidating power in one person makes weak leadership. According to Ecclesiastes:

> Although an assailant may overpower one person,
> two can withstand him.
> Moreover, a three-stranded cord is not quickly broken. (Ecc 4:12)

So that's it; in the book of Acts, we find no pastors, priests, bishops, church buildings, orders of worship, or sermons. But we find example after example of the miraculous power of the Holy Spirit and relationship to the true head, Jesus Christ.

No wonder churchianity claims that the book of Acts is just history.

Chapter 22

# Let's Play
# "Find the Bishop"

In the last two chapters we reviewed every instance of "elder," "bishop," "disciple," "brother," and "saint" in the book of Acts. During that period of about thirty years, Jesus' Ekklesia had apostles and elders but no pastors, priests, or bishops. Yet churchianity claims that bishops (or pastors) were instituted by the apostles and existed from the earliest days of the church. (That's a trick statement; we'll find out why at the end of this chapter.)

Luke never mentions pastors, priests, or bishops in Acts, but what about the rest of the New Testament? Before we can be certain that first-century congregations had no single, visible head, we'd need to consider every mention of pastors or bishops. But going verse by verse through the entire New Testament would take too long. Is there an easier way?

Yes there is. Strong's Concordance contains every Greek word in the New Testament in alphabetical order. Each word has a unique ID number along with a list of every verse where it appears. In the case of bishops just three Greek words are involved: *episkopeo* (ep-ee-skop-EH-oh)—to supervise or oversee; *episkope* (ep-is-kop-AY)—supervision, overseership; and *episkopos* (ep-IS-kop-oss)—supervisor, overseer. All three words appear only eleven times in total. There's just one word for pastor, and it turns up only once.

Ephesians 4:11 is the only instance of the word "pastor" in the entire New Testament. The Greek word is *poimen* (poy-MANE, NT:4166) and means shepherd. *Poimen* occurs eighteen times in the New Testament and in every other instance is correctly translated "shepherd." Seven of those instances refer to literal shepherds; ten instances refer to the Lord Jesus Christ. If the KJV translators had been consistent, Ephesians 4:11 would read "*shepherds and teachers*" instead of "pastors and teachers." Everywhere else, it is translated into English as shepherd; in Ephesians 4:11 it's translated into Latin as pastor.[1]

> It was he who gave some to be apostles, some to be prophets, some to be evangelists, and some to be *pastors and teachers*, to prepare God's people for works of service . . . (Eph 4:11-12 NIV, emphasis mine)

With that quick overview of *poimen* or *shepherd*, we can effectively eliminate it, and we're going to now examine all eleven instances of the three words related to bishops. We'll use Strong's Concordance to locate them. To define them, we'll use the Bauer-Danker-Arndt-Gingrich (or BDAG) New Testament Greek-English lexicon, third edition.

Finally, to make our word study enjoyable as well as educational, we'll make a game out of it. The game is called "Find the Bishop." Find the Bishop consists of three rounds—one round for each Greek word. If we can't find the bishop as defined by churchianity, we can conclude he *doesn't exist*. If he does exist, we will sure find him in one of these eleven rounds.

Round one covers *episkopeo*, and it's an easy round because the word appears only twice.

**ROUND 1:**

**EPISKOPEO (NT:1983)—TO OVERSEE**

*Episkopeo* is defined as:

> **to accept responsibility for the care of someone, oversee, care for** . . . hence in a distinctively Christian sense of the activity of church officials **1 Pt 5:2**, esp. of one entrusted with oversight . . .[2]

This word occurs just twice in the New Testament. In Hebrews 12:15, episkopeo does not refer to the person or office of an overseer and may be disregarded in this context:

**1. Hebrews 12:15:**

*See to it* that no one comes short of the grace of God, that no one be like a bitter root springing up and causing trouble, and through him many become defiled. (Heb 12:15, emphasis mine)

So Hebrews 12:15 has been eliminated. That leaves just ten references to the bishop in the entire New Testament.

**2. 1 Peter 5:1-2:**

The only other instance of *episkopeo* is in Peter's first letter, where he explicitly states that elders (*presbuteros*) serve as overseers (*episkopeo*):

> So as your fellow elder and a witness of Christ's sufferings and as one who shares in the glory that will be revealed, I urge the elders among you: Give a shepherd's care to God's flock among you, *exercising oversight* . . . (1 Peter 5:1-2, emphasis mine)

Uh-oh! Peter writes to his fellow *elders*, not bishops, and then proceeds to undermine Ignatius' definition of a single bishop by instructing the elders (plural) to serve as overseers. If Peter had any idea that such a thing as a bishop-CEO existed, or that he was one himself (and of Rome, no less!), he gives no evidence of it in his letter written circa AD 65. So Peter didn't help us find the bishop.

That's the end of round one, and Ignatius' bishop-CEO is nowhere in sight. And now, with just nine references remaining, we move on to round two . . .

## ROUND 2:
### EPISKOPE (NT:1984)—OVERSEERSHIP

*Episkope* is defined as:

> **engagement in oversight, supervision,** of leaders of Christian communities . . .[3]

This word occurs four times in the New Testament. Two of these instances refer to God, not to any man, and may be disregarded in this context:

**1. Luke 19:44:**

> They will demolish you - you and your children within your walls - and they will not leave within you one stone on top of another, because you did not recognize the time of your *visitation from God*." (Luke 19:44, emphasis mine)

**2. 1 Peter 2:12:**

> and maintain good conduct among the non-Christians, so that though they now malign you as wrongdoers, they may see your good deeds and glorify God *when he appears*. (1 Peter 2:12, emphasis mine)

Two of our remaining nine references have just been eliminated, leaving only seven to go. But the other two instances of *episkope*, translated "bishoprick" and "office of a bishop" in the KJV, sound quite promising. Let's consider the earliest instance, spoken by Peter soon after Jesus' ascension. Here it is, first from the KJV, then from the NET Bible:

**3. Acts 1:20:**

For it is written in the book of Psalms, Let his habitation be desolate, and let no man dwell therein: and his *bishoprick* let another take. (Acts 1:20 KJV, emphasis mine)

For it is written in the book of Psalms, 'Let his house become deserted, and let there be no one to live in it,' and 'Let another take his *position of responsibility.*' (Acts 1:20 NET, emphasis mine)

In Acts 1, the eleven apostles were considering a replacement for Judas Iscariot, and Peter quoted Psalm 109:8. The Old Testament Hebrew word *pequddah* (pek-ood-DAW, NT:6486) is translated into the New Testament Greek word *episkope*—"supervision, oversight." Judas and the rest of the twelve held official positions of oversight; but were they bishop-CEOs as Ignatius defined the term and as we understand it today? Peter answers that question in his very next sentence, where he provides a job description of the apostolic office:

Thus one of the men who have accompanied us during all the time the Lord Jesus associated with us, beginning from his baptism by John until the day he was taken up from us - one of these must become a *witness* of his resurrection together with us. (Acts 1:21-22, emphasis mine)

Peter could have said "For one of these must become a *ruler* of God's flock," but he didn't. Instead, Peter wanted someone who had witnessed Jesus' entire public ministry, from John's baptism to the resurrection. It looks as though Peter intended to fulfill Jesus' words in Acts 1:8:

. . . you will be my *witnesses* in Jerusalem, and in all Judea and Samaria, and to the farthest parts of the earth. (Acts 1:8, emphasis mine)

So Acts 1:20 is inconclusive as far as proving the existence of bishops as church CEOs. *Episkope* here refers to the apostles of Christ, not to leaders of a local Ekklesia. It indicates only what is already obvious: that the twelve held positions of leadership and oversight to fulfill Jesus' commission in Matthew 28:18-20. If bishop-CEOs do exist in the New Testament, we ought to find a job description of the office. And that brings us to our fourth and last instance of *episcope*: 1 Timothy 3:1 (again, first the KJV, then the NET Bible):

### 4. 1 Timothy 3:1:

This is a true saying, if a man desire the *office of a bishop*, he desireth a good work. (1 Tim 3:1 KJV, emphasis mine)

This saying is trustworthy: "if someone aspires to the *office of overseer*, he desires a good work." (1 Tim 3:1 NET, emphasis mine)

Paul goes on in verses 2 through 7 to list the qualifications for the office of overseer. So *episkope* is an official position, not just some informal function. But we still have no job description—we still don't know what an overseer does.

We've now reviewed six of our eleven New Testament references to the bishop. Three of those references were eliminated, one referred to elders and bishops synonymously, and two were inconclusive. There are only five more references to the bishop in the entire New Testament! The clock is running out on nineteen centuries' worth of churchianity's holiest tradition, and we still haven't found Ignatius' pastor-bishop-CEO.

We're about to start round three. If Ignatius' bishop-CEO doesn't turn up in the next five verses, we may be forced into overtime—searching for the bishop in documents written after the first century—documents without apostolic authority—writings that failed to make the New Testament cut! But there's still hope. Round three, the final round, is the longest; and now we're focusing on *episkopos*—the Big Guy himself!

ROUND 3:

EPISKOPOS (NT:1985)—OVERSEER

*Episkopos* is defined as:

> **one who has the responsibility of safeguarding or seeing to it that something is done in the correct way, guardian** . . . The term was taken over in Christian communities in ref. to one who served as **overseer** or **supervisor** . . .[4]

This word occurs five times in the New Testament. The instance in 1 Peter 2:25 refers to Jesus Christ and may be disregarded in this context:

**1. 1 Peter 2:24-25:**

> He himself bore our sins in his body on the tree, that we may cease from sinning and live for righteousness. By his wounds you were healed. For you were going astray like sheep but now you have turned back to the shepherd and *guardian* of your souls. (1 Peter 2:24-25, emphasis mine)

In Acts 20:28, Paul addressed the elders of the church of Ephesus. He stated that the Holy Spirit had made them overseers, and exhorted them to be shepherds of the church of God:

**2. Acts 20:17-18, 28:**

> From Miletus he sent a message to Ephesus, telling the elders of the church to come to him.

> When they arrived, he said to them . . . "Watch out for yourselves and for all the flock of which the Holy Spirit has made you *overseers*, to shepherd

the church of God that he obtained with the blood of his own Son." (Acts 20:17-18, 28, emphasis mine)

Uh-oh! As late as AD 60, Paul stated that elders are overseers and used the terms synonymously. Or rather, Paul is telling us that *elder* is the *office*, and *oversight* is the *function*. We now have two scriptures, 1 Peter 5:1-5 and Acts 20:28 that agree that elders are overseers. Our next scripture indirectly confirms this understanding of *episkopos*:

### 3. Phillipians 1:1:

From Paul and Timothy, slaves of Christ Jesus, to all the saints in Christ Jesus who are in Philippi, with the *overseers* and deacons. (Phil 1:1, emphasis mine)

Philippi has more than one overseer! Elders are not mentioned; yet we know from Titus 1:5 that Paul appointed elders (plural) in every town (singular). So the town of Philippi would have had multiple elders, and now we learn that the town of Philippi had multiple overseers! All of which is perfectly consistent with 1 Peter 5:1-5 and Acts 20:28, but utterly inconsistent with the notion of a single bishop-CEO as the visible head of every congregation.

Does the fact that Paul here names "overseers and deacons" separately suggest that the Philippian Ekklesia was divided into clergy and laity? The Philippian letter itself provides a better explanation in 4:15-18:

It is altogether probable, as has frequently been pointed out, that they (overseers and deacons) are specifically addressed in this particular letter because Paul has just received the gift of money from the Philippian church which these administrators and workers have been largely responsible for raising and sending."[5]

We noted previously that 1 Timothy 3:1-7 lists the qualifications for an overseer, and 1 Timothy 3:2 is our fourth instance of *episkope*:

### 4. 1 Timothy 3:2-7:

The *overseer* then must be above reproach, the husband of one wife, temperate, self-controlled, respectable, hospitable, an able teacher, not a drunkard, not violent, but gentle, not contentious, free from the love of money. He must manage his own household well and keep his children in control without losing his dignity. But if someone does not know how to manage his own household, how will he *care for the church of God?* He must not be a recent convert or he may become arrogant and fall into the punishment that the devil will exact. And he must be well thought of by those outside the faith, so that he may not fall into disgrace and be caught by the devil's trap. (1 Tim 3:2-7, emphasis mine)

So an overseer takes care of the Ekklesia, and God considers good family management as the preeminent job qualification. Paul goes on in verses 8-15 to list the qualifications for deacons, but never mentions elders. That's because, as we have seen, the terms elder and overseer (bishop) were used synonymously, and everybody in the first century Ekklesia knew it.

And now let's conclude our game of "Find the Bishop." The fifth and final instance of *episkope* in the New Testament is Titus 1:7, where Paul again lists the qualifications of an overseer. Here's the larger context:

### 5. Titus 1:5-9:

> The reason I left you in Crete was to set in order the remaining matters and to appoint elders in every town, as I directed you. An elder must be blameless, the husband of one wife, with faithful children who cannot be charged with dissipation or rebellion. For the *overseer* must be blameless as one entrusted with God's work, not arrogant, not prone to anger, not a drunkard, not violent, not greedy for gain. Instead he must be hospitable, devoted to what is good, sensible, upright, devout, and self-controlled. He must hold firmly to the faithful message as it has been taught, so that he will be able to give exhortation in such healthy teaching and correct those who speak against it. (Titus 1:5-9, emphasis mine)

In his first letter to Timothy, Paul lists the qualifications for overseers and deacons but doesn't mention elders. In the letter to Titus, Paul uses the term elder and overseer in the same list of qualifications. Therefore it is obvious that . . .

Well, according to churchianity, it's obvious that in his letter to Timothy, Paul inexplicably omitted the qualifications for elders, and that in his letter to Titus, Paul awkwardly conflated the qualifications for elder and overseer in the same paragraph. But that's upside-down. It imposes churchianity's myth-theology on Paul's letters. It's another example of how churchianity makes God's written Sacred Communication hard to understand.

If we take these passages at face value and interpret them in their normal sense, they become easy to understand. The puzzling omissions and combinations disappear and we see—for the third time—that elders are overseers, and that a local Ekklesia always has more than one of them.

And that concludes our game of "Find The Bishop." We've reviewed every reference to "bishop" in the entire New Testament, and . . .he isn't there?

WAIT A MINUTE! You mean, that's it? There's no bishop-CEO anywhere in the New Testament?

That's correct. The New Testament mentions only two offices in the Ekklesia—elder and deacon—and any one Ekklesia always has multiple elders and deacons.

### CHURCHIANITY'S TRICK STATEMENT

At the beginning of this chapter, I said that churchianity's claim about the church having pastors or bishops from its earliest days is a trick statement. The trick consists of changing the definition of the word bishop. In the New Testament, the terms elder, bishop, and shepherd are used interchangeably. Elder is the job title; bishop (overseer) and pastor (shepherd) are the job description. But Ignatius changed the definition of bishop. To the apostles of Christ, an elder was an overseer (bishop) and every local Ekklesia always had multiple elders with no president or head elder. But to Ignatius, and to most of us today, a pastor or bishop is a CEO who presides over elders, deacons, and the congregation.

So yes, the apostles appointed multiple overseers (bishops) in every local Ekklesia, and Jesus' Ekklesia had supervisors from the beginning. But no, until the second century there were never any pastors or bishops as we understand the term today.

### FORCED INTO OVERTIME

Our game of "Find the Bishop" has been forced into overtime. If we actually want to find the bishop, we must search for him in Christian writings from after the first century. But that presents a HUGE problem for churchianity.

Churchianity's problem has to do with divine revelation. Christianity has twenty-seven documents that are recognized as inspired by God—the twenty-seven books of the New Testament written or approved by the apostles of Christ—and nowhere in any of those twenty-seven documents is there any mention of church government. All attempts to explain God's "silence" disregard the obvious meaning of God's written Sacred Communication and impose a foreign meaning—organized religion's myth-theology—on God's Word, as our church historian noted earlier:

> One may account for this virtual silence by saying either that the writers did not regard such forms as important or that they took them for granted; but the silence itself is undeniable.[6]

But churchianity's predicament is much worse than it first appears—as we're about to discover. As Thomas Lindsey points out,

> All this shows us that during the last decades of the first century each Christian congregation had for its office-bearers a body of deacons and a body of elders—whether separated into two colleges or forming one must remain unknown—and that the elders took the "oversight" while the deacons performed the "subordinate services." These, constituted the local ministry of each Christian church or congregation—for these terms were then equiva-

190

lent. These men watched over the lives and behaviour of the members of the community; they looked after the poor, the infirm, and the strangers; and in the absence of members of the prophetic ministry they presided over the public worship, especially over the Holy Supper.[7]

**Endnotes**

1    Wuest's Expanded Translation: "pastors who are also teachers"; The Message: "and pastor-teacher"; World English Bible: "shepherds and teachers"; ESV note: "or the pastor-teachers"; Darby: "shepherds and teachers."

2    Bauer, *BDAG*, 379.

3    Bauer, *BDAG*, 379.

4    Bauer, *BDAG*, 379.

5    Niebuhr at al, *The Ministry In Historical Perspectives*, 10.

6    Niebuhr et al, *The Ministry In Historical Perspectives*, 3.

7    Lindsay, *The Church And The Ministry In The Early Centuries*, 154-155.

Chapter 23

# Four Answers

We're now ready to address our fundamental question: what does God think about organized religion? Was the body of Christ an infant that grew up over several centuries as church government developed? Does the New Testament comprise God's complete and permanent plan for Jesus' Ekklesia, or does it reveal only a partial and temporary plan? Which parts, if any, of our twenty-seven New Testament documents should be disregarded because they were temporary? What specific examples and instructions, recorded in writing by Jesus' apostles and their associates, no longer apply to Christians today?

In the previous sections of this book we established the following:

- Jesus promised to build His Ekklesia but delegated the details to His apostles.

- Jesus promised His eleven apostles that the Holy Spirit would guide them into all truth.

- These same eleven apostles unanimously and completely approved of Paul's teaching.

- The Apostle Paul stated that he was a wise master builder and that he had declared the whole purpose of God.

- Paul's letters contain specific instructions and examples detailing the purpose, design, and functioning of Christ's body.

- Nothing in the New Testament indicates that any of Paul's instructions were temporary.

- The truth that the Holy Spirit revealed, and which all of the apostles knew, taught, practiced, and documented, included <u>none</u> of the following:

  o The office of the bishop or pastor

  o Clergy and laity

  o Ordination

  o Salaried clergy

  o Temples ("church" buildings)

  o Worship services and the Order of Worship

  o Sermons

Our question is *not* whether Christianity departed from documented New Testament teaching and practice after the first century, but rather: did God authorize the changes, or at least permit and approve of them? As Dr. Bruce Shelley succinctly states:

> These changes in the structure and functioning of the church, especially the role of bishops, raise crucial and controversial questions. Christians of nearly every denomination admit that these changes took place. The question is: What do the changes mean, and what authority, if any, do they have for the church of later times, especially our own?[1]

The Church Infancy Myth's original version claims that God authorized organized religion after the New Testament was completed—by giving divine revelation via unwritten tradition and the selected writings of "church fathers" who were not apostles of Christ.

The Myth's stealth version claims that either (A) the New Testament's silence about church government means that God permits Christians to organize however they wish; or else that (B) God approves of organized religion but cannot or does not communicate clearly and normally; consequently we must infer the purpose, design, and functioning of Jesus' Ekklesia from a handful of cherry-picked, out-of-context proof texts.

There is, of course, a third, non-mythical explanation for organized religion: that it's a counterfeit, invented after AD 100. God never authorized it, and He neither permits nor approves of it.

If God rescinded multiple elders, overlapping leadership, and all of Paul's instructions about how the body parts of Christ's body function when they meet together, then much of the New Testament is now obsolete. And if God instituted church government and ritual temple worship after AD 100, then the New Testament—which is silent on those subjects—reveals only a partial and temporary plan for Jesus' Ekklesia.

On the other hand, if God didn't revoke any of the truth recorded in the New Testament—truth promised by Jesus, revealed by the Holy Spirit, and recorded and approved by the apostles of Christ—then the New Testament presents a complete and permanent plan for Jesus' Ekklesia, and all of Paul's instructions are still in force.

Thus we have a multiple choice question with three possible answers:

1.) What does God think of organized religion?
   A) He authorized it.
   B) He permits and approves of it.
   C) None of the above.

Put another way, do or do we not agree with the Church Infancy Myth which states:

> . . . the apostles and early Christians . . . were looking for the speedy return of Christ, and consequently did not *organize the church in its infancy*, as it was afterward found necessary to do.[2] (emphasis mine)

Do we agree with those to whom Bruce Shelley refers when he says:

> Still other Christians argue that the Holy Spirit so dwelt in the church and guided its decisions that the developments of the early centuries in doctrine and church structure were the work not of men but of God. They are, therefore, permanently binding for the church.[3]

Do we agree with the stealth version of the myth which says:

> At first, church organization and government in the New Testament was flexible to meet changing needs. But as the church became better established, it gave attention to the right structures and procedures that would help it accomplish its mission…Thus, numerous forms of church government are used today to provide order and structure for the work of churches.[4]

Whatever our views on this controversy may be, we should be able to agree that one of the following statements must be true: either: (1) God intended at least some of the examples and instructions in the New Testament to be temporary, or else (2) He intended all of them to be permanent.

And based on Jesus' promise to His eleven apostles in John 16:13, we should also be able to agree that either (1) Jesus' apostles knew that at least some of what they taught, practiced, and documented in the New Testament was temporary, or else (2) they knew that all of it was permanent.

Stating a problem correctly is half the solution. With our question put in the form of two either-or, true-or-false statements like we have just done, we can use a handy technique called a truth table to identify all logically possible answers. The truth table below displays our question from God's perspective down the left-hand side, and from the apostles' perspective across the top:

| The purpose, design, and functioning of Jesus' Ek-klesia which is documented in the New Testament . . . | . . . was known by the apostles to be temporary. | . . . was known by the apostles to be permanent. |
|---|---|---|
| . . . was intended by God to be temporary. | 1 | 2 |
| . . . was intended by God to be permanent. | 3 | 4 |

TABLE 23-1: NEW TESTAMENT INSTRUCTIONS AND EXAMPLES: TEMPORARY OR PERMANENT?

As the table shows, there are just four ways to combine our two true-or-false statements. These four possible answers to our question are represented by table cells 1 through 4. We can now state all the logically possible answers clearly and examine each one individually. Only one of these answers is true; the other three are false. We'll start with answer number one.

### ANSWER NUMBER ONE

1. "The truth that the apostles believed, taught, practiced, and documented in the New Testament was intended by God to be temporary, and was known by the apostles to be temporary."

Christ's apostles, as we have seen, knew all the truth, not just partial, temporary, or first-century truth. If answer number one is true, then all of Jesus' apostles knew that His permanent design for the Ekklesia included:

- A paid, professional CEO as the visible, acting head of each congregation instead of multiple elders, overlapping leadership, and Jesus as the invisible, acting head of His body;

- The division of Christ's body into a ruling clergy and a submitting laity;

- A formal ceremony (ordination) to make the clergy-laity division apparent;

- Salaried clergy;

- Meetings in temples (i.e. "church" buildings) instead of homes;

- Meetings consisting of ceremonial "worship" rituals;

- The body parts of Christ's body passively listening to an oration (sermon) by the CEO instead of actively functioning in every meeting.

**If answer number one is true**, not only did all the apostles of Christ fail to teach, practice, and document God's permanent design; they taught, practiced, and documented something entirely different from and incompatible with God's permanent design. Instead of correcting Paul's temporary version of the Gospel when they had the opportunity, they gave it their written approval—twice! And all of Jesus' apostles kept God's permanent truth secret and took it with them to their graves. They thus completely nullified Jesus' promise and wasted the Holy Spirit's guidance.

**If answer number one is true**, then when John, the last of the Twelve, died in AD 100, one of two things had to happen: either (A) the Holy Spirit had to duplicate His effort and once again reveal all the lost truth to succeeding generations of "church fathers" (men who were not apostles of Christ) so that they could finally implement God's permanent design for the church; or else (B) the Holy Spirit did not give further revelation about God's permanent design for Jesus' Ekklesia, and since that time the structure and functioning of the body of Christ has been a matter of political preference.

Maybe you noticed that (A) and (B) above aren't hypothetical. View (A) is the Myth's original version, aka the Rule of Faith, and is the official position of churches for whom the Bible is God's *primary* revelation. View (B) is the Myth's stealth version and is held explicitly or implicitly, in one form or another, by churches for whom the Bible is God's *only* revelation. Christians may disagree over whether God's written Sacred Communication is *prima* or *sola*, but actions speak louder than words, and so far our actions demonstrate that we all agree that the divine revelation recorded in the New Testament is partial and temporary.

### ANSWER NUMBER TWO

2. "The truth that the apostles believed, taught, practiced, and documented in the New Testament was intended by God to be temporary, but was known by the apostles to be permanent."

If God intended for the apostles' teaching and practice to be temporary but they didn't know it, then they didn't know all of the truth. Answer number two thus accuses Jesus of error and the Holy Spirit of failure. It is self-evidently false.

### ANSWER NUMBER THREE

3. "The truth that the apostles believed, taught, practiced, and documented in the New Testament was intended by God to be permanent, but was known by the apostles to be temporary."

In addition to being false for the same reason that answer number two is false, answer number three is absurd. The New Testament gives no indication whatsoever that the apostles considered any of their teaching and practice to be anything other than permanent.

### ANSWER NUMBER FOUR

4. "The truth that the apostles believed, taught, practiced, and documented in the New Testament was intended by God to be permanent, and was known by the apostles to be permanent."

**If Answer number four is true**, then the apostles of Christ did not fail to teach, practice, and document God's permanent design for Jesus' Ekklesia; rather, they fulfilled Jesus' promise to build His Ekklesia because they were both authorized and empowered by the Holy Spirit to do so. They did not nullify Jesus' promise, waste the Holy Spirit's guidance, or keep God's permanent truth secret; rather, they taught and practiced God's design and gave their unanimous written approval to the apostle Paul, who documented God's whole purpose.

**If Answer number four is true**, then all of the New Testament's detailed instructions and examples regarding the purpose, structure, and functioning of Jesus' Ekklesia are still in effect; none of them have been rescinded or revoked. The New Testament documents God's complete and permanent design for Jesus' Ekklesia, and that design includes:

- Jesus as the invisible, acting head of each congregation, multiple elders, overlapping leadership, and no bishop or pastor CEO;

- No division of Christ's body into clergy and laity;

- No formal ceremony (ordination) to formalize the clergy-laity division;

- No salaried leadership;

- Meetings in private homes instead of temples ("church" buildings);

- Meetings consisting of active participation by *each* of the body parts of Christ's body.

**If Answer number four is true**, then the New Testament's examples and instructions are also unalterable. Since the apostles of Christ knew all the truth, there was zero truth remaining to be revealed later. Thus, any teaching or practice that deviates from the apostolic instructions and examples documented in the New Testament cannot be valid.

**Finally, if answer number four is true**, then the myth of the church's infancy is a lie, and the term "church fathers" is a misnomer: the apostles of Christ were the true and only church fathers. The men who developed church government after the first century were really the *churchianity fathers*.

## Endnotes

1   Shelley, *Church History In Plain Language: Updated 2nd Edition*, 71.

2   Orr, *International Standard Bible Encyclopedia*, "Bishop"

3   Shelley, *Church History In Plain Language: Updated 2nd Edition*, 72.

4   Youngblood, *Nelson's Bible Dictionary*, "Church Government"

Chapter 24

# NT Reliability:
# The Best Evidence
# You've *Never* Heard

Now that our argument to disprove churchianity is complete, and we have once and for all busted the myth, there is one last thing I'd like to cover. While I did write this book in order to guide my fellow believers *out* of churchianity and *into* relationship with Jesus, I also know that each of you will be coming from varying backgrounds. Some were raised to trust the Bible as God's divinely-inspired written communication, some of you may be new Christians. Some of you may merely be curious, or seeking truth, but do not yet know whether you believe in the Bible or not. Yet if you are curious, and if you are seeking truth, you may be wondering, *can we trust that the Bible wasn't forged?* If the Bible itself is a forgery, then our whole argument fails and we're back to nothing. But if it *is* the original, then how do we know?

There is a simple way to prove that the New Testament was written during the lifetimes of Christ's apostles and not altered afterwards. It's the *strongest possible* evidence for New Testament reliability and accuracy. And it's hiding in plain sight on practically every page of the New Testament itself.

### CRITICS CHARGE THE NEW TESTAMENT WITH FORGERY

The New Testament makes it clear that the apostles' reliability is based entirely on Jesus Himself. If Christ's apostles aren't reliable, then neither is the Lord Jesus Christ.

Today, however, all we know about what the apostles believed, practiced, and taught comes from the New Testament's twenty-seven books and letters. What if some of those books and letters were forgeries—written after the apostles' lifetimes—after the first century? And even if all the original documents were authentic, today all we have are copies. How can we be certain they weren't changed over the centuries?

If the New Testament itself isn't reliable, then Jesus' promises to His apostles aren't reliable either. And many critics of Christianity contend that the New Testament does not reliably record the teaching of the apostles. Critics charge that at least some, if not most, of the New Testament was either forged or altered after the first century.

This criticism turns up, for example, in Dan Brown's wildly popular novel *The Da Vinci Code*. Brown's fictional historian Sir Leigh Teabing asserts that the Bible was altered numerous times over the centuries and that the New Testament was rigged to advance the political agenda of the Roman Catholic Church:

> "The Bible is a product of *man* . . . and it has evolved through countless translations, additions, and revisions. History has never had a definitive version of the book."[1]

> "Of course, the Vatican, in keeping with their tradition of misinformation, tried very hard to suppress the release of these scrolls. And why wouldn't they? The scrolls highlight glaring historical discrepancies and fabrications, clearly confirming that the modern Bible was compiled and edited by men who possessed a political agenda—to promote the divinity of the man Jesus Christ and use His influence to solidify their own power base."[2]

These accusations are not new nor have they gone unanswered. For over a century scholars have been researching and publishing the evidence that refutes them. Lee Strobel's *The Case For Christ* (1998), and Mark D. Roberts' *Can We Trust The Gospels* (2007), both present overviews of the abundant evidence for New Testament reliability, and both books include references for further study.

But the strongest possible evidence for New Testament reliability isn't mentioned in either of those books—or anywhere else, to my knowledge. It proves that the New Testament's books and letters were written during the apostles' lifetimes and not changed afterwards. It utterly refutes fictional historian Sir Leigh Teabing's accusations.

That such powerful evidence for New Testament reliability exists and yet has gone unnoticed is astonishing. But what's even more surprising is *where* it exists: it's right in plain sight on practically every page of the New Testament!

The New Testament itself contains the strongest possible evidence that its books and letters could not have been written or changed after the first century.

What is this mysterious proof of New Testament reliability, and why haven't we heard about it?

### ORGANIZED RELIGION'S POLITICAL AGENDA

Critics charge that after the first century, church authorities forged or altered the New Testament documents to advance their political agenda. Well, *was* there a political agenda after AD 100 that was promoted by church authorities? History has already answered that question for us as Bruce Shelley illustrates:

> These local leaders were of two sorts. One group was called elders or presbyters (from the Greek for "elders"). These same men were also known as bishops (overseers) or pastors (shepherds). The other group of leaders was called deacons . . . This general picture, however, soon changed. After the turn of the century Ignatius, the pastor of the church at Antioch, wrote a series of letters. In these he speaks habitually of a single bishop (or pastor) in each church, a body of presbyters, and a company of deacons. God's grace and the Spirit's power, he teaches, flow to the flock through this united ministry.[3]

> The beginnings of the change date from the early decades of the second century; by the end of the century it was almost complete . . . the "prophetic" ministry passed away, its functions being appropriated by the permanent office-bearers of the local churches; and every local church came to supplement its organization by placing *one* man at the head of the community, making him the president of the college of elders.[4]

> By the late second century, however, the unchallenged leader in church affairs was the bishop.[5]

To summarize:

- During the first century, each local Ekklesia had two kinds of leaders: elders and deacons.

- Elders were also called presbyters, bishops (overseers), and pastors (shepherds).

- Every local Ekklesia had multiple elders but no "head" elder.

- Shortly after AD 100, Ignatius of Antioch wrote a series of letters advocating a single visible leader: a "head" elder. He called this individual the bishop.

- Within two generations, all the churches had adopted this change.

So there *was* a political agenda after AD 100 that was promoted by Christian leaders. It comprised three major changes to first-century Christianity:

1. One elder became the official head over the other elders, deacons, and the congregation.

2. The new regime claimed control over relationship with God and the Holy Spirit's power.

3. Political authority replaced spiritual authority, making prophets and prophecy not just obsolete, but subversive as well.

All of this is history, not mythology.[6]

### THE EVIDENCE YOU'VE NEVER HEARD

And now, if you haven't already guessed it, here's how the New Testament itself proves that it couldn't have been written or altered after the first century: If any of the twenty-seven books and letters of the New Testament were written or changed after AD 100, *what would we expect to find in them?* We'd expect to find:

1. The bishop as the visible head over the other elders, deacons, and the congregation.

2. Church leadership in control of God's grace and the Spirit's power.

3. Prophetic ministry restricted or prohibited.

But what we actually find is precisely the opposite.

If the accusations against New Testament reliability were valid, we would expect to find the apostles of Christ appointing a single bishop (or pastor) over each church, along with injunctions to "do nothing without the bishop." We would expect to find manifestations of God's supernatural power limited to church officers. We would expect to find, in those supposedly first-century writings, the same sort of instructions that we find in the second-century letters of Ignatius of Antioch.

Instead, we find precisely the opposite. Both Peter and Paul use the terms "elder" and "bishop" synonymously. Every local church has multiple elders and there's no mention of a single "head" elder. Peter proclaims that prophecy is part of the gift of the Holy Spirit, given to "as many as the Lord our God will call to himself" (Acts 2:14-39). Paul declares that God gives supernatural spiritual gifts to every believer (1 Cor 12:7), encourages everyone to prophesy (1 Cor 14:1, 5), and even warns against despising prophecy (1 Thes 5:20).

Finally, the entire book of Acts documents about thirty years of church history during which believers did *everything* without "the bishop."

It's strikingly obvious that the New Testament documents could not have been forgeries, nor could they have been altered to harmonize with second-century church politics. And so far we've considered only the changes that a forger or fabricator from about AD 220 or earlier would likely have made. At the very least, a forger ought to have changed Jesus' promise in John 16:13 to apply to "the church" instead of just His eleven apostles who were with Him in the room.

### CONFIRMED BY CHURCH HISTORY

How can I be so certain what we'd find if the New Testament had been written or changed after AD 100? That's easy: all these changes actually happened by the early third century (AD 201):[7]

> The Church, which was in earlier days a "brotherhood of saints," became a community *over whom a bishop presided.* It was defined, not so much by the manner of life led by its members, as by the government which ruled over them . . .[8] (emphasis mine)

> The early freedom of worship no longer existed. The reading, prayers, and exhortations were all in the hands of the clergy. The people shared in the singing only.[9]

> Those men who possess the "gift" of healing are to be ordained presbyters after careful investigation be made that the "gift" is really possessed and that the cures do really come from God. The leaders of the churches seem to be anxious to enrol (sic) within the regular ministry of the congregation, and to prevent them from overshadowing its authority, all who are possessed of "gifts" . . .[10]

> The final form which the new organization of the congregation took, says Harnack, "was characterized . . . by the dying out, *that is by the extermination,* of the last remains of the *charismata*, which under the new ideas were dangerous, seldom appearing, and often compromising and discrediting as far as they rose above the ranks of harmless."[11] (emphasis mine)

### KNOWN FOR OVER A CENTURY

I think it's accurate to say that this powerful internal evidence for New Testament reliability isn't commonly known—or even known at all. For several years I wondered if I was the first person to recognize it. But it turns out that someone else knew about it over one hundred years ago.

German theologian Theodor Zahn published his *Introduction to the New Testament* in 1897. It proved so popular that it was translated and published as a three-volume English edition in 1909. In Volume II, professor Zahn explained why Paul's letters to Timothy and Titus could not have been forgeries and could not have been changed after Paul wrote them:

> Now, however, from Revelation, the Epistles of Ignatius, and the tradition concerning the disciples of John, we learn that by the close of the first century the monarchical episcopate had been generally introduced and firmly established in the Churches of Asia Minor, which was the destination of 1 Tim., and that after the middle of the second century this form of government became more and more common in the Churches of Europe. How could a pseudo-Paul, writing in the year 100 or 160 with a view to exerting some influence upon the system of Church organisation in his time, ignore so completely the Church life which he observed about him, and present Paul and his helpers so entirely in the dress and language of 50-70 in all that affected the essential forms of Church organisation? The aim on the forger's part in this way to avoid all telltale anachronisms would directly contradict his other purpose, namely, in Paul's name to influence the Church of his own time; while everyone acquainted with ancient literature, particularly the literature of the ancient Church, knows that a forger or fabricator of those times could not possibly have avoided anachronisms.[12]

That long quotation isn't easy to follow, so let's unpack it. Zahn's argument goes as follows:

- A second-century forger would have had no experience of first-century Christianity. His only knowledge of church life would be organized religion's version.

- Yet the letters to Timothy and Titus contain no hint of the bishop or any other second-century changes. How could a forger manage to completely ignore the only church life he had ever experienced?

- Obviously then, if the letters are bogus, our hypothetical forger took great care to avoid any mention of second-century changes. Now why would he do that?

- Why, he'd do it to cover his tracks; to make us believe his forgeries were actually written by Paul. Because since all of the second-century changes occurred after Paul's lifetime, Paul couldn't have written about them.

- But that would defeat the forger's purpose, which was to convince us that Paul believed in, practiced, taught, and documented all those second-century changes.

- No forger would be that stupid. But in any case, no forger of that era could have covered his tracks that well.

At the end of that quotation Zahn mentions anachronisms. An anachronism is someone or something that is chronologically out of sequence. For example, a story about George Washington sending a telegraph would be an obvious anachronism since the electrical telegraph wasn't invented until after Washington's lifetime. Likewise, any account of Paul or Peter advocating a single "head" elder over every local congregation would be an obvious anachronism since "*the* bishop" wasn't invented until after their lifetimes.

Professor Zahn's point was that the internal evidence proves Paul's letters to Timothy and Titus could not possibly have been forgeries. But his logical argument applies to every other book and letter of the New Testament. This is the strongest possible evidence for New Testament reliability. And it was published in English over a century ago. So why haven't we ever heard about it?

### WHY HAVEN'T WE BEEN TOLD?

I can think of just two reasons why we've never heard about this evidence for New Testament reliability. Either Zahn's logical argument was disproven, or else it has been ignored and suppressed. I haven't found any indication that the argument was disproven. But what possible reason could there be for ignoring or suppressing such monumentally important evidence?

## Endnotes

1    Brown, *The Da Vinci Code*, 231.

2    Brown, *The Da Vinci Code*, 234.

3    Shelley, *Church History In Plain Language: Updated 2ⁿᵈ Edition*, 70.

4    Lindsay, *The Church And The Ministry In The Early Centuries*, 169.

5    Shelley, *Church History In Plain Language: Updated 2ⁿᵈ Edition*, 71.

6    "These changes in the structure and functioning of the church, especially the role of bishops, raise crucial and controversial questions. Christians of nearly every denomination admit that these changes took place." (Shelley, *Church History In Plain Language: Updated 2ⁿᵈ Edition*, 71.)

7    "Pictures of this ministry which ruled in the end of the second and in the earlier part of the third century, have been preserved for us in early ecclesiastical manuals." (Lindsay, *The Church And The Ministry In The Early Centuries*, 245.)

8    Lindsay, *The Church And The Ministry In The Early Centuries*, 266.

9    Lindsay, *The Church And The Ministry In The Early Centuries*, 251.

10   Lindsay, *The Church And The Ministry In The Early Centuries*, 248.

11   Lindsay, *The Church And The Ministry In The Early Centuries*, 354.

12   Zahn, *Introduction to the New Testament*, 93.

http://www.archive.org/details/introductiontone03zahnuoft

Epilogue

# The Wheelbarrow

by Mike Zuehlke

The author of this book was a very close friend of mine. I will start from the beginning and end at the end. As a boy I was taken to church on the holidays. I said things to make the church folks happy, because it was expected of me. But I was an atheist because of all the hypocrisy that I saw in the churches.

I didn't like Christians because they would ask questions and if I didn't give the right answers, it would turn into hours of lectures. I was abused as a child, but I survived. I grew up filled with hatred, rage, and lots of anger. I started working out and studied survival skills. I smoked, and used drugs and alcohol to escape. I was a bad boy in general. The funny thing was that I always sought the truth in everything. I always had a burning desire to know what was really true and really right (correct). I used drugs to delve deep into my mind to see what made me tick. They helped me to see life from other people's point of view. Drugs gave me compassion for the folks that were having a tough time with life. But I had no use for the lazy and truly bad apples. I was given a small booklet: Norman Vincent Peale's *Quotations from Jesus Christ*. I liked some of the things that Jesus said, but denied His deity.

I was given *The Living Word Bible* and started reading it when I was twenty-five to show Christians that they were wrong. I was going to show them all the things wrong with their beliefs and their book. I had decided to read the Bible literally from cover to cover. I started with the Library of Congress

Number and continued onward from there. I had read all the Old Testament, Matthew, Mark, Luke and three quarters of John. On a Wednesday night in early June of 1972, I was sitting alone on my couch with all the doors and windows locked. I was completely straight; no drugs or alcohol.

I was reading John, when God said to me, "Hey Mike!"

*Uh-Oh.* "Is that you God?" I asked.

"Yes" was the reply.

"But I don't believe in you."

"Well, here I am."

"What do you want with me?"

"I don't do this to everyone, but you have read all about me and tonight you must make a choice. Are you going to accept me or reject me?"

I said, "Man, that is a heavy trip to lay on a guy. I need time to think this over. So, I will tell you what; I will meet you in church on Sunday and give you an answer. Hello? Hello? Are you still there?" Just silence.

The rest of the week was spent walking around kicking the carpet and swearing. When Sunday arrived, I went to this Pentecostal church where I heard that God was doing miracles. I heard a message that I had never heard before. The preacher was talking about how much God loved me and cared about me. How His love for me was so great that He gave His son to pay the price that I could not pay to put me in a right relationship with Him. It was an awesome message about the love and compassion of God for mankind. But I was a tough guy sitting in the last row of pews right next to the door. After the message and the alter call, when the building was almost empty, I was still sitting there and was trying to understand what I had just heard. The preacher came to the back, kneeled in the pew in front of me, rested his arms on the back of it, and looked deep into my eyes and said "Son, why is there so much pain in the eyes of someone so young?" Tears were running down my face and I told him that life had been extremely hard on me, and that I was trying my best to cope with it. He asked if I wanted God to take it away. I replied that is what I wanted. He prayed with me, and I told God yes, I accepted Him.

I went home and sat on my couch meditating on what had just happened to me. I have always searched for truth and reality. I questioned myself about what I knew to be true and real about the experience that I had just had. I knew that there is an all-powerful entity that exists, regardless of what you wish to call it (I choose to call it "God," or "my Father.") I also knew that the entity had started a dialog with me. So, in my mind it was perfectly ok to talk to it.

I said, "Hey God, are you there?" He replied "Yes, I am." I almost fell off the couch! Holy cow! God is talking to me! I told God that I wanted to get to know Him as much as is humanly possible. He asked me if that is what I really wanted. I replied, "You know my heart and what is in my mind, I have no secrets from you." He told me, "then go for it!" That has been my pursuit since then.

I now know who I am and what I am supposed to do. I am God's man Mike and God is a very close personal friend of mine! I am His relationship guy. I am supposed to tell people about who God is and what He is really like. God is loving and gentle; He is not the big guy in the sky waiting for you to make a mistake so that He can punish you. Let me ask you a question; how many of your sins (errors, mistakes, whatever) were in the future when Jesus died on the cross? All of them, right.

Jesus did not die for them up until you turned twenty-one, or thirty, or sixty. He died for every sin that you have already committed and even the ones that you are going to commit in the future. When Jesus said "It is finished," what He meant was, IT IS FINISHED! You ARE holy and blameless before God now. So having said that, you can see that God has no desire to punish you anymore because of your acceptance of what Jesus did for you. Jesus came to fulfill the LAW and did it. There are no more rules or ten commandments to follow to enter the Kingdom of God.

In my pursuit of God, I read hundreds of Christian and non-Christian books, and went through many religions, churches, and everything else in the hope of gleaning out bits of truth and wisdom from everything. I was collecting pieces of truth from all the experiences that I had and the things that I had read. Throughout all of this, I stayed in touch with God by chatting with Him. I find that He talks to me but is usually very brief and to the point. I would ask God for something or to do a favor for me, and He would do it sometimes. Let me share some true stories that I experienced.

My biological father was an alcoholic who lived a day's drive away. I went to see him and shared what I had found. He rejected it. A few months later my stepmother called me and told me that my dad was in the hospital dying and that I should pray for him. I think that she was listening to what I had been telling my dad. I got on my stomach with my face in the carpet and cried out to my Father, "please don't let him die yet. Please give me another chance to share with him." He got up and walked out of the hospital and went home. I drove up the next week and shared once again. He still rejected what I told him. A few months later I got another call that was the same thing. So, I asked God to please give me another shot at him. Again, he got up and walked out of the hospital and went home. I made the trip once more with the same message. His response was that he was still not buying it.

Several months later I got the call again. Back to God I went with the same request. But this time I did not know that my dad had died. The priest gave him the Last Rites. The doctor filled out the death certificate. He was in the morgue getting ready to be embalmed when he sat up and scared the wits out of the guys in there with him! He left the hospital and went home with the death certificate as a souvenir.

I went up once again but with a different message this time. I told him that God had granted him three extensions to his life, but there would not be another. And I still wanted him to see the truth that I was presenting to him. My dad told me that he believed me and wanted to accept God. He accepted God's offer and his life completely changed; he was a different man. He lived for a couple of years more and finally died. I wasn't notified until after he had been dead for three days and already embalmed. When I found out I cried out to God and asked why I was notified so late. God told me very lovingly that it was time to let him go.

In 1980 my Jewish neighbor Mr. L was an alcoholic. I had gone to AA and got dried out. Mrs. L came to me one day to ask if I would get her husband to straighten out. I told her that if I did, she would not like him. She insisted that it would be fine. I told her three times that he would be very different. She claimed it would be fine. He came over a few hours later; he said she had told him if he didn't come and talk to me, she would take his son and go back to the east coast to live with her parents. I asked him if he was serious because I did not want to waste my time or his. He said that he was very serious. So, I took him to AA.

He asked me to be his sponsor and I said that I would on one condition. I get to pick his higher power. I said that his higher power was going to be the God of his forefathers: the father of Abraham, Isaac, and Jacob. He said that was fine because although he was born Jewish, he was an atheist. I assured him that was ok. I kept telling him about God when we were together on the daily trips back and forth to the AA meetings.

After around a week or so he asked me: if my God is who I claimed He is, then could He cure his alcoholism? I replied of course He can. I said that we should pray and ask God to do that for us. He told me that he did not believe in God. I said that it was fine because I believe in Him. He said that he had no faith. I told him that he did not need to have any faith because I would give him mine. We prayed and asked God to remove alcohol from his life and BANG! He was instantly cured. We stopped going to AA because he was cured. Another week passed and he showed up at my house again and asked if my God could cure his drug habit. Again, I replied yes. He said that he still did not believe and had no faith. I replied that I believed and again he would not need any faith because I would give him my faith. We prayed again and BANG - his drug problem was gone. A couple of weeks later he was at my house again telling me that he was a very heavy smoker and wondered if that God of mine could cure his tobacco habit. I replied of course he can.

Now in my mind I was having this serious conversation with God. I am telling God that I am sure we got him if He would please do just this one more miracle. Mr. L said his thing about nonbelief and no faith. Smiling, I told him that he should know the drill by now. We prayed and I believed for him and gave him my faith once again and guess what…BANG. He was healed of tobacco.

So now guess what; a few days later, my doorbell is ringing and there he is on my stoop hopping from foot to foot with his eyes twinkling. "Mike," he says, "if we could bottle this stuff and sell it, we could become gazillionaires!" I told him that we have to give it away or it doesn't work. Well, the sorrowful look on his crestfallen face was a sight to behold. He became a believer and is a great brother to this day. He has experienced God's power in his life many times since then, and God has performed many miracles on his behalf as well.

By the way, his wife left him and took his son and went back east because she didn't like him anymore. We prayed his son back (but that is another story for another time).

One beautiful windless summer day, I was driving in the mountains talking to God. I had been fasting for ten days because I was a bit troubled and wanted some answers. I asked God if He was actually in control and if He really loved me, and He said yes. I asked if He really truly loved me, and He said yes. I asked if He cared about my everyday life, and He said yes. I then asked if He cared about every teensy-weensy tiny detail of my everyday life. He said "Mike, do you see the pinecone in the middle of the road ahead? I want you to run over it."

I replied, "HA, watch this." Now I was extremely aware of where each one of my tires were at every moment. You could put a dime in the road and tell me to run over it and I would ask which tire do you want me to run over it with. Well, Just as I got to the pinecone, and on this completely windless day, a big gust of wind came up and blew it off the road! "NO FAIR," I cried! That was cheating! The rest of the day remained windless. Then I remembered what I had asked just before God had asked me to run over the pinecone. "Hello?" I said, and was greeted by silence. I didn't hear from God for the rest of the day. He left me to meditate on what I had just experienced. Yes, He is in charge and in control. God is not old and senile; He isn't off in outer space attending to more important matters. He is right here with us all the time.

Jesus said that the Kingdom of God is at hand. What that means is that it is for right here and right now! Not in the sweet by and by after we die. God created us to have a relationship with Him. He loves us and wants to spend time with us. God's kingdom is here, and we have access to it right now. I think that Andrew Farley's book *The Naked Gospel* is an excellent book to read to help us understand our relationship with God. Over many decades I collected many puzzle pieces of the truth, but did not see the big picture of how they fit together. That book showed me the picture on the cover of the box with all my puzzle pieces in it. I now know how they all fit together. Another awesome book is *The Practice of the Presence of God* by Brother Lawrence.

God has performed a great many miracles on my behalf. He is my Father, and He loves me. Let me share a story about a tightrope walker. There was a tightrope stretched across Niagara Falls with a fellow who was going to walk across it. He asked the crowd if they thought he could walk across it. Many were unsure. He walked across and then asked if they thought he could walk back. There were still doubters. He returned to the original side. Then he took a wheelbarrow and asked if they thought he could cross pushing the wheelbarrow. More people were unsure again. He then crossed pushing the wheelbarrow. He asked if they thought that he could come back with it. The folks mostly said yes. He came back to a wildly cheering crowd. He then asked if they thought that he could do it again. Everyone screamed YES, for they had seen him do it and return. He said to them, "if you truly believe I can do it, get into the wheelbarrow!"

God wants us in the wheelbarrow and to trust him completely. My Jewish friend who is a believer told me one day that God said to him, "When you work, I rest; and when you rest, I work!"

What this is all about is everyone's personal relationship to God. God created us to hang out with Him. God is my Father, just like the father in the Bible story whose son took his share of the family fortune, left the farm, went to town, spent it all on wine, women, and song. He ended up sleeping with the pigs and remembered that the servants at the farm were treated better than what he was experiencing. When he returned to the farm, he wanted to be one of the servants. But when the father saw his son returning, he ran down the driveway calling for a robe and a ring for his lost son. "Kill a fattened calf," he said, "and let us have a feast, for my wayward son has returned!" That is my Father, the God whom I serve. My Father wants to have the same kind of relationship with you as well. Do you want to experience the power lost by the early Christians? Get in the wheelbarrow with no holding back and no reservations. God can, will, and still does answer prayers and still performs miracles!

The more time that you spend with God the easier it becomes to recognize His voice. A good rule of thumb is to listen twice as much as you talk. So, if you talk for ten minutes then listen for twenty minutes. It gets easier to quiet your mind from all the stuff running rampant in there. It just takes a while is all.

Does God answer all my prayers? Absolutely not, but He does answer a lot of them. When I pray, I just talk to God the same way I talk with all my friends. I don't use any fancy language or verbose verbiage. I just talk normal with God and relax and be myself. Prayer is not tying a note to a rock and tossing it up into the air hoping that God will notice it. It is not tying a note to a rock and throwing it over the wall between you and Him hoping that He will stub His toe on it while walking on the other side and pick it up and read it. You can't lie to God; he knows you completely. And never make promises to God; inevitably, you will not have the ability to keep them, and the Devil will use that as a foothold to smother you with guilt. It is about having a close personal relationship with Him (i.e.: being in the wheelbarrow). I talked to people that said that they tried out prayer and God never answered them. When you get to really know God, then you are able pray in harmony with His spirit. I have no power. What I do have is relationship. I simply ask my Father and He performs the miracles according to His will. That is why it is very important to be in harmony with His spirit. So that you do not pray amiss (wrongly). That is when things get real and that is where the rubber meets the road.

God is not something that you try out like taking a car for a test drive to see if it works for you. Get in (the wheelbarrow) or get in not, there is no try (with apologies to Yoda). It is a whole lifetime commitment. Do you have to change and get all religious? No, you can still be yourself. If God wants you to change something about yourself then He will tell you. God will tell you what He would like for you to change. You can relax and not worry about SINS, because Jesus has already paid for them. If you become aware of something undesirable that you are doing or not doing, then ask God to help you to change. Ask God for wisdom. He *will* give it to you if you ask Him. Remember that there are no hard fast rules that you have to follow; relax and enjoy hanging out with God. Try to use common sense and always try to do the loving, kind, merciful things.

Always remember to maintain an attitude of gratitude; never forget to say thank you. I am happy to share that the author of this book got into the wheelbarrow. I feel very honored and blessed that he considered me a close friend. Please feel free to reread and meditate on this as much as it takes to sink in.

I pray that you can find peace and truth in what has been shared here,
   ~*God's man Mike*

## P.S.: THE WAR

*This is about spiritual warfare, the battle for your mind.*

In 2 Kings 6:11-17, Elisha's servant's eyes were opened to the spiritual realm. This is a real story about the spiritual realm affecting the physical realm. The story of Job is an example of spiritual conflict that was in the physical realm. The spiritual realm exists even if we can't see it. The first step is to recognize that spiritual warfare exists. If the enemy can influence your mind, he can affect your actions. Those of us that are aware of the spiritual war, find that the fight is usually in our minds. Relationship with God and prayer is the answer to being able to win the war. We ask you to please pray for wisdom and insight in order to help others along their path through life.

# APPENDIX

The following seven practices are the most obvious visible changes that became necessary and inevitable once second-century congregations accepted a single, visible head.

None of these practices can be found in the New Testament. All of them were invented after AD 100—after the lifetimes of Christ's apostles. First-century Christians never heard of any of them.

## THE OFFICE OF THE BISHOP OR PASTOR

(with the possible exception of Christians in the eastern Roman Empire)

> ...the pattern of a single bishop, or pastor, at the head of each church...does not clearly emerge till the opening years of the second century. The first witness to it is Ignatius, a prophet of the church of Antioch in Syria, who has become the bishop in the sense of the single head, of the church in that city.[1]

> During the 2nd century the ministry was subject to a change. The ruling body of office-bearers in every congregation received a permanent president, who was called the pastor or bishop, the latter term being the commoner.[2]

> Paul made sure, however, that the churches planted in the path of his missionary journeys had pastoral leaders to care for the spiritual needs of believers in a given place. These local leaders were of two sorts. One group was called elders or presbyters (from the Greek for "elders"). These same men were also known as bishops (overseers) or pastors (shepherds). The other group of leaders was called deacons.[3]

> The meeting described by the apostle is not to be taken as something which might be seen in Corinth but was peculiar to that city; it may be taken as a type of the Christian meeting throughout the Gentile Christian Churches; for the Apostle, in his suggestions and criticisms, continually speaks of what took place throughout all the churches.[4]

> ...(Timothy) will remind you of my ways in Christ, *as I teach them everywhere in every church.* (1 Cor 4:17 NET, emphasis mine)

> ...I give this sort of direction *in all the churches.* (1 Cor 7:17 NET, emphasis mine)

If anyone intends to quarrel about this, *we have no other practice, nor do the churches of God.* (1 Cor 11:16 NET, emphasis mine)

...As in *all the churches of the saints*...(1 Cor 14:33 NET, emphasis mine)

## CLERGY AND LAITY

We do not find a common term in general use to denote the former class until the beginning of the 3rd century. In the west the word was ordo, and in the east clerus, from which come our "orders" and "clergy."[5]

## ORDINATION

Ordination is not to be confused with consecration. Ordination is the conferring of holy orders: "The division of the congregation into clergy and laity and the common mode of making the difference apparent in daily ecclesiastical life were both borrowed from the usages of the civil society round them. The laity were called *plebs* and the clergy the *ordo*—the names applied to the commons and the senate of the Italian and provincial towns."[6]

### SALARIED CLERGY

Pictures of this ministry which ruled in the end of the second and in the earlier part of the third century, have been preserved for us in early ecclesiastical manuals. Perhaps the *Canons of Hippolytus* may be most fitly selected to furnish them...[7]

The Canons forbid any of these offerings being reserved for the clergy, as was the custom in later times...[8]

...Cyprian seems to have been the first to make payments to the clergy...[9]

### CHURCH BUILDINGS

The earliest trace we find of buildings set apart exclusively for Christian worship dates from the beginning of the third century (202-210): Clement of Alexandria, *Stromata*, vii. 5.[10]

## Worship services and the Order of Worship

...the New Testament does not instruct worshipers in a specific procedure to follow in their services...[11]

## Sermons

The early freedom of worship no longer existed. The reading, prayers, and exhortations were all in the hands of the clergy. The people shared in the singing only.[12]

**Endnotes**

1   Niebuhr at al, *The Ministry in Historical Perspectives*, 23.

2   Orr, *International Standard Bible Encyclopedia,* "Ministry"

3   Shelley, *Church History In Plain Language: Updated 2nd Edition*, 70.

4   Lindsay, *The Church And The Ministry In The Early Centuries,* 48.

5   Orr, *International Standard Bible Encyclopedia,* "Ministry"

6   Lindsay, *The Church And The Ministry In The Early Centuries*, 245, (footnote 2).

7   Lindsay, *The Church And The Ministry In The Early Centuries*, 245.

8   Lindsay, *The Church And The Ministry In The Early Centuries*, 255.

9   Lindsay, *The Church And The Ministry In The Early Centuries*, 304.

10   Lindsay, *The Church And The Ministry In The Early Centuries*, 43, (footnote 3).

11   Youngblood, *Nelson's Illustrated Bible Dictionary,* "Worship"

12   Lindsay, *The Church And The Ministry In The Early Centuries*, 251.

# GLOSSARY

**Allegorizing** – assigns to the text a symbolic meaning different from its literal, normal meaning. This is sometimes called the deeper or spiritual meaning. It's a seductive and insidious way to impose a foreign meaning on God's words; to put words in God's mouth; to make God appear to say things He never said. See also: Spiritulizing.

**Apostle** – "the formal structure of the apostolate is derived from the Jewish legal system in which a person may be given the legal power to represent another. The one who has such power of attorney is called a Sjaliach (apostle). The uniqueness of this relationship is pregnantly expressed by the notion that the Sjaliach (apostle) of a man, is as the man himself" (Ridderbos and Gaffin 1988). See also: Shaliach.

**Aramaic** – from *Encyclopedia Britannica*: "Semitic language of the Northern Central, or Northwestern, group that was originally spoken by the ancient Middle Eastern people known as Aramaeans. It was most closely related to Hebrew, Syriac, and Phoenician and was written in a script derived from the Phoenician alphabet."

**Bind** – in Matthew 16:15-19, Jesus was speaking as a Jewish rabbi and using rabbinical figures of speech. His first-century Jewish audience understood precisely what He meant. To "bind" meant to prohibit something; to "loose" meant to permit it. See also: Loose.

**Bishop** – (Literally: Overseer). Shortly after AD 100, Ignatius of Antioch wrote a series of letters advocating a single visible leader: a "head" elder over all the churches. He called this individual the bishop.

**Body of Christ** – the organismic entity that God uses to continue His work on earth, made up of the church, or Ekklesia – people who form the *parts* of the body. "From him the whole body, joined and held together by every supporting ligament, grows and builds itself up in love, as each part does its work," (Eph 4:16 NIV). See also: Church, Ekklesia.

**Burden** – (Greek: *Phortion*: far-TEE-on; Matthew 11:30; NT:5413): translates as "Burden" in the KJV, "Load" in the NET: In first century Israel, yoke and burden were rabbinical figures of speech. A rabbi's yoke was his teaching. His burden meant his commands and prohibitions. See also: Yoke.

**Casting Lots** – Making a decision through chance by casting lots, such as dice, straw, pebbles, etc. This has much precedence in the Bible: Numbers 26:55-56, Numbers 33:54, 1 Samuel 14:41, and Jonah 1:7 are just a few examples.

**Catholic (Church)** – (Literally: Universal). In his letter to the Smyrneans, Ignatius first coined the term: "Wherever the bishop shall appear, there let the multitude [of the people] also be; even as, wherever Jesus Christ is, there is the Catholic Church."

**Charisma** – (KHAR-is-ma; NT:5486). Refers to one of the three Greek words that Paul uses to distinguish three different kinds of gifts. In 1 Cor 12:4-6 Paul explains that there are three distinct categories of gifts and three different givers. See also: Diakonia, Energema.

**Charybdis** – in Homer's Odyssey, Charybdis, which manifests as a large whirlpool, was one of two monsters blocking the sea route that Odysseus must take. Being stuck between Charybdis and Scylla is used as a metaphor, similar to being "stuck between a rock and a hard place," or, choosing "the lesser of evils." See also: Scylla.

**Church** – in the New Testament, *Ekklesia*, often translated as "church," means the company of believers in Jesus. But today, the word church means a building for religious meetings. See also: Body of Christ, Ekklesia.

**Church Fathers** – from *Encyclopedia Britannica*: "any of the great bishops and other eminent Christian teachers of the early centuries whose writings remained as a court of appeal for their successors, especially in reference to controverted points of faith or practice."

**Church Government** – not found in the New Testament. Implemented by setting up one man as the visible head over every congregation brought political power and control into Christianity. Once second-century Christians accepted a visible head, everything else about Jesus' Ekklesia had to change to follow suit. Instead of an *organism*—the body of Christ—Christianity became a political *organization*. See also: Churchianity, Organized Religion.

**Church Infancy Myth** – A myth used to legitimize church government that says Jesus' Ekklesia began as an infant; the New Testament documents only the Church's infancy; after the New Testament was completed, God authorized and guided the development of church government as the Ekklesia grew to maturity.

**Churchianity** – the name churchianity highlights the fact that there is something that claims to be Christianity but is different; something that professes to love and serve the Lord Jesus Christ but actually has an entirely different agenda. Churchianity is hijacked Christianity and has been masquerading as Jesus' Ekklesia for about 1,900 years. See also: Organized Religion, Church Government.

**Clergy** – those who are to be obeyed. "As the members of the senate or the ordo had a special bench called the *concessus,* in the basilica or court-house, so the clergy had special seats in church. 'It is the authority of the Church...'" (Lindsay 1903). "In the west the word was ordo, and in the east clerus, from which come our 'orders' and 'clergy'" (Orr 1996). See also: Laity.

**College of Elders** – "the first century each Christian congregation had for its office-bearers a body of deacons and a body of elders—whether separated into two colleges or forming one must remain unknown—and that the elders took the 'oversight' while the deacons performed the 'subordinate services,'" (Lindsay 1903).

**Congregation** – *Merriam-Webster*: "a gathering, especially an assembly of persons met for worship and religious instruction." See also: Laity.

**Constantine** – Constantine was acclaimed Roman emperor by the army in 306; became the western emperor in 312; eastern empire 324.

**Denomination** – *Merriam-Webster*: "a religious organization whose congregations are united in their adherence to its beliefs and practices." Examples of Christian denominations are Baptist, Catholic, or Methodist.

**Devotionalizing** – one of three types of non-normal interpretation, devotionalizing comes in two forms, both of which are also types of universalization. A *devotion* typically consists of a verse, a reflection, and a prayer. The problem occurs when one misses the larger context of a passage and assumes that all promises, even if made specifically to the apostles, were made to *everyone, for all time*. The other form treats the Bible as a kind of divine Ouija Board or Magic 8-Ball: a mystic oracle that provides daily personal direction and guidance. See also: Spiritualizing, Universalizing.

**Diakonia** – (Greek: dee-ak-on-EE-ah; NT:1248) service gifts. The purpose of the *diakonia* gifts is to prepare the body parts of Christ's body for works of service. The job of apostles, prophets, evangelists, and shepherd-teachers is to prepare the rest of us to function as Christ's body on earth. When Jesus' body parts function as intended, the body of Christ grows up and becomes mature. See also: Charisma, Encrgcma.

**Disciple** – (Distinct from: Apostle). *Merriam-Webster*: "a pupil or follower of any teacher or school." The terms apostle and disciple are not synonymous. Jesus had many other disciples besides the Twelve.

**Divine Energy** – "…there are different distributions of **divine energy** (*energema*) motivating these gifts in their operation, but the same (Father) **God** who by His divine energy operates them all in their sphere" (1 Cor 12:4-6 WET, emphasis and parenthetical material mine). See also: Energema.

**Doctrine** – *Merriam-Webster*: "a principle or position or the body of principles in a branch of knowledge or system of belief."

**Eidetic** – *Merriam-Webster*: "marked by or involving extraordinarily accurate and vivid recall especially of visual images."

**Eisegesis** – *Merriam-Webster*: "eisegesis is the interpretation of a text (as of the Bible) by reading into it one's own ideas."

**Ekklesia** – (Greek: ek-klay-ZEE-ah; NT:1577). *Ekklesia* is the English equivalent of the New Testament Greek word translated as church. In the New Testament, Ekklesia means the company of believers in Jesus. But today, the word church means a building for religious meetings. The Apostle Paul refers to the Ekklesia as Christ's body fourteen times in his thirteen letters. And Paul meant that literally, not figuratively. See also: Body of Christ, Church.

**Energema** – (Greek: en-ERG-ay-mah; NT:1755). One of three technical terms Paul uses to describe different kinds of gifts: "…there are different distributions of **divine energy** (*energema*) motivating these gifts in their operation, but the same (Father) **God** who by His divine energy operates them all in their sphere" (1 Cor 12:4-6 WET, emphasis and parenthetical material mine). See also: Charisma, Diakonia, Divine Energy.

**Epistle** – letters written by the apostles to other Christians. For instance, thirteen books in the New Testament were epistles written by the Apostle Paul.

**Eucharist** – from *Encyclopedia Britannica:* "Eucharist, also called Holy Communion or Lord's Supper, in Christianity, ritual commemoration of Jesus' Last Supper with his disciples. The Eucharist (from the Greek *eucharistia* for 'thanksgiving') is the central act of Christian worship and is practiced by most Christian churches in some form. Along with baptism it is one of the two sacraments most clearly found in the New Testament."

**Evangelical** – *Merriam-Webster:* "of, relating to, or being in agreement with the Christian gospel especially as it is presented in the four Gospels." (The Gospels are the first four books of the New Testament, i.e., Matthew, Mark, Luke, and John.)

**God's Flock** – God's flock (symbolizing a *flock of sheep*) are *people* under the care of a shepherd, namely Jesus. Jesus said "My sheep listen to my voice, and I know them, and they follow me" (John 10:27). "Give a shepherd's care to God's flock among you, exercising oversight not merely as a duty but willingly under God's direction, not for shameful profit but eagerly. And do not lord it over those entrusted to you, but be examples to the flock. Then when the Chief Shepherd appears, you will receive the crown of glory that never fades away" (1 Peter 5:2-4).

**Gospel, The** – (Literally: good news). "Passages like 1 Samuel 31:9 and 2 Samuel 18:19 indicate that when these words were used in reference to kings and kingdoms, they signified the good news of *victory in battle*. This observation is important because the 'good news' in the New Testament is so often associated with victory for God's kingdom" (Thirdmill 2014).

**Hermeneutics** – from *Encyclopedia Britannica:* "the study of the general principles of biblical interpretation. For both Jews and Christians throughout their histories, the primary purpose of hermeneutics, and of the exegetical methods employed in interpretation, has been to discover the truths and values expressed in the Bible."

**Hupotasso** – (Greek: hoop-ot-AS-so; NT:5293). "Primarily a military term, 'to rank under' (hupo, 'under,' tasso, 'to arrange'), denotes (a) 'to put in subjection, to subject,'…(b) in the middle or passive voice, to subject oneself, to obey, be subject to…" (Vine 1984).

**Ignatius of Antioch** – from *Encyclopedia Britannica:* "known mainly from seven highly regarded letters that he wrote during a trip to Rome, as a prisoner condemned to be executed for his beliefs. He was apparently eager to counteract the teachings of two groups—the Judaizers, who did not accept the authority of the New Testament, and the docetists, who held that Christ's sufferings and death were apparent but not real. The letters have often been cited as a source of knowledge of the Christian church at the beginning of the 2nd century."

**Inimical** – *Merriam-Webster:* "being adverse often by reason of hostility or malevolence…For example, high inflation may be called 'inimical' to economic growth."

**Kosmos** – (Greek: KAHZ-mahs; NT:2889). "The whole circle of earthly goods, endowments riches, advantages, pleasures, etc, which although hollow and frail and fleeting, stir desire, seduce from God and are obstacles to the cause of Christ" (Thayer 1999).

**Laity** – those who are to obey. "…borrowed from the usages of the civil society round them. The laity were called *plebs* and the clergy the *ordo*—the names applied to the commons and the senate of the Italian and provincial towns" (Lindsay 1903). See also: Clergy.

**Logos (of God)** – (Greek: LOW-gahs; John 1:14; NT:3056). A word (as embodying an idea), a statement, a speech. Jesus, the Son of God, the Word (*Logos*) of God in the flesh (John 1:14).

**Loose** – In Matthew 16:15-19, Jesus was speaking as a Jewish rabbi and using rabbinical figures of speech. His first-century Jewish audience understood precisely what He meant - to "bind" meant to prohibit something; to "loose" meant to permit it. See also: Bind.

**Monepiscopacy** – the pattern of a single bishop, or pastor, at the head of each church. See also: Church Government.

**Myth-Busting** – *Cambridge Dictionary:* "saying or showing that something generally thought to be true is not, in fact, true, or is different from how it is usually described."

**Myth-Interpretation** – interpreting the Bible in a non-normal or mystical manner. Becomes a vicious circle: a self-reinforcing and self-perpetuating trap of circular reasoning. We myth-interpret the Bible because we believe it is mystical. But myth-interpretation is what makes the Bible mystical in the first place. See also: Allegorizing, Devotionalizing, Spiritualizing, Universalizing, Myth-theology.

**Myth-Theology** – mostly mythology with just enough bad theology thrown in to make it appear plausible as long as we don't look too closely. See also: Myth-interpretation.

**Ordained** – from *Merriam-Webster*: "...from Latin, to put in order, appoint, from *ordin-, ordo* order." Formally appointing someone to an official church office or title.

**Order of Worship** – from *Merriam-Webster*: "the arrangement of the various parts of a worship service within Protestant Christianity."

**Org Chart** – a diagram breaking down the organization's structure and relationships and the relative ranks of its parts or members.

**Organized Religion** – *Merriam-Webster:* "a belief system that has large numbers of followers and a set of rules that must be followed." God has already told us, in writing, in the New Testament, that He neither authorized nor does He approve of church government and its practices. See also: Church Government, Churchianity.

**Orthodox (Christianity)** – Christian denomination. From *Encyclopedia Britannica*: "(from Greek *orthodoxos,* 'of the right opinion'), true doctrine and its adherents as opposed to heterodox or heretical doctrines and their adherents."

**Papal Infallibility** – from *Encyclopedia Britannica*: "in Roman Catholic theology, the doctrine that the pope, acting as supreme teacher and under certain conditions, cannot err when he teaches in matters of faith or morals."

**Pastor** – (Literally: shepherd). *Merriam-Webster*: "a spiritual overseer, especially : a clergyperson serving a local church or parish."

**Pentecost** – a feast day (described in Leviticus 23:15-21). Pentecost means "fiftieth" and took place on the 50$^{th}$ day after Passover. Jews from all over the Roman empire had traveled to Jerusalem to participate.

**Poimen** – (Greek: poy-MANE; NT:4166. Literally: shepherd). Eph 4:11 is the only instance of this word being translated into the latin "pastor" in the entire NT. Every other instance is correctly translated "shepherd." Seven of those instances refer to literal shepherds; ten refer to the Lord Jesus Christ. If the KJV translators had been consistent, Eph 4:11 would read "*shepherds* and teachers" instead of "pastors and teachers."

**Prima Scriptura** – (Distinct from: Sola Scriptura). The doctrine that holds that the Bible is the "first" or "primary" authority for Christian faith and practice. See also: Sola Scriptura.

**Proistamenous** – (Greek: pro-is-TAH-men-os; 1 Thess 5:12 KJV; NT: 4291). Translated as "over you" in the KJV (1 Thess 5:12).

**Proof Text** – Biblical passages adduced as proof, such as proof of a teaching, position, or argument.

**Protestant Reformation, Protestantism** – The movement of 16$^{th}$ century Europe whose followers believed in freedom to relate directly and individually with Jesus, which was in direct opposition to the Roman Catholic Church and subsequently caused another branch of Christianity called *Protestantism.*

**Rabbi** – from *Encyclopedia Britannica*: "(Hebrew: 'my teacher' or 'my master') in

Judaism, a person qualified by academic studies of the Hebrew Bible and the Talmud to act as spiritual leader and religious teacher of a Jewish community or congregation."

**Request For Proposal** – a public document describing a project, soliciting bids from contractors to complete it.

**Sanhedrin** – from *Merriam-Webster*: "the supreme council and tribunal of the Jews during postexilic times headed by a High Priest and having religious, civil, and criminal jurisdiction."

**Scylla** – In Homer's Odyssey, Scylla, a six-headed monster, was one of two monsters blocking the sea route that Odysseus must take. Being stuck between Charybdis and Scylla is used as a metaphor, similar to being "stuck between a rock and a hard place," or, choosing "the lesser of evils." See also: Charybdis.

**Seminary** – from *Merriam-Webster*: "an institution for the training of candidates for the priesthood, ministry, or rabbinate."

**Shaliach** – (Hebrew: shah-LEE-akh): an apostle. "the formal structure of the apostolate is derived from the Jewish legal system in which a person may be given the legal power to represent another. The one who has such power of attorney is called a Sjaliach (apostle). The uniqueness of this relationship is pregnantly expressed by the notion that the Sjaliach (apostle) of a man, is as the man himself" (Ridderbos 1988). See Also: Apostle.

**Sola Scriptura** – (Dinstinct from: Prima Scriptura). A doctrine that holds that the Bible is the only (sole) authoritative source for all Christian faith and practice. See Also: Prima Scriptura.

**Spiritualizing** – one of three forms of non-normal interpretation. Assigns to the text a symbolic meaning different from its literal, normal meaning. This is sometimes called the deeper or spiritual meaning. It's a seductive and insidious way to impose a foreign meaning on God's words; to put words in God's mouth; to make God appear to say things He never said. See also: Allegorizing, Devotionalizing, Universalizing.

**Tithe** – (Literally: one tenth). *Merriam-Webster*: "to pay or give a tenth part of - especially for the support of a religious establishment or organization."

**Universalizing** – one of three forms of non-normal interpretation. The notion that the entire Bible—every promise, command, prohibition, instruction, and example in the Old and New Testaments—applies to every Christian at all times. See also: Devotionalizing, Spiritualizing.

**Westminster Confession of Faith** – from *Encyclopedia Britannica*: "produced by the Westminster Assembly, which was called together by the Long Parliament in 1643, during the English Civil War, and met regularly in Westminster Abbey until 1649."

**Yoke** – (Greek: *Zygos*: zoo-GAHS; Matthew 11:30; NT:2218). In Matthew 11:30, Jesus was speaking as a Jewish rabbi and using rabbinical figures of speech. His first-century Jewish audience understood precisely what He meant. A rabbi's "yoke" was his teaching. See also: Burden.

# BIBLIOGRAPHY

Alcorn, Randy C. 2008. *Heaven*. Carol Stream, Ill.: Tyndale House Publishers.

Bauer, Walter. 2000. *A Greek-English Lexicon of the New Testament and Other Early Christian Literature*. Chicago: University of Chicago Press.

Bell, Charles M. 1994. *Discovering the Rich Heritage of Orthodoxy*. Light & Life Publishing Company.

Bell, Rob. 2009. *Velvet Elvis*. Zondervan.

Berkhof, Louis. 1986. *Principles of Biblical Interpretation*. Grand Rapids, MI: Baker Book House.

Bethke, Jefferson. 2012. "Why I Hate Religion but Love Jesus." https://www.youtube.com/watch?v=1IAhDGYlpqY.

Brown, Dan. 2013. *The Da Vinci Code : A Novel*. New York: Anchor Books.

Cambridge University Press. 2019. "Cambridge Dictionary: Find Definitions, Meanings & Translations." Cambridge Dictionary. 2019. https://dictionary.cambridge.org/us/.

Carroll, Lewis, and Parragon Publishing. 2010. *Alice in Wonderland*. Bath, UK: Parragon.

Chadwick, Henry. 1993. *The Penguin History of the Church*. Penguin UK.

Encyclopædia Britannica, Inc. n.d. "Find Definitions & Meanings of Words." Britannica Dictionary. https://www.britannica.com/dictionary.

Farley, Andrew. 2009. *The Naked Gospel : The Truth You May Never Hear in Church*. Grand Rapids, MI: Zondervan.

———. 2011. *God without Religion : Can It Really Be This Simple?* Grand Rapids, MI: Baker Books.

Fausset, A R. 1984. "Church." In *Fausset's Bible Dictionary*. Grand Rapids, MI: Zondervan.

Felder, Don, Glenn Frey, and Don Henley. 1976. *Hotel California*. Vinyl.

Los Angeles, CA: Asylum Records.

Freedman, David Noel, Gary A Herion, David F Graf, John David Pleins, and Astrid Billes Beck. 2008. *The Anchor Bible Dictionary. Volume 1 A-C.* New Haven, CT: Yale University Press.

Howard, Thomas. 1984. *Evangelical Is Not Enough : Worship of God in Liturgy and Sacrament.* San Francisco, CA: Ignatius Press.

Ignatius. Letter to Polycarp. 110ADa. "Ignatius, to Polycarp," 110AD.

———. Letter to The Ephesians. 110ADb. "Ignatius, to the Ephesians," 110AD.

———. Letter to The Magnesians. 110ADc. "Ignatius, to the Magnesians," 110AD.

———. Letter to The Philadelphians. 110ADd. "Ignatius, to the Philadelphians," 110AD.

———. Letter to The Romans. 110ADe. "Ignatius, to the Romans," 110AD.

———. Letter to The Smyrneans. 110ADf. "Ignatius, to the Smyrneans," 110AD.

———. Letter to Trallians. 110ADg. "Ignatius, to the Trallians," 110AD.

Keck, Leander E. 1995. *The New Interpreter's Bible. Volume VIII : General Articles on the New Testament, the Gospel of Matthew, the Gospel of Mark.* Nashville, TN: Abingdon.

Kittel, Gerhard, and Geoffrey William Bromiley. 1966. *Theological Dictionary of the New Testament. 3.* Grand Rapids, MI: Wm. B. Eerdmans.

Lawrence, Brother. 2020. *The Practice of the Presence.* Parables.

Lindsay, Thomas Martin. 1903. *Church and the Ministry in the Early Centuries.* London: Hodder and Stoughton.

McCranie, Steve. 2006. *Love Jesus, Hate Church : How to Survive in Church-- or Die Trying!* Gastonia, NC: Back2acts Productions.

Mearns, William Hughes. 1899. *Antigonish.* Poem.

Merriam-Webster. 2014. *Merriam Webster's Collegiate Dictionary.* Springfield: Merriam-Webster.

Niebuhr, Helmut R, and Daniel D Williams. 1956. *The Ministry in Histori-*

*cal Perspectives*. New York: Harper.

Orr, James. 1996. "Church Government, Ministry, to Know the Depths." In *The International Standard Bible Encyclopaedia*. Peabody, MA: Hendrickson Publishers.

Ramm, Bernard L. 1970. *Protestant Biblical Interpretation; a Textbook of Hermeneutics*. 3rd Revised. Grand Rapids, MI: Presbyterian and Reformed Publishing Company.

Ridderbos, Herman N, and Richard B Gaffin. 1988. *Redemptive History and the New Testament Scriptures*. Presbyterian & Reformed Publishing Company.

Roberts, Mark D. 2007. *Can We Trust the Gospels? : Investigating the Reliability of Matthew, Mark, Luke, and John*. Wheaton, IL: Crossway Books.

Robertson, A T. 1930. *Word Pictures in the New Testament*. Grand Rapids, MI: Baker Book House.

Santayana, George. (1905) 2006. *The Life of Reason*. United States: Echo Library.

Scofield, C I. 1998. *The New Scofield Study Bible*. Getty Center for Education in.

Shelley, Bruce L. 1995. *Church History in Plain Language*. 2nd ed. Nashville, TN: Thomas Nelson.

Stone, Larry. n.d. "Chapters and Verses." The Story of the Bible. Accessed October 27, 2022. http://www.storyofbible.com/chapters-and-verses.html.

Strobel, Lee. 2016. *Case for Christ*. Zondervan.

Strong, James. 2010. *The New Strong's Exhaustive Concordance of the Bible*. Nashville, TN: Thomas Nelson.

Sullivan, Louis H. 1896. "The Tall Office Building Artistically Considered." *Lippincott's Magazine*, 1896.

Thayer, Joseph Henry, and Christian Gottlob Wilke. 1999. *Greek-English Lexicon of the New Testament : Being Grimm's Wilke's Clavis Novi Testamenti*. Peabody, MA: Hendrickson.

Thirdmill. 2014. *Kingdom & Covenant in the New Testament: The Kingdom of*

*God*. Vol. 2. Casselberry, FL: Third Millennium Ministries, Inc.

Vincent, Marvin R. 1991. "1 Thessalonians 5:12, Romans 12:8." In *Word Studies in the New Testament*. Peabody, MA: Hendrickson.

Vine, W E. 1984. *Vine's Complete Expository Dictionary of Old and New Testament Words*. Nashville, TN: Thomas Nelson.

Waldron, Samuel E. 2015. *To Be Continued : Are the Miraculous Gifts for Today?* Greenville, SC: Calvary.

Walker, Williston. 1985. *A History of the Christian Church*. New York: Scribner.

Westminster Assembly. 1646. *The Westminster Confession of Faith*. Westminster Assembly.

Wiersbe, Warren W. 1992. *Wiersbe's Expository Outlines on the New Testament*. Wheaton, IL: Victor Books.

Wight, Fred. n.d. "Manners & Customs: Customs at Mealtime | AHRC." Ancient Hebrew Research Center. Accessed December 11, 2022. https://www.ancient-hebrew.org/manners/customs-at-mealtime.htm.

Willard, Dallas. 1998. *The Divine Conspiracy : Rediscovering Our Hidden Life in God*. New York: HarperCollins Publishers.

Youngblood, Ronald F, F F Bruce, R K Harrison, and Thomas Nelson Publishers. 2014. "Church Government, Worship." In *Nelson's Illustrated Bible Dictionary*. Nashville, TN: Thomas Nelson.

Zahn, Theodor. 1953. *Introduction to the New Testament*. Grand Rapids, MI: Kregel.

(This page intentionally left blank)

(This page intentionally left blank)

Made in the USA
Monee, IL
26 April 2023

32502851R00144